Supplement to Judicial Remedies in the European Communities

Supplement to Judicial Remedies in the European Communities

A Case book

L. J. BRINKHORST

Professor of Law, University of Groningen

H. G. SCHERMERS

Professor of Law, University of Amsterdam

1972

KLUWER B.V. - DEVENTER

STEVENS & SONS LTD - LONDON

Printed in The Netherlands by Hooiberg nv, Epe

ISBN 90 268 0641 8 and SBN 420/96580
Library of Congress Catalog Card Number: 71-92205

TABLE OF CONTENTS

The law of the European Communities is in continuous evolution.

Although the Case book *Judicial Remedies in the European Communities* appeared only three years ago (1969), so many new judgments of importance have since been delivered both by the Court of Justice and by the courts of the member States, that a new publication was deemed necessary so as to update the original materials. Particular jurisprudential tendencies have become more established and certain new developments have occurred.

The overall picture is that the autonomy of the legal order of the Communities has now generally been recognised; the direct effect and the supremacy of Community law is becoming an accepted fact even in those countries where the dualist approach to the relationship between international law and national law is solidly entrenched. The acceptance of the jurisprudence of the Court of Justice can be said to be furthered by the Court's acknowledgment of the fact that the fundamental legal principles of the member States, such as the protection of basic human rights, are to be safeguarded also within the framework of the Communities.

Thus by mutual cooperation and by respect for one another's competences, Community structures and national structures are becoming increasingly interwoven. In the context of the subject of this casebook this conclusion is not without significance. In the final analysis the effectiveness of judicial remedies before the Court of Justice depends on their being understood and accepted in municipal law.

In view of the expected expansion of the European Communities, materials are included which may shed light on the constitutional situation with respect to the relationship between international law and municipal law in the acceding countries: Denmark, Ireland, Norway and the United Kingdom. In each of these countries the securement of an effective and smooth integration of Community law into the national legal spheres presents specific constitutional problems.

It is hoped, that the materials introduced may illuminate some of the key problems, which these countries are encountering.

The system of the Case book has been preserved as far as possible. Thus, all cases bear names prefixed by the name of a State when the judgment has been delivered by a national court (e.g. the *German Lütticke* Case is a judgment of a German Court; the *Lütticke Case* of the Court of Justice).

The same titles and subtitles have been used and they bear the same letters and numbers. Only in some instances (e.g. Chapter One, Part II B 2; Chapter Three, parts III C and IV, Chapter Four, parts I, II A, II C 2) have new subtitles been added. The new indices are cumulative, covering both the original work and the supplement.

In the Case book references have been given to the Dutch, French and German texts of the cases (Jur., Rec. and Samml. respectively). Since 1969 the official language texts have used the same page numbering. After that date, therefore, only the pages in Jur. have been given.

The authors wish to thank Mr. H. M. van Niftrik, Miss Elizabeth A. Hay and Mr. Kieran Coonan for their assistance in translating foreign texts and in correcting the English used. Again they thank the staff of the Europa Instituut of the University of Amsterdam for their help and, in particular, Mr. G. Borchardt, who contributed much to the editing of the book. They also acknowledge the help of Mr. A. W. H. Meij, who prepared the cumulative index. Finally the participants of the International Course on European Integration, who used most of the material in mimeographed draft, are to be acknowledged for their valuable comments.

Cases and other materials have been included until July 1972.

August 1972   H. G. SCHERMERS Amsterdam
                                                         L. J. BRINKHORST Groningen

Chapter One

Actions against member States before the Court of Justice

LITERATURE: Gaudet, The European Communities, *The effectiveness of international decisions*, (Ed. Schwebel) Leiden 1971 *pp.309-329*; Eynard, l'Article 169 du traité de Rome, douze ans d'application de la procédure d'infraction à l'égard des Etats membres de la CEE, *Riv.dir.eur.1970, pp.99 et seq.*; Mertens de Wilmars and Verougstraete, Proceedings against member States for failure to fulfil their obligations, *7CMLRev.1970, pp.385-407*. Amphoux and Marechisini, Recours en constatation des manquements des Etats membres, *Les Novelles, Droit des Communautés Européennes*, Brussels 1969 *pp.367-377 and 379-389*.

I. GENERAL PROVISIONS

'The Commission devotes special attention to the performance by member States of their obligations. Article 169 of the EEC Treaty, together with judicial cooperation of the kind contemplated by Article 177 of the EEC Treaty... represents an important means of ensuring the effective and uniform application of Community law. The scope of these provisions, and of Article 141 of the Euratom Treaty and Article 88 of the ECSC Treaty, which are intended to achieve the same result, goes far beyond the scope of the rules hitherto accepted in traditional international law to ensure that States perform their obligations. So during the last few years, the effectiveness of these procedures has resulted in their acquiring an ever-growing importance, especially in the field of the EEC Treaty. ... Breaches of Community law may result either from a direct violation of the Treaties or from failure to respect the provisions (regulations, directives and decisions) adopted under the Treaties.

If the Commission considers that a member State has failed to perform its obligations under the Treaties, it begins by explaining its point of view to the State concerned and by giving it a chance to make comments. A large number of cases are settled during this first 'pre-judicial' stage.'[1]

II. IMPLEMENTATION

A. Supervision by member States

'....

Article 169 concerns actions against member States initiated by the Commission;

[1] Fourth General Report on the Activities of the Communities, Brussels-Luxembourg 1971, paras.553-554.

Article 170, actions initiated by other member States. No such proceedings have so far been brought. It seems that governments anyway prefer to have the Commission take the initiative in the proceedings; the said governments quite often inform the Commission about the failures they think important.

The procedure of Article 170 differs from the procedure of Article 169 although the finality of the procedure appears to be exactly the same in both cases. The plaintiff State cannot act immediately. Before instituting proceedings against another member State, it must first bring the matter before the Commission. The latter shall deliver a reasoned opinion after the States concerned have been given the opportunity both to submit their own cases and to reply to each other's case both orally and in writing. The compulsory character of this preliminary procedure of inquiries into the cases of both parties forms the main distinction between the procedure of Article 170 and that of Article 169. In the former type of procedure there are certain formal requirements which must be fulfilled with a view to assure the legality of the procedure.

These special features of the procedure also have a bearing on the scope of the reasoned opinion that there is a violation of the Treaty or that no such violation exists. The latter possibility has not been envisaged in an Article 169 procedure.

A third hypothesis, contemplated in Article 170, should also be considered here: if the Commission refuses to act and does not give any reasoned opinion within three months from the date on which the matter was brought before it, the absence of such opinion shall not preclude the plaintiff State from bringing the matter before the Court.'[1]

B. Supervision by Community organs

In reply to questions from the European Parliament, the European Commission has provided surveys of the state of application of Articles 169 EEC, 88 ECSC and 141 Euratom respectively until January 1, 1970.[2] Since the entry into force of the Treaty until 1 January 1970 the Commission has engaged the action of Article 169 EEC against member States in 214 Cases. During 1969 alone 46 such actions were commenced as compared with 20 and 18 in 1968 and 1967 respectively. A similar increase in the number of reasoned opinions issued can be observed: 5 in 1967; 12 in 1968 and 21 in 1969. The same is true for the number of proceedings begun in the Court of Justice: 0 in 1966 and 1967; 2 in 1968 and 11 in 1969.[3]

There exists a widespread variation in the time periods which elapse in the in-

---

[1]Mertens de Wilmars and Verougstraete, 7CMLRev. 1970, pp.392-393, Nos.12 and 13. [2]Questions No.310/69 (Vredeling), OJ 1969, No.C159/6 and No.501/69 (Vredeling), OJ 1970 No.C73/1. [3]According to Table 26 of the Fifth General Report on the Activities of the Communities, a total of 27 appeals were brought before the Court under Articles 169 and 93 until 31 December 1971, of which 2 in 1970 and 1 in 1971 (see also table 24 and table 29 of the Fourth General Report).

dividual cases. The Commission indicates in its answers to the above questions that the time-limits imposed may be extended, 'either to find solutions together with the governments, which are in accordance with the law of the Community, or because the compliance with Community law leads to legislative procedures which may encompass quite some time.'[1] The Commission will only engage an action before the Court when it has reached the conclusion that the fulfilment of the Treaty cannot be obtained by mutual consultation.

The periods of time during which cases are pending before the Court of Justice also differ considerably. According to the Commission the period varies between 6 and 36 months.

The total number of cases under the EEC Treaty until 1 January 1972 in which the Court has rendered judgment amounts to 19:

1961—case 7/61
1962—cases 10/61 and 2 and 3/62
1964—consolidated cases 90 and 91/63
1965—case 45/64—interlocutory judgment
1968—case 7/68
1969—cases 45/64—final judgment, 24/68, 6/69, 16/69
1970—cases 7/69, 26/69, 28/69, 31/69, 33/69, 38/69, 77/69, 8/70
1971—none

As far as the ECSC Treaty is concerned, the former High Authority did not make a systematic inventory of the procedures under Article 88 ECSC.

In total 4 judgments have been rendered under this provision:

1960—cases 3/59, 20/59, 25/59
1969—case 11/69

In 1971, for the first time, a case was rendered under Article 141 Euratom, case 7/71.

In the Rediscount Rate Case (6 and 11/69, see below pp.7, 29 and 165 the question was raised *inter alia* whether in support of its appeal under Article 88 ECSC a member State was entitled to invoke the illegality of the original decision addressed to the member State, the non-observance of which had formed the very reason for the action under Article 88 ECSC. The Court of Justice confirmed its previous holding in the Railway Tariffs Case (3/59. Jud.Rem.p.87) that a decision by the Commission under Article 88 ECSC is of a declaratory nature and cannot impose new obligations which did not exist before. The appeal against the original decision must be instituted within the time-limits prescribed by Article 33, para 3 ECSC.

[1]*OJ 1970, No. C73/2.*

1.Supervision under the ECSC Treaty

....

2.Supervision under the EEC Treaty

'Whenever it is said that a State 'fails to fulfil any of its obligations under this Treaty' the words 'obligations under this Treaty' do not refer exclusively to obligations proceeding from the Treaty itself but also to obligations following from secondary law— regulations, directives and decisions—issued by the Council or the Commission. Moreover the general principles of law implied by Community law should also be observed by the member States.

Such a failure may result from divergent opinions on the interpretation of Community law. Quite often the Court will have to decide whether there is a contradiction between a Treaty provision (or secondary law) and municipal law. The decisions of the Court will rest frequently on a certain interpretation of such provisions. In these cases, the question to be decided is largely similar to the question to be decided in preliminary rulings: experience teaches that, in the scope of a question for preliminary rulings, the national court often wants a solution of a conflict between municipal and Community law.

A second example of such failure stems from conflicts of legislative jurisdiction (*ratione materiae*) between municipal and Community autohrities. The Court's decision of 19 December 1969 (Commission of the EC *v.* French Republic, Rediscount Rate Case, see below, pp.7, 29 and 156) provides a good instance of this kind of failure. The Court had to define the limits of permissible Community intervention in monetary matters.

Finally such failure may result from an action or default of action by national administrations. In this case the Court's decision will not rest exclusively on considerations of pure legality.

Violation of obligations incumbent upon member States often does not result from the drafting of a particular national statute or regulation. Such obligations are, *inter alia*, the obligations resulting from Article 86 ECSC and Article 5 EEC by which, in similar terms, member States undertake that they will take all steps needed to discharge their obligations resulting from formal measures by the Community's institutions, that they will assist the Community to carry out its tasks and that they shall abstain from measures which could jeopardize the attainment of the objectives of the Treaty.'[1]

---

[1]Mertens de Wilmars and Verougstraete, 7 *CMLRev. 1970, pp.388-389, Nos.5 and 6.*

*a.*Author of violation

CASES

(1)WOOD CASE
Commission of the EC *v.* Belgium, Case 77/69, Judgement of 5 May 1970.
(Rec.XVI, p.244; 8 CMLRev.1971, pp.79-80).
Notes: Schermers, *AA 1970, pp.430-434;* Winter, *8 CMLRev.1971, pp. 80-81.*

Facts: Belgium levied a tax on imported wood, which, according to the Commission, violated Community law. The Belgian Government thereupon presented to the Belgian parliament a draft law which was intended to conform to the Treaty requirements. This draft law lapsed however when a new Parliament had to be elected on 2 March 1968.

On 28 November 1968, the Commission again started the procedure of Article 169, which caused the new government again to present a draft-law to Parliament. When this law had not been adopted by 30 June 1969, the Commission instituted proceedings before the Court on 22 December 1969. The Belgian government submitted that it had used its best efforts in order to obtain a change in the legislation. Under the circumstances it could, therefore, not be held responsible for the negligence of the Belgian Parliament. The question before the Court was, whether Article 169 is only intended to be used against *governments* which violated the Treaty or whether the action would also be possible in cases where the Treaty is alleged to have been violated by other independent institutions of the member State.

The Court held:

....

'The obligations under Article 95 of the Treaty incumbent upon the member States as such, and the responsibility of a member State under Article 169 subsist, whatever may be the government agency whose action or inaction is the cause of the failure, even if it involves an institution that is independent under the constitution. The plea raised by the defendant is therefore not sustained.
Under these conditions, the Kingdom of Belgium has failed in the obligations incumbent upon it under Article 95 of the Treaty.'[1]

....

Note: The Court confirmed this decision in Case 8/70 (Commission of the EC *v.* Italy, Rec.XVI (1970), p.967).

---

[1]Reproduced by permission from Common Market Reports, published by and copyright 1965, Commerce Clearing House, Inc., Chicago, Illinois.

The question has been raised whether the procedure of Article 169 EEC can also be used in other situations, e.g. when a municipal court has not observed its obligations under Article 177 EEC. In its replies to written questions from the European Parliament[1], the European Commission indicated that this could indeed be the case. When the *Conseil d'Etat* in a judgment of 1 March 1968 (Semoules Case, Jud.Rem. p.160) had applied a municipal act irrespective of any prior Community law obligations the Commission stated that it was of the opinion 'that Article 169 EEC is applicable whenever a court of a member State violates Article 177 of the (EEC) Treaty'.[2] When further questioned whether it had taken the necessary steps in the case cited pursuant to its obligation under Article 155 EEC to ensure that the Treaty provisions are observed[3], the Commission gave the following answer:

'As the Commission has observed... before, it is certainly not excluded to engage the procedure under Article 169 EEC in the cases mentioned... However, the Legal Commission of the Parliament[4] is of the opinion that the application of such a procedure would undoubtedly go against the independence of the judiciary vis-à-vis the executive. On these grounds the Commission's view is that the procedure referred to in Article 169 EEC ought not be engaged in all cases in which a decision of a municipal court violates the object of the law of the Community.'[5]

*b.*Precontentious proceedings

....

There is some disagreement on the nature and effect of the reasoned opinion.

This so-called opinion is obviously not one in the sense of Article 189 under which 'recommendations and opinions shall have no binding force'. Indeed the reasoned opinion has a binding force because it compels the State concerned to comply with a certain obligation and it specifies a time-limit to do so. On the other hand, the opinion has still another purpose: it may provide for measures to be taken by the member State in order to put an end to its failure, and it may indicate measures which could facilitate that task. According to Advocate-General Lagrange, the Commission has wide discretion in prescribing such measures as might alleviate the requirements which a complete respect of the relevant Treaty obligation might imply. These features lead to consider the reasoned opinion as the administrative stage of an enforcement procedure which, if not successful, will result in a trial.

[1]*Nos.101/67* (Westerterp), *OJ 1967, No.270/2 and 28/68* (Deringer), *OJ 1968, No.C71/1.* [2]*OJ 1968, No.C71/ 2.* [3]Written question *No.349/69* (Westerterp), *OJ 1970, No.C20/3.* [4]Report Merchiers concerning the questions relating to the application of art. 177 EEC. Documents Eur. Parl. 94/69, p.25. This report observed furthermore that the fault of a municipal Court does not engage *ipso facto* the international liability of the State in question. [5]*OJ 1970, No.C20/5.* Translation by the authors.

If, however, the State complies in due time, there will no longer be a failure and the procedure of Article 169 cannot be continued. In such case another problem arises, *viz.* whether the compliance has only effect for the future (*ex nunc*) or also for the past (*ex tunc*).

This question can be of extreme importance when the failure happened to consist of an infringement of provisions of Community law producing direct effects in the legal relations between the member States and their citizens.'[1]

....

CASE

(1) REDISCOUNT RATE CASE

Commission of the EC *v.* French Republic, Consolidated cases 6 and 11/69, Judgment of 10 December 1969.

(Rec.XV, pp.543, 544; CMLR 1970, p.67; 7 CMLRev.1970, p. 482; See also pp.29 and 156).

Notes: Brinkhorst and Verougstraete, *6 CMLRev.1970, pp.483-489;* Cahier, *CDE 1970, pp. 576-584,* Schermers, *AA 1970, pp.173-175;* VerLoren van Themaat, *SEW 1970, pp.650-658;* Knöpfe, *EuR 1970, pp.255-266.*

Facts: In this case the French Government disputed, *inter alia*, the legality of the reasoned opinion which the Commission had issued under Article 169. The question arose whether such an opinion could be annulled by the Court.

The Court held:

'This opinion constitutes only a pre-contentious phase of the proceedings which may eventually lead to an action before the Court of Justice and a consequent review of the well-foundedness of this opinion coincides with the well-foundedness of the appeal itself which the Commission has instituted before the Court of Justice pursuant to Article 169. Therefore the argument taken from the illegality of the reasoned opinion must be rejected. Consequently the maintenance after November 1, 1968, of a gap greater than 1.5 points between the preferential rediscount rate on exports to other member States and the ordinary rate constitutes a breach of the obligations under the decision 68/301/EEC of July 23, 1968.'[2]

[1] Mertens de Wilmars and Verougstraete, *7CMLRev. 1970, p. 391, No.10.* [2] Translation by CMLRev.

*c.*Discretion to invoke Article 169

CASES

(1)FIRST ART TREASURES CASE
Commission of the EC *v.* Italian Republic, Case 7/68, Judgment of 10 December 1968. (Rec.XIV, p.597, CMLR 1969, p.8).

Facts: The Commission instituted an action under Article 169 EEC requesting the Court of Justice to declare the Italian Government in violation of its obligations under Article 16 EEC by having imposed duties on the export of *inter alia* objects of artistic value and interest. The defendant questioned the admissibility at the appeal, since the Commission had instituted the proceedings before the Court only four days before the dissolution of the Italian Parliament, at a time when draft legislation for the repeal of the disputed measure was already pending.

The Court held:

....

'It is for the Commission, under Article 169 of the Treaty, to judge the moment at which it shall choose to bring an action before the Court, and the considerations which determine such choice may not affect the admissibility of the action, which follows only objective rules.
Besides, in the present case, the action of the Commission was preceded by a pro-longed exchange of views, begun before the expiry of the second stage of the tran-sitional period with the Italian Government, to bring the competent authorities of the Republic to do what was necessary to amend the provisions criticised by the Commission.
The action is therefore admissible.'[1]

....

(2)WOOL IMPORTS CASE
Commission of the EC *v.* Italian Republic, Case 7/69, Judgment of 10 March 1970. (Jur.XVI/2, pp.117-118; CMLR 1970, pp.108-109).
Notes: Winter, *7 CMLRev.1970, pp.489-492.*

Facts: In 1969 Italy had not yet introduced the system of value added tax. It levied a turnover tax on all sales of goods based on their total value. On imported wool a tax was levied to compensate the taxes on national wools when they were transferred between different stages of production.

[1]Translation by CMLR.

In practice, however, Italian wool was not transferred between stages of production since virtually all wool remained with the same owner during the entire process. The Commission considered that the compensatory taxes (which did not compensate anything) were protective taxes in violation of Article 95 of the EEC Treaty.

By letter of 12 July 1966 the Commission instituted proceedings under Article 169. The Italian government remedied the situation to a large extent, but not entirely.

On 16 July 1968 the Commission issued a reasoned opinion (as provided for by Article 169, para 1). The Italian government did not comply with the opinion. On 4 February 1969 the Commission brought the matter before the Court of Justice. On 2 July 1969 the Italian government issued a new law which in their view fully redressed the situation.

The Commission considered in the first place that the law of 2 July 1969 did not entirely terminate the violation. Both parties discussed in detail whether this submission was correct. The Commission furthermore considered that the Court should in any case declare that Italy was in violation of its obligations until 2 July 1969.

The Court held:

....

'(3)However, the parties have devoted since then the major part of their arguments to the effects and incidence of the tax system brought into operation by the said decree-law.

The Commission has not referred to any objective other than that of putting an effective end to the specific failure alleged against the Italian Government, so that its only aim is to bring to a close this alleged failure in so far as it exists.

(4)It follows from these circumstances that, although the parties still disagree about the effects of the aforementioned decree-law, they nevertheless consider that this measure substantially affects the outcome of the present dispute and they have requested the Court to consider the situation as a whole.

In so doing the applicant has as a result changed the subject-matter of its application so that it is no longer concerned only with the question whether at the time the application was filed, there was failure on the part of the Italian Republic to fulfil the obligations which bind it under Article 95, but mainly with the question whether this failure continued after the coming into force of the decree-law.

(5)In the present case, the Court could not possibly decide whether the situation created by decree-law No. 319 is compatible with the obligations which rest upon member-States under Article 95 of the Treaty.

Because of the importance given by the Treaty to the action for failure to fulfil an obligation, which is at the Commission's disposal, Article 169 has surrounded this procedure with guarantees which may be ignored all the less because of the obligation

imposed by Article 171, as a consequence of this action, on member-States to take all
necessary measures for the execution of the judgment of the Court.

The Court cannot therefore give any decision in this case as to whether there has been
any failure to fulfil an obligation subsequent to changes brought about by legislative
action in the course of the proceedings, without infringing the rights of the member-
State to submit its defence pleas on the basis of a written statement of the grounds of
complaint within the framework of the procedure laid down in Article 169.

(6) In these circumstances, it is for the Commission to set in motion again, as regards
the effects of decree-law No.139, the procedure provided for in Article 169, and
possibly to refer to the Court the precise failure to fulfil an obligation which it wants
condemned.

In view of the change in the subject-matter of this dispute, the request as originally
set out in the application should be dismissed.'[1]

....

(3) OLIVE OIL CASE

Commission of the EC *v.* French Republic, Case 26/69, Judgment of 9 July 1970.
(Jur.XVI/6, p.577; Rec.XVI, p.576; CMLR 1970, p.458).

Facts: According to Council Regulation No.136/66 of 22 September 1966 concerning
the establishment of a common market organisation for oils and fats, levies are imposed on the importation of olive oil from third countries. By publication in the
Journal Officiel of 3 December 1966 the French government declared these levies to
be inapplicable in the case of imports of a certain quota of olive oil originating in and
deriving from Tunisia.

As Tunisia had belonged to the French customs territory there had never been such
levies on Tunisian olive oil. The French announcement was subsequently extended a
number of times in the following years.

The Commission was of the opinion that the French measures were contrary to the
said regulation and instituted an action under Article 169, leading to the institution
of proceedings in the Court on 14 June 1969. Pending the appeal before the Court the
association convention between the EEC and Tunisia entered into force on 1 September 1969. Pursuant to this convention Regulation No.1471/69 was enacted which replaced the existing system concerning imports of olive oil from Tunisia by a new
regime.

The Court inquired *ex officio* whether that new situation affected in any way the
admissibility of the appeal.

[1]Translation by CMLR.

The Court held:

I.As to the interest of the action

....

'(3)It therefore appears that the Commission's application was lodged at a time when the failure alleged against the respondent had virtually lapsed as a result of the substitution of the system laid down in Article 5 of Annex I of the association agreement for the import system in force in the French Republic.

Now in these conditions and not being able to assess the Commission's motives in making this application under Article 169, the Court has to consider whether this action still has a sufficiently subsisting subject-matter.'[1]

After a summary review of the merits the Court decided that the application should be dismissed.

(4)EXPORT REBATES CASE

Commission of the EC *v*. Italian Republic, Case 31/69, Judgment of February 17, 1970.

(Jur.XVI, p.34; AA1970, pp.430-434; CMLR 1970, p.188; 8 CMLRev.1971, pp.74-76).

Notes: Schermers, *AA 1970*, pp.433-434.

Facts: Many Common Market organisations for agricultural products require the payment of a rebate in case of export to third countries. For nearly a year the Italian government did not pay any such rebates to Italian exporters. The Commission, considering this a breach of Italy's obligations initiated the procedure of Article 169. During the oral proceedings the Italian Government added the submission that Article 169 could not be applied where the failure of a member State consists in the non-implementation of directly applicable rules of Community Law. In such cases interested parties should invoke these rules directly before the municipal courts.

The Court held:

....

'Although this point was argued only at a late stage in the proceedings, it concerns the jurisdiction of this Court, which should examine it of its own motion.

An abstention to act, just as much as a positive action, is capable of constituting, on the part of a member State, the non-fulfilment of a duty by which it is bound. Moreover the existence or non-existence of remedies before national courts can have no influence whatever on the exercise of the remedy provided in Article 169, the two remedies having different objects and different effects.'[1]

[1]Translation by CMLR.

....

There is a fundamental difference between the action of Article 169, which is the application of the international law principle of responsibility of a State for violation of its obligations to Community law and the action on the basis of a Treaty provision which has direct effect. The Court of Justice confirmed this in a holding in the case 28/67, Molkereizentrale, when it said:

'For an action instituted by a private person is aimed at the maintenance of individual claims in a particular case, while the purpose of the intervention of the Community authorities is to favour the general and uniform observance of the rule of Community law;

For this reason individual legal guarantees, which private persons can draw from the Treaty, and the powers conferred upon the Community organs in order to enforce fulfilment of the obligations undertaken by the member States, differ in object, purpose and consequences and cannot be compared with each other.'

*D.*Non-Compliance with previous judgement

CASE

(1)SECOND ART TREASURES CASE
Commission of the EC *v.* Italian Republic, Case 48/71, Judgment of 13 July 1972. (not yet published)

Facts: In the First Art Treasures Case (see above, p.8) the Court of Justice had held that Italy had failed to fulfil its obligations under Article 16 of the EEC Treaty by continuing after 1 January 1962 to impose a tax on the exportation of art treasures to other member States of the Community pursuant to an Italian law of 1 June 1939. When, more than two years later, the Italian law had still not been repealed and continued to be enforced by the Italian customs authorities, the Commission on 23 July 1971 lodged a new appeal against Italy before the Court of Justice for failure to fulfil its obligations. This time a violation of Article 171 EEC was argued, which requires member States 'to take the necessary measures to comply with the judgment of the Court of Justice'.

The Italian Government objected that the tax could only be withdrawn by law and that it had introduced a draft-law for the repeal of the 1939 law; however, the Italian parliament had not yet had occasion to approve it because of its early dissolution on 28 February 1972.

In the meantime the non-applicability of the Italian tax had been invoked by a private party before a municipal court. Upon a request for a preliminary ruling by the president of the Tribunal of Turin the Court of Justice had held that Article 16 EEC had direct effect in the relations between member States and their subjects since 1 January 1962 and created rights in favour of private persons, which municipal courts must safeguard. (Eunomia Case, see below, p.43).

After the conclusions of the advocate-general and just before the judgment was to be rendered, the Italian Government on 4 July 1972 informed the Court of Justice that it had formally repealed the tax (by a decree!) with retroactive effect as of 1 January 1962.

The Court held:

....

'5.As the case concerns a directly applicable Community rule, the argument that the violation could be terminated only by the adoption of constitutionally appropriate measures which would repeal the provision onder which the tax had been instituted, would amount to the assertion that the application of a common rule is subject to the law of each member State and, more specifically, that this application would be impossible as long as a municipal law would be in conflict with it.

6.In the present case, the effect of Community law which had been determined by a final court decision with regard to the Italian republic, implied for the competent national authorities the legal prohibition to apply a municipal provision which was recognised to be incompatible with the Treaty, and, equally, the obligation to take all measures in order to enable Community law to obtain its full effect.

7.The realisation of the objectives of the Community requires that the rules of Community law, under the Treaty itself or by virtue of procedures established by it, apply as of right at the same time and with identical effect on the whole territory of the Community without the member States being able to oppose any kind of obstacles.

8.The member States' attribution of rights and powers to the Community in accordance with the provisions of the Treaty entails a definitive limitation of their sovereign rights against which no provisions of municipal law, whatever their nature, can be legally invoked.

9.It must therefore be found that the Italian Republic has failed to fulfil its obligations under Article 171 of the Treaty by not abiding by the judgment of the Court of 10 December 1968 in the Case 7/68.

10.By communication of 4 July 1972 defendant has informed the Court that the imposition of the tax has been discontinued and that its effects have been cancelled as of 1 January 1962, the date on which the levy had to be abandoned.

....

The Court

1. notes: that the failure to fulfil its obligations under Article 171 EEC has been brought to an end by the Italian Republic with effect as of 1 January 1962,
2. holds: defendant is condemned to pay the costs.

3.Sanctions

Judgments of the Court of Justice given under Article 169 EEC are of a declaratory nature. Article 171 requires the member State concerned to take the necessary measures for their implementation. These measures may vary from the repeal of existing legislation in violation of Community law to the introduction of new laws to bring the municipal legislation in line with Community rules.

The question also arises whether, to what extent and under which circumstances private parties—having suffered damages from the failure of the State to fulfil its obligations—may institute an action before a municipal court invoking the judgment of the Court of Justice in support. Obviously the possibility of obtaining damages through a national judiciary can constitute an important sanction against Treaty violations by a State.

The answer depends on the national provisions concerning judicial protection and the legal ranking of decisions of international organisations in municipal law.

Art.67, para 2 of the Netherlands Constitution confers, e.g., explicit preeminence to decisions of international organisations over conflicting rules of municipal law. It is generally acknowledged that these include decisions by judicial organs.

CASES

(1) BELGIAN FROMAGERIE LE SKI CASE (FIRST INSTANCE)
Etablissements Détry *v.* Belgium, Minister of Economic affairs, *Tribunal de Bruxelles*, Decision of 6 February 1967.
(Unpublished. Excerpts of the most important parts are printed in Eversen & Sperl, Répertoire de la Jurisprudence de la Cour de Justice 1967, Nos.2718-2722, 2782-2783, 2872, 2876-2877, 2893; RTDE 1969, p.705; EuR 1970, pp.62, 63, see also 8 CMLRev.1971, pp.92 *et seq.*).
Notes: Schrans, *RW 1968-1969, col.537-538; id. SEW 1970, pp.518-528; id. 8 CMLRev.1971, pp.92-97.*

Facts: Bij Royal Decree of 3 November 1958, the granting of import licences for certain dairy products (which included cream cheese) was made dependent upon payment of certain duties to the State.

In an action by the Commission under Article 169 EEC concerning the conformity of this decree with Community law, the Court of Justice found Belgium guilty of a violation of Article 12 EEC (see Dairy Products Case, November 13, 1964, Jud.Rem. pp.12-14).

Thereupon the firm of Détry (later: Fromagerie Franco Suisse 'Le Ski'), traders in dairy products, brought an action before the Civil Tribunal of Brussels, claiming restitution from the Belgian state of Bfrs. 60 million for duties paid pursuant to the Belgian decree. The Plaintiff's claim was dismissed on the following ground of Community law (the grounds of municipal law will not be discussed here):

The Tribunal held:

....

'Considering that by establishing the duty which is the subject of litigation the Royal Decree of November 3, 1958 failed to fulfil the obligations undertaken by Belgium under Article 12 of the Treaty of March 25, 1957;

and that the Belgian government thus brought about the action which it lost on November 13, 1964;

that since the Court's judgement on that date the Belgian legislature had neither been able to maintain nor re-establish the duties on import licences...;

Considering that only since the Court gave its judgement has Belgium failed in its obligations under Article 12 of the Treaty and that persons with an interest could personally bring an action against the subsequent demand for the illegal duties;

that the appellant was not, in this particular case, entitled to exercise an individual right to have the effects of the domestic law prior to November 13, 1964 (date of the Court's judgement) declared non-applicable to him;

that the claim by the appellant for restitution of the duties paid during that period (i.e. the period prior to the judgement) was not well-founded in so far as it was for reimbursement of an alleged amount which was not owed.'[1]

(2) BELGIAN FROMAGERIE LE SKI CASE (SECOND INSTANCE)

S.A. Fromagerie Franco-Suisse 'Le Ski' *v.* Belgium, Ministry of Economic Affairs, *Cour d'Appel de Bruxelles* (Court of Appeal) (*2nd ch*), Decision of 4 March 1970.

(JT 1970, pp.413-415; RTDE 1970, pp.369-373; CMLR 1970, pp.222, 224, 225).

Notes: Goffin and Burlion, JT 1970, pp.347-348; Schrans 8 CMLRev. 1971, pp.95-97; SEW 1971, pp. 518-525.

Facts: After the Dairy-Products Case (see Jud.Rem.pp.12-14) the Royal Decree of 3 November 1958 had been withdrawn. Belgian legislation requires parliamentary approval of decrees of the executive concerning import duties, even if they have been subsequently withdrawn.

After the plaintiff had appealed, the contentious Royal Decree of 1968 was ratified, as from the date of its coming into force, by an Act of Parliament of 19 March 1968.[2]

[1]Translation by Europa Instituut. [2]*Mon. Belge 21 March 1968.*

The Act stipulated that amounts paid in application of the 1958 Decree were definite, irrecoverable and could not give rise to any dispute before any national authority whatsoever.

In addition to its task of reviewing the decision of the Tribunal, the Court of Appeal was also bound to examine the impact of this Act—and in particular the clause above—on the dispute before it. After stating that Article 12 EEC has direct effect and creates rights for citizens of the member States which municipal courts must safeguard.

The Cour d'Appel held:

....

'The procedure for a declaration of failure to fulfil obligations is one initiated by the Commission against a member State under Articles 169 and 171 of the Treaty. It does not require the violated provision to be 'self-executing' (*i.e.* directly applicable). It does not concern the rights of individuals which citizens may elicit from a 'self executing' provision and enforce before internal courts. The State's argument fails to take into account that the aforesaid Article 12 has such a character.

The law of 19 March 1968 validated indiscriminately all levies of special duties established by the *arrêtés royaux*, which it is ratifying for the period in which they were applied. It is incompatible with Article 12 of the Treaty in so far as the latter forbade the introduction of such duties.

States have the duty of ensuring that a norm of internal law which is incompatible with a norm of international treaty law which embodies undertakings which they have made, may not validly be set up against the latter.

This obligation should have as corollary the superiority of the treaty norm over the internal norm.

The superiority of international law applies both for reasons of social morality and because the superiority of internal law would be to condemn international law, since it would embody a constant menace weighing upon the general character of the latter, through the impossibility for the rules of international law to attain and maintain that character.

The respondent in vain retreats behind the requirement of the Law of 19 March 1968 which, it says, is categorical when it decrees that the payments are due and shall be retained by the Treasury.

This statutory text certainly does not express the wish to impose its provisions in despite of the contrary provisions, directly applicable of the EEC Treaty.

In the absence of any constitutional—as is the case here—or legislative provision requiring expressly the courts to apply in any case, even in case of conflict, a Law subsequent in time to a treaty which had been approved and published and was still in force, it is not for the courts to create such an obligation.

An implied determination to compel the application of the internal law conflicting with obligations under an international treaty could not be accepted unless it was absolutely clear.

Such a determination does not appear *ipso facto* from the fact that the Law under consideration here forbids any dispute with regard to the sums levied. The text of the Law does not say that the prohibition also applies where it would run counter to the EEC Treaty.

. . . .

Contrary to the objection of the respondent, the appellant's claim does not lead to a declaration that a Law is null and void but to a finding that its effects are stopped in so far as it is in conflict with a directly applicable provision of international treaty law.'

. . . .

The Court, for these reasons, hereby decides:
'The appellant is in principle justified in claiming repayment of the special duties which it paid under the *Arrêté Royal* of 3 November 1958 and the subsequent *arrêtés royaux*, on the importation of milk products from member States of the European Economic Community.'[1]

Note: The *Cour d'Appel* came to the conclusion that the plaintiff should in principle be regarded as having a right to obtain reimbursement of the charges it had previously paid. It reserved a final decision on the merits until after the parties had had an opportunity to present further evidence as to the amounts actually paid.

The Belgian State subsequently appealed *en cassation* to the *Cour de Cassation*, which on 27 May 1971 in line with the conclusions of its Procureur-Général Ganshof van de Meersch refused to review the judgment of the Cour d'Appel. See for the opinion of the *Cour de Cassation*, below p.57-58.

[1]Translation by CMLR, footnotes omitted.

Chapter Two

Actions against Community institutions before the Court of Justice: Administrative Jurisdiction

I. CONTROL OF THE LEGALITY OF COMMUNITY ACTS

LITERATURE: Lauwaars, Lawfulness and Legal Force of Community Decisions, 1973, 450 pp., thesis. (Rechtmatigheid en rechtskracht van gemeenschapsbesluiten) Leiden, 1970, 363 pp.; Bebr, La Cour de Justice, Recours en annulation et en carence, *Les Novelles*, Droit des Communautés Européennes, Brussels, 1969, *pp.309-331; Empfehlt es sich, die Bestimmungen des Europäischen Gemeinschaftsrechts über den Rechtsschutz zu ändern und zu ergänzen?*, Deutscher Juristentag 1967, München und Berlin, 1967, 167 pp.

A. Appeals for annulment

1.Acts, susceptible of appeal

LITERATURE: Van Empel, L'acte public inexistant et le droit Communautaire, *CDE, 1971, pp. 251-284; idem*, Vernietiging en nietigheid van onrechtmatig overheidshandelen in de Europese Gemeenschappen, *R.M.Themis, 1971, pp.389-416;* Morand, Les recommandations, les résolutions et les avis du droit communautaire, *CDE 1970, pp.623-644.*

*a.*Acts considered as binding and therefore susceptible of appeal.

CASE

(1)ERTA CASE
Commission of the EEG *v.* Council of the EEC, Case 22/70, Jugdment of 31 March 1971.
(Jur.XVII (1971), *pp.263-296*; CMLR, 1971, *pp.357-362*; EuR 1971, *pp.242-249*; 8 *CMLRev., pp.* 392-401; see also *pp.550-556*).
Notes: von Arnim, *AWD 1972,pp.215-222;* Schermers, *AA 1972, pp.108-110*; Brinkhorst, *SEW 1971, pp.479-484, RMC 1971, pp.211;* Louis, *CDE 1971, pp.479-490;* Sasse, *EuR 1971, pp.208-241;* Waelbroeck, *Integration 1971,pp.81-89;* Winter, 8 *CMLRev.1971,pp.550-556*; Constantinesco,RTDE 1971, *pp.796-809*; Collinson, Stanf. Law Rev. 1971, *pp.956-972*; Kovar, AFDI 1971, *pp.386-418*; Raux, RGDIP 1972, *pp.36-68*; Werbke, NJW 1971, *pp.2103-2109*; Ganshof van de Meersch, CDE 1972, *pp.127-159.*

Facts: In the present case the Commission appealed against deliberations by the Council of 20 March 1970, according to which the Member-States would take a particular common position in the negotiations on a new European Agreement concerning the work of crews of vehicles engaged in International Road Transport (the European Road Transport Agreement (ERTA) of 1 July 1970).

The Council objected that its deliberations of 20 March 1970 did not amount to a measure in the sense of Art.173, against which an appeal would be possible. In its submission, the acts concerned were not open to review as they formed not a regulation, directive or decision in the sense of Article 189. Only political consultations had taken place.

The Court held:

....

'39.Since the only matters excluded from the ambit of the appeal for annulment open to the Member States and the institutions are 'recommendations or opinions'—which by the final paragraph of Art.189 are declared to have no binding force—Article 173 treats as acts open to judicial review all measures taken by the institutions designed to have legal effect;

40.This review tends to ensure, as required by Article 164, observance of the law in the interpretation and application of the Treaty;

41.It would be inconsistent with this aim to interpret the conditions in which the application is admissible so restrictively as to limit the availability of this procedure merely to the categories of acts envisaged by Article 189.

42.The procedure must be available in the case of all measures taken by institutions, whatever their nature or form, designed to produce legal effects.

....

55.Hence, the discussion on 20 March 1970, had definite legal effects both in the relations between the Community and the Member States, and in the relationship between institutions.

....

97.The Commission submits furthermore that the act in question lacks any reference to its legal grounds and any reasoning.

98.The requirements made by Article 190 for regulations, directives and decisions do not also apply for acts of a special character such as the act of 20 March ,1970.

99.Since it participates in the activities of the Council, the Commission receives the legal protection which Article 190 provides for third parties affected by the acts mentioned in the Article.'[1]

*b.*One appeal against several decisions

...

---

[1]Translation by CMLR.

*c.*Appeal against parts of a decision

. . . .

2.Capacity to lodge an appeal

*a.*Appeals by member States and Community institutions

For the first time, in 1970, an appeal was instituted by a Community institution against the act of another. In the ERTA-case (Case 22/70, see above p.18) the Commission asked the Court to annul the deliberations of the Council of Ministers.

*b.*Appeals by private parties

> LITERATURE: Mertens de Wilmars, Het onderscheid tussen beschikking en reglement in het legaliteitscontentieux van de EEG, *Tijdschr. Bestuurswetenschappen en Publiekrecht* 1970, pp. 440-449.

   (i)ECSC

. . .

   (ii)EEC

a.Admissibility of appeals against decisions

CASES

   (i)ALCAN CASE
Alcan Aluminium Raeren and others *v.* Commission of the EC, Case 69/69, Judgment of 16 June 1970.
(Jur. XVI (1970), pp.393-395; CMLR 1970, pp.345-346).

Facts: The appeal was lodged by several aluminium refining companies against a refusal by the Commission to grant a request (based on Protocol XII of 2 March 1960) of the Belgian and Luxembourg Governments for additional national tariff quotas of aluminium. This Protocol provided for the possibility of reduced duty quotas to be granted by the Commission for unwrought aluminium imported into certain member States of the Community, and was modified as a result of the Kennedy Round negotiations of 1967. The Commission contested the admissibility of the appeal on the grounds that the companies were not directly and individually concerned in the sense of Article 173, para 2, EEC.

The Court held:

. . . .

'(2)The aim of this provision is to ensure the judicial protection of individuals in all cases where they are directly and individually concerned by a Community act, which is not directed to them, in whatever form it appears.

Under these conditions, it is necessary to examine whether the decision of 12 May 1969, which is the subject-matter of the present case, concerns the applicants directly and individually, although it was addressed to Belgium and Luxembourg.

(3)It should be noted that the challenged decision was taken under powers conferred on the Commission by Protocol XII on onwrought aluminium, attached to the Agreement of 2 March 1960 on compilation of the part of the Common External Tariff relating to products on 'List G.'. Under this protocol and subject to the conditions therein prescribed, 'the Commission may authorize on their request... Benelux countries to open annual tariff quotas subject to a duty of 5 per cent. to cover the import needs of their refining industries'.

It follows that the decision made by the Commission, in pursuance of the provision quoted above, has no effect other than to create a power in favour of the member States concerned, and does not confer any rights on possible beneficiaries of any measures which the said States might later take under the said decision. Consequently it appears that the award, under Protocol XII, of a tariff quota carrying a reduced rate of duty in favour of Belgium and Luxembourg, could not have effects directly concerning undertakings which might benefit from this award.

(4)However, the applicants have submitted that the decision under attack was a negative decision and not one granting an authorisation and that, as such, it directly concerned them by depriving them of any possibility of enjoying a reduced rate of duty under a tariff quota.

Furthermore, it was argued that, as the decision had been taken after expiry of the period of time covered by it, the identity of importers who might have benefited from the said quota, was definitively established, so that the decision rejecting the said request individually concerned the importers in question.

(5)Nevertheless, the annulment of the decision of 12 May 1969 cannot confer on the applicants the benefits they seek, as such benefits can only result from the opening of tariff quotas by the national authorities, after the member State concerned has obtained the relevant authorisation from the Commission.

It appears therefore that the application aims in fact at bringing the Commission to take a measure, the effects of which, under Protocol XII, can only affect member States. Consequently, the decision rejecting the request does not concern the applicants in any different manner than would the positive decision, which they wished to obtain.

It follows that the application should be dismissed as inadmissible, the applicants not having established that they were concerned within the meaning of Article 173 (2).'¹

....

(2) APPLES CASE

N.V. International Fruit Company and others *v.* Commission of the European Communities, Consolidated Cases 41-44/70, Judgment of 13 May 1971.
(Jur.XVII (1971), pp.420-423).

Facts: In the framework of the Common Market organization for fruit and vegetables, the Commission enacted Regulation No. 459/70² which introduced a system of import licences, obtainable from national authorities in order to restrict imports of dessert apples from third countries into the Community for the period of 1 April 1970 to 30 June 1970 inclusive. Each week the national authorities had to total all demands and inform the Commission of the amount of apples for which import licences were requested. On the basis of this data the Commission then decided the precise percentage the national authorities could grant the requests.

By Commission Regulation No. 565/70 of 25 March 1970, it was decided that requests for import licences filed before 20 March 1970 could be granted up to 80 per cent of a certain reference quantity. In the following months this system was repeated in a number of further regulations. Regulation No.983/70 of 28 May 1970, applied to import licences filed before 22 May 1970.

The plaintiffs appealed against the refusal by the Dutch authorities (the *Produktschap voor Groenten en Fruit,* hereafter called P.G.F.) to grant import licences for which they had filed requests on 19 May 1970. The Commission submitted that the appeal was inadmissible as it had not addressed any decision to the plaintiffs, but that the refusal was issued by the *P.G.F.* and was therefore a national administrative act. Moreover no appeal was possible against measures with a general effect such as Regulation No.983/70.

By decision of 19 October 1970, the Court joined the plea of inadmissibility to the merits.

The Court held:

'The applicants seek annulment of a decision issued by the Commission pursuant to Article 2 (2) of Regulation Nos.459/70 dated 11th March 1970 (JO 1970, No.L 57), whereby the Commission refused to grant them licences for the import of dessert apples from non-Member countries, and which was notified to them through the agency of the 'Produktschap voor Groenten en Fruit' at The Hague.'

¹Translation by CMLR. ²*OJ 1970-L57.*

As to the admissibility

. . . .

'16.It is obvious that Regulation No.983/70 was adopted with one eye on the state of the market, and the other on the quantities of dessert apples for which import licences had been applied for in the week ended 22nd May 1970.

17.It follows that at the moment of adoption of the said Regulation the number of applications which could be affected by it was fixed.

18.No new application could be added.

19.To what extent, in percentage terms, the applications could be granted, depended on the total quantity for which applications had been submitted.

20.Accordingly the Commission, by deciding that the system introduced by Article 1 of Regulation No.565/70 should be maintained in the relevant period, decided to grant every application submitted, albeit by merely taking note of the quantities requested.

21.Consequently, Article 1 of Regulation No.983/70 is not a provision of general application within the meaning of the second paragraph of Article 189 of the Treaty, but must be regarded as a bundle of individual decisions taken by the Commission under Article 2 (2) of Regulation No.459/70, each of which, although taken in the form of a Regulation, affects the legal position of one of the applicants.

22.Thus, the decisions are of individual concern to the applicants.

23.Moreover, it is clear from the system introduced by Regulation No.459/70—and particularly from Article 2 (2) of this Regulation—that the decision on the grant of import licences was a matter for the Commission.

24.According to this provision, the Commission alone is competent to appraise the economic situation in the light of which the grant of import licences must be justified.

25.Article 1 (2) of Regulation No.459/70, providing that 'the Member States shall, in accordance with the conditions prescribed by Article 2, issue licences to each interested party who submits an application therefore', makes it clear that the national authorities do not enjoy any discretion in the matter of the grant of licences and the conditions on which applications by interested parties should be granted.

26.The duty of such authorities is merely to collect the data necessary to put the Commission in a position to reach a decision in accordance with Article 2 (2) of this Regulation, and subsequently to adopt the national measures needed to give effect to that decision.'[1]

(3) CHINESE MUSHROOM CASE

Werner A.Bock *v.* Commission of the EC, Case 62/70, Judgment of 23 November 1971. (Jur.XVII (1971), pp.907-910; CMLR 1972, pp.170, 171).

[1]Translation by Court of Justice.

Facts: In 1970, the German Federal Republic, for various reasons, prohibited imports of mushrooms into its territory from the People's Republic of China.

This prohibition was easy to enforce when the German importer intended to import direct from China or a non-member country into Germany.

On the other hand, the problem was much more complex when the importer wanted to buy Chinese mushrooms put into free circulation in one of the countries of the Community.

In fact, since the adoption of Regulation 865/68 of 28 June 1968, the German authorities had been obliged normally to issue the permit requested automatically and within a very short period because the goods were in free circulation in a member-State. They could only refuse the permit if they had already received from the Commission the authorisation mentioned in Article 115 (1) of the Treaty—an authorisation which in exceptional cases, and particularly in a case of deflection of trade, permits a member-State to exclude from Community treatment certain products originating in non-member countries but already in free circulation in one or more of the other member-States.

However, such authorisation in respect of mushrooms from China was not requested by Germany until 11 September 1970 and was not granted by the Commission until 15 September.

On 4 September 1970 the firm Werner A.Bock applied for an import permit for a consignment of Chinese mushrooms with a value of DM 150.000 for which it had a firm offer and which according to its declaration, was in free circulation in Holland.

On 9 September 1970 it reminded the appropriate German authority, the Federal Office for Food and Forestry, of this application.

Finally, on 11 September it repeated its request by telex. This telex launched a brisk activity on the part of the German authorities. In fact, on the same day:

(1)the German delegation at Brussels, alerted by the German Ministry of Agriculture, informed the Commission by telex that the German authorities had received an application for an import permit for a consignment of Chinese mushrooms to a value of DM 150.000 and that the German Government was asking the Commission urgently to authorise Germany to exclude from Community treatment such imports 'including the import envisaged' in the application mentioned above;

(2)the German authority informed Messrs. Bock that it had decided to reject their application for a permit as soon as 'the Commission has given its authorisation under Article 115 of the Treaty'.

Messrs.Bock took further measures which remained unsuccessful.

On 15 September the Commission adopted the decision requested authorising Germany to exclude from Community treatment mushrooms originating in China in free circulation in the Benelux States. This decision included a sentence which concerned applications for permits 'at present and duly pending before the German authorities'.

On 12 November 1970 Bock lodged an appeal against this Decision.

The Commission claimed that the appeal was inadmissible as it was not of direct and individual concern to the plaintiff.

The Court held:

....

'In the present case it suffices to state that the German Government, which had justified its initiative by referring to an application submitted to it at the time, was able to assume that the provision in issue was intended to cover precisely applications that had already been submitted. The Commission was, on 15 September 1970, the date when the challenged decision was adopted, aware that the authorisation was to extend, according to the wishes of the German Government, to applications for permits which were already pending before the German authorities before 11 September 1970, the date on which the German Government had addressed its request to the Commission. Therefore if the Commission intended to exclude these applications from the protective measure it should have expressed this clearly, instead of using the words 'this decision also covers...' with which it implicitly extended the scope of application of Article 1 (1) of the decision.

Accordingly, since the second sentence of this Article must be so interpreted that it covers the applicant firm's case, the firm is affected by the provision which it seeks to have annulled.

2.The Commission contends that the applicant firm is not in any event directly concerned by an authorisation granted to Germany as Germany had been free to refrain from using it.

The appropriate German authorities had nevertheless already informed the applicant firm that they would reject its application as soon as the Commission had granted them an appropriate authorisation. They had requested the authorisation with precisely the applications already before them at that time in view.

It follows from this that the applicant firm was directly concerned.

3.The Commission further maintains that the decision in issue did not concern the applicant firm individually, but referred in an abstract manner to all market participants who intended to import the goods in question into Germany during the period of validity of the decision.

However, the applicant firm has merely challenged the decision to the extent that it covers imports for which applications for import permits were already pending at the date of its entry into force. Nevertheless, the number and persons of the importers affected to this extent were already ascertainable before this date. The Commission knew 'that the provision of the decision in issue would only affect the interests and the legal position of these importers. In these circumstances these importers were, compared with all other persons, just as individualised as the addressee.'[1]

....

The Court, declaring the appeal admissible and well founded, annulled the Decision in as far as it concerned products for which requests for licences were pending on the date the Decision was made.

β. Admissibility of appeals against regulations

CASES

(1)ZUCKERFABRIK WATENSTEDT CASE

Zuckerfabrik Watenstedt GmbH *v.* Council of the EC, Case 6/68, Judgment of 11 July 1968.

(Jur.XVI (1968), pp.569-588; Rec.XIV (1968), pp.595-615; Samml. XIV (1968), pp.611-631; CMLR 1969, p.37).

Facts: The *Zuckerfabrik* lodged an appeal against Regulation No.1009/67/EEC of the Council of the European Communities. The Council invoked the exception of inadmissibility as the *Zuckerfabrik* was not competent to appeal against regulations. The *Zuckerfabrik* replied that the category of sugar producers to which it belonged was so clearly defined that it would be possible to individualize the persons affected. It contended furthermore that it was affected differently from than others owing to particular circumstances.

The Court held:

....

'The measure in issue, therefore, determines the pattern of prices for a product and, in consequence, the rights and obligations of buyers and sellers of the product, including its producers. Such a measure is of general application within the meaning of Article 189 of the Treaty because it applies to objectively determined situations, and has legal effects on classes of persons defined in a general and abstract manner. It applies to the applicant only by virtue of the applicant's capacity as a seller of raw beet sugar, without any further specification. Furthermore, a provision like Article 9 (3) of the regulation, which revokes or sets a time limit to a provision of general application, has the same general character as the provision which it qualifies.

Nor is the regulatory character of a measure lost because it is possible to determine

---

[1]Translation by CMLR.

with more or les precision the number or even the identity of the persons to which it applies at a given moment, provided that the measure clearly applies by virtue of an objective factual or legal situation defined by the measure itself.

The respondent has not contravened those requirements by regulating the price system for one product in a different way from that of other products. If one were to refuse to characterise a system of price control as a regulation, for the sole reason that it concerns a particular product and affects its producers by reason of a situation which distinguishes them from all other persons, the concept of a decision would be enlarged to such an extent as to endanger the system of the Treaty, which permits individual persons to apply for an annulment only of specific decisions directed to them or measures which affect them in an analogous manner.

The application must therefore be dismissed as inadmissible.'[1]

(2)Compagnie Française Case

La Compagnie Française Commerciale et Financière, S.A. *v.* Commission of the European Communities, Case 64/69, Judgment of 16 April 1970.

(Jur.XVI (1970), pp.221-228; Rec.XVI (1970), pp.221-228; Samml., pp. 221-228).

Notes: Lauwaars, *SEW 1970, pp.658-668.*

Facts: On 11 August 1969, The French Franc was devalued. The Council of the European Communities decided on the same day not to change the Unit of Account of the European Communities but to allow France to take temporary measures to cope with the sudden rise in prices of agricultural products expressed in French Francs, as the prices of such products are expressed, officially, in Units of Account. France was permitted to lower the intervention price (so that it would come to the same amount in French Francs as before the devaluation), to subsidize imports and to impose a levy on exports (thus compensating the decrease in the existing French prices when expressed in Units of Account). The Commission was authorized by the same Regulation to take further measures.

On 22 August 1969, the Commission issued Regulation 1660/69.[2] Article 2 of this regulation made provisions for contracts concluded before 1 August and expressed in French Francs. For these contracts the levy on exports to third States would be diminished, except with respect to exporters who could have made use of the opportunity of previous establishment of export restitutions and had not done so.[3]

---

[1]Translation by CMLR. [2]*OJ 1969, no. L213/1.* [3]According to the agricultural policy of the EEC export restitutions are granted for most agricultural products in order to compensate the difference between the high EEC price level and the lower level of world market. The amount of the restitution depends on world market prices. In some cases exporters have a choice of having this amount fixed before or after finishing their contract.

The *Compagnie Française*, one of the exporters affected by this exception, lodged an appeal against the Articles 2 and 3 of Regulation 1660/69. The Commission submitted a preliminary objection of non-admissibility to which the Compagnie Française replied that the attacked provision was of concern only to the group of exporters who had concluded export contracts in French Francs and who had not made use of the opportunity of previous establishment of the normal export restitutions. It was possible to determine the number and identity of these exporters before the date on which the contested regulation was adopted. The Compagnie Française considered itself directly and individually concerned.

The Commission denied that the situation was parallel to the Toepfer Case, since in the latter case a small and actual known group of traders was concerned, while in the present case a regulatory rule of transitory law was promulgated which affected the *Compagnie Française* as a member of the abstract group to which the regulation applies.

The Court held:

....

'3.It must therefore be considered whether, in the light of Article 173 of the EEC Treaty, the disputed provisions merely have the appearance of a regulation and are really of individual concern to the plaintiff.

4.As laid down in Article 8 of the Council's Regulation (EEC) 1586/69 of 11 August 1969 relating to certain measures setting up the contingency plan to be followed in the agricultural sector after the devaluation of the French Franc, the regulation which is the subject of the present dispute is part of a group of provisions designed to adapt the operation of the intervention mechanisms of the common organization of the agricultural markets to the devaluation of the French Franc which took place on 8 August 1969.

....

11.In our opinion, the regulative nature of an instrument is not brought into question by the possibility of deciding more or less precisely the number of identity of the class to which it applies, in as much as it is clear that its application takes effect in terms of an objective situation of law or fact defined by the instrument in relation to this end.

12.Moreover, the fact that a transitory regulation purports to apply only to certain situations arising prior to a date fixed by it, those situations thus being often formed before its entry into force, does not prevent such a regulation from being an integral part of those former and new provisions which it is attempting to conciliate, nor from participating in the general character of those provisions.

13.The regulative character of Article 3 of Regulation 1660/69, which provides that Articles 1 and 2 are to take effect from 11 August 1969, is not in doubt.

14.The provision in question fixes the date from which the new regulations are to take effect.

15.Save where there is a détournement de pouvoir it shares the general character of the regulations which it brings into effect.

....

18.In the premises, the claim must be rejected as inadmissibile.'

3.Grounds of appeal

LITERATURE: Soell, *Zur Ermessensbindung der Kommission der Europäischen Gemeinschaften am Beispiel des EGKS-Vertrags, AWD 1970, pp.297-302;* Van Der Esch, *Pouvoirs discrétionnaires de l'exécutif européen et contrôle juridictionnel, Deventer 1968;* Clever, *Ermessensmissbrauch und détournement de pouvoir nach dem Recht der Europäischen Gemeinschaften im Licht der Rechtsprechung ihres Gerichtshofs,* Berlin 1967, pp.185.)

a.Lack of powers (incompetence)

CASES

(1)REDISCOUNT RATE CASE

Commission of the EC *v.* France, Consolidated Cases 6 and 11/69, Judgment of 10 December 1969.

(Jur.XV (1969), pp.523-557; Rec.XV (1969), pp.523-557; Samml.XV (1969), pp.523-557; CMLR 1970, pp.43-76; 7 CMLRev.1970, p.479. See also pp. 7 and 156.)

Notes: Brinkhorst and Verougstraete, *7 CMLRev.1970, pp.483-489;* Cahier, *CDE 1970, pp.576-584;* Schermers, *AA 1970, pp.173;* Lemaitre, *RMC 1969, pp.57-59.*

Facts: After the May 1968 crisis in France, which caused serious difficulties in the French economy, the Commission of the EC, in two decisions of 6 July 1968 (for ECSC products) and of 23 July 1968 (for EEC products) authorized the French government (in the latter case under Article 108 (3) EEC) to maintain a difference of three points between re-discount rates for credits on internal and on external transactions.

This safeguard measure was granted until 31 October 1968, while France was authorized to keep a difference of 1.5 points from 1 November 1968 to 31 January 1969. The French government, in November 1968, rather than reducing the difference between the two rates as prescribed by the decisions, increased (although temporalily) the margin between the two. Consequently, the Commission instituted an action under Article 169 (Case 6/69).

The Court held:

....

A. Appeal 6/69 (EEC).

'10.Against the procedure followed by the Commission within the framework of the EEC Treaty the Government of the French Republic invokes 'the insufficiency of the Treaty Rules in the monetary field' and submits that the adjustment of the re-discount rate belongs directly to the monetary policy—which falls within the sole jurisdiction of the Member States—and that therefore, by instituting the actions which have resulted in the decision of 23 July 1968, the Commission has acted without a right (*sans droit*), by claiming a competence which the Treaty denies it.

11.The decision of 23 July 1968, must be considered as definitive, since no appeal for annulment has been instituted against it within the time limit laid down in Article 173, para 3, of the Treaty.

12.The French Government, while not disputing that it let the time pass, submits nevertheless that this decision was taken in a field which falls within the exclusive competence of the Member States, invoking on the one hand Community public policy (ordre public communautaire) and arguing on the other hand that 'too close an attachment to forms would be just as contrary to the true Community spirit as their neglect'.

13.If that submission were founded, the above-mentioned decision would lack all legal basis in the Community order and, in proceedings where the Commission, in the interests of the Community, brings any action against a State for violation of the Treaty, it is a basic requirement of the legal order that the Court should examine whether this is the case.'

(2)ICI CASE

Imperial Chemical Industries Ltd. *v.* Commission of the EC, Case 48/69, Judgment of 14 July 1972, Considerations nos 126-142. See also below p.155.
(not yet published)

Facts: By a decision of 24 July 1969 the Commission imposed a penalty of 50.000 E.U.A. on plaintiff, for violation of Article 85, para.1 which prohibits *inter alia* concested practices by private parties.

ICI objected that it was situated outside the Community and that the Commission had therefore no power to impose a penalty upon it because of the mere fact that acts which it had committed the Community had effects within the Common Market.

The Court held:

....

On the competence of the commission

'The applicant, whose registered office is outside the Community, contends that the Commission has no competence to impose fines upon it by reason merely of the effects produced in the Common Market by acts it may have committed outside the Community.

In a case of concerted practice, it is first necessary to ascertain whether the behaviour of the applicant manifested itself in the Common Market. It follows from what has been said that the increases in question took effect in the Common Market and concerned competition between manufacturers operating therein. Hence, the actions for which the fine in question has been imposed constitute practices carried on directly within the Common Market.

It follows from what has been said in examining the plea relating to the existence of concerted practices, that the applicant company decided on increases of sale prices of its products to users in the Common Market, increases which are uniform in relation to the increases decided upon by the other manufacturers involved. By making use of its power of direction over its subsidiaries established in the Community, the applicant was able to have its decision applied on this market.

The applicant objects that this behaviour is the behaviour of its subsidiaries and not of itself.

The fact that the subsidiary has a distinct legal personality does not suffice to dispose of the possibility that its behaviour might be imputed to the parent company. Such may be the case in particular when the subsidiary, although having a distinct legal personality, does not determine its behaviour on the market in an autonomous manner but essentially carries out the instructions given to it by the parent company. When the subsidiary does not enjoy any real autonomy in the determination of its course of action on the market, the prohibitions imposed by Article 85 (1) may be considered inapplicable in the relations between the subsidiary and the parent company, with which it then forms one economic unit. In view of the unity of the group thus formed, the activities of the subsidiaries may, in certain circumstances, be imputed to the parent company.

It is well-known that the applicant held at the time the whole, or at any rate the majority, of the capital of these subsidiaries.

The applicant was able to influence, in a decisive manner, the sale price policy of its subsidiaries in the Common Market, and it in fact made use of this power on the occasion of the three price increases under discussion. The telex messages relating to the 1964 increase, which the applicant had addressed to its subsidiaries in the Common Market, determined, in a manner binding on their addresses, the prices and other conditions of sale which they must impose in relation to their customers. In the absence of contrary indications, it must be assumed that on the occasion of the 1965 and 1967 increases the applicant did not act otherwise in its relations with its subsidiaries established in the Common Market.

In these circumstances, the formal separation between these companies, arising from their distinct legal personality, cannot, for the purposes of application of the competition rules, prevail against the unity of their behaviour on the market. Thus, it is indeed the applicant which carried out the concerted practice within the Common Market.

The plea of incompetence raised by the applicant must, therefore, be held unfounded.'

*b.*Violation of basic procedural rules

....

*c.*Infringement of the Treaty

....

*d.*Misuse of powers (*détournement de pouvoir*)

....

4.Consequences of annulment

....

B. Appeal against inaction

LITERATURE: Soldatos, L'introuvable recours en carence devant la Cour de Justice des Communautés Européennes, *CDE (1969), pp.313-334;* Bebr, Recours en carence, *Les Novelles, Droit des Communautés Européennes*, Brussels 1969, *pp.*320-331; Reuter, Le recours en carence de l'article 175 du traité de la CEE dans la jurisprudence de la Cour de Justice des Communautés Européennes, *CDE* 1972, *pp. 159-175.*

CASES

(1)STEEL SUBSIDIES CASE

Netherlands *v.* Commission of the EC, Case 59/70, Judgement of 6 July 1971. (Jur.XVII (1971), pp.653-654.)

Facts: In the framework of its Fifth Economic and Social Development Plan, the French Government granted the French steel industry some low interest loans in order to enable this industry to improve its competitive position vis-à-vis foreign steel companies. The High Authority was informed of these measures in September

¹Translated by Court of Justice.

1966 and concluded provisionally in June 1967, that these loans were not prohibited under Article 4 (c) ECSC nor entailed the need to issue a recommandation pursuant to Article 67 ECSC.

The newly formed Commission of the EC definitely confirmed this opinion in a letter of 4 December 1968 to the French Government, of which the Dutch Government was informed on 9 December 1968.

The latter Government, not content with this reply, requested the Commission on 24 June 1970 to issue a decision pursuant to Article 88 ECSC, declaring that France had violated its obligations under Article 4(c) ECSC, and subsidiarily, to issue a re-commendation under Article 67 ECSC. When the Commission did not take the requested measures, the Dutch Government, on 12 October 1970, lodged an appeal under Article 35 against the implicit refusal of the Commission to act.

The Commission asked the Court to declare the appeal inadmissible on the grounds that the prescribed time periods had elapsed.

The Court held:

....

'Article 35, which seeks to bring even those cases where the Commission gives no decision or makes no recommendation under the scrutiny provided for testing the legality of the Commission's acts, affords an opportunity of applying to the Court on the basis of the fiction, arising on expiry of a period of two months, of an implied refusal in the cases where the Commission is required or empowered by a provision of the Treaty to give a decision or make a recommendation, but fails to do so. On expiry of this period of inaction, the interested party has a further month to apply to the Court.

However, the Treaty provides no fixed period for the exercise of the right to apply to the Commission under Article 35 (1) and (2).

It follows, however, from the common purpose of Articles 33 and 35 that the requirements of legal certainty and continuity of Community action underlying the time limits laid down for applications under Article 33 must likewise—having regard to the special difficulties which the silence of the competent authorities can involve for the interested parties—be taken into account in the exercise of the rights conferred by Article 35.

These requirements cannot lead to such contradictory consequences as the duty to act within a short period in the first case and the absence of any time limit in the second. This reflection finds support in the system of time limits in Article 35, which allows the Commission two months to define its attitude, and the interested party one month to apply to the Court.

Thus, it is implicit in the system of Articles 33 and 35 that the exercise of the right to apply to the Commission cannot be indefinitively delayed. If the interested parties are thus restricted to a reasonable time in a case where the Commission is silent, such is the case *a fortiori* when it is unmistakable apparent that the Commission has decided to take no action.

In the present case, when the letter addressed to the French Government on the 4th December 1968 was brought to the notice of the Dutch Government on 9th December 1968, there could no longer be any doubt about the Commission's attitude to the matter, especially since this had been expressed in response to the request made by the Dutch Government at the Council meeting, and the Dutch Minister of Economic Affairs had again placed his Government's objections before the Commission by letter dated 5th April 1968.

Furthermore, the duty of co-operation imposed on Member States by Article 86 must impel a Member State which regards a system of loans as contrary to the Treaty to resort to the procedures and opportunities of legal action placed at its disposal by the Treaty in sufficient time to ensure that effective intervention is still possible, and that the position of third parties is not needlessly prejudiced.

Having regard to these circumstances, a period of 18 months between the communication of 9th December 1968 and the request addressed to the Commission on 24th June 1970 by way of commencement of the procedure of Article 35 cannot be regarded as reasonable. It is all the more unjustifiable because the communication of 9th December 1968 had no new or unforeseen character in any respect whatever. Thus, the Dutch Government on 24th June 1970 could no longer take action under Article 35 of the Treaty.

The application must be declared inadmissible.[1]

(2) COMPOSERS CASE

Deutscher Komponistenverband *v.* Commission of the EC, Case 8/71, Judgment of 13 July 1971.
(Jur.XVII (1971), pp.710-711.)

Facts: In an anti-trust suit against the German Association for the protection of the rights of authors of music (GEMA), the Deutscher Komponistenverband had requested the Commission that it, as an interested party, be consulted.

The Commission had replied that the *Komponistenverband* had no legal interest in being heard in the oral proceedings as it had been authorized to comment in writing. The *Komponistenverband* then lodged an appeal for inaction, submitting that the Commission, in violation of its obligations, had neglected to hear it. The Commission raised preliminary objection under Article 91 Rules of Procedure.

[1]Translated by Court of Justice.

The Court held:

....

'Under Article 175 para.3 any natural or legal person may, under the conditions laid down in the preceding paragraphs, lodge a complaint before the Court of Justice that an institution of the Community has failed to address to that person any act other than a recommendation or an opinion. It is clear from the context, especially from the first paragraph, that the words '... has failed to address to that person any act' refer to a failure to act in the sense of failure to take a decision or define a position; they do not refer to an act different from the one sought or deemed necessary by the interested parties.

By a telex message of 13 November 1970 the applicant submitted a claim to be heard under Article 19 (2) of Regulation No.17, in conjunction with Article 5 of Regulation No.99/63, in the various proceedings instituted against GEMA. By letter of 17 November 1970 the applicant was informed that the Commission, without prejudice to the question whether the applicant had a sufficient interest within the meaning of the said provisions, would afford it the opportunity of submitting its views in writing within a month; this period was extended twice. The Commission has therefore acted in accordance with Article 5 of Regulation No.99/63 'concerning hearings under Article 19 (1) and (2) of Regulation of Council No.17'. Thus it has not in the present case failed to deal with the applicant's claim, so that the provisions of Article 175 are not in point.

The application must therefore be rejected as inadmissible.'

C. Exception of illegality

....

II. PLENARY JURISDICTION

A. Actions for non-fulfilment of Treaty obligations

....

B. Non-contractual liability of the Communities

LITERATURE: Goffin, La Cour de Justice. La responsabilité non-contractuelle des Communautés, and *idem*, Recours en indemnité, *Les Novelles, Droit des Communautés Européennes*, Brussels, 1969 pp.141-158, resp. pp.333-340; van den Burg, De niet contractuele aansprakelijkheid der Europese Gemeenschappen en de Jurisprudentie van het Hof van Justitie, SEW 1969, pp.198-237.

1.ECSC

....

2.EEC

CASES

(1)THIRD LÜTTICKE CASE

Lütticke *v.* Commission of the EC, Case 4/69, Judgment of 28 April 1971.
(Jur.XVII (1971), pp.336-340; EuR 1971, pp.370-374.)
Notes: Goffin and Mahieu, *CDE 1972, pp.64-93.*

Facts: Lütticke imported dairy products into Germany. Until 1 January 1968, the Federal Republic levied a compensatory turnover tax on such imports. Lütticke had informed the Commission that this tax had become illegal after the end of the first stage of the transitional period (1 January 1962). He had asked the Commission to take action against Germany; when the Commission refused to do so he appealed to the Court. His appeal was declared inadmissible (see Jud.Rem., p.75, First Lütticke Case). Before the German courts Lütticke appealed against the tax. This appeal, finally, led to a request for a preliminary ruling by the *Finanzgericht Saarland.* The preliminary ruling given by the Court of Justice clearly demonstrated that the German taxes were no longer valid (see Jud.Rem., p.111, Second Lütticke Case). Lütticke had suffered considerable damages for which he blamed the Commission, submitting that it should have followed a more active policy against Germany. In the present case he sued the Commission for these damages.

The Court held:

On the admissibility

....

'5.The defendant contests the admissibility of the appeal on the additional ground that its real objective, although brought pursuant to Arts 178 and 215 para 2, is not merely to establish negligence on the part of the Commission but also indirectly to force the Commission to initiate the procedure of Art.97 para 2 and—possibly—that of Art.169 against the Federal Republic of Germany. According to the defendant, the conditions stipulated by Art.175 for an appeal for inaction are thereby circumvented.

6.A claim for damages, as defined in Arts.178 and 215 para 2 was provided in the Treaty as an independent form of redress. It has a specific function within the system of remedies and its application—on account of its special objective—is subject to particular conditions.

The fact that a claim for damages under certain circumstances leads to a result similar to that arizing on a claim pursuant to Art.175 does not cause its inadmissibility. Such a rule would be in conflict both with the independence of the claim and with the efficacy of the whole system of remedies as provided by the Treaty.

Consequently, this exception of inadmissibility must be rejected.'

....

On the merits

....

'10.According to Article 215 para.2 and the general principles referred to in this provision, a number of conditions must be fulfilled for the liability of the Community, to wit the existence of damages, the causal link between the asserted damage and the disputed behaviour of the institutions and the illegality of this behaviour.

11.In the first place it has to be established in this case whether the Commission has not observed by its action its obligations under Art.97 para.2.

....

13.The function of Art.97 ensures that—with regard to imports—compensatory turnover taxes levied under a cumulative cascade system are in conformity with the principles of Art.95. Such a system necessary implies that both the estimate of the tax burden on domestic production—which determines the level of the average percentages—and the method of levy employed—having regard to the entire system of the relevant tax law—are within the discretion of the states which apply that system.

14.The commission exercises a special supervision pursuant to Art.97 para 2 in view of Art.95 and 97 para 1, which implies that it may have regard to those factors which are taken into account by the State.

....

17.Already in 1962 it became an established practice for the Commission together with the experts of the member States to check the tax percentages issued pursuant to national legal provisions against Arts.95 and 97 para 1.

At that time the Commission discussed the percentage applicable to this product with the German Authorities and also with those of the other member States involved in the milk powder trade;

After having taken note of the German Government's explanation the Commission informed it that the percentage of 4% applicable to the import of milk powder into Federal Republic was considered to be excessive.

On account of this intervention this percentage was reduced to 3% by the Federal Republic effective as from April 1st 1965—later advanced to January 1st 1962. In view of a further reduction the Commission did not find cause to issue a directive or decision pursuant to Art.97.

Moreover, no mention has been made of any objection by those Member States whose exports might have suffered from the tax system now objected to by the petitioner.

It appears from the above, therefore, that the Commission has not been shown to be lacking in its supervisory duties.

19.The petitioner has not demonstrated that an average percentage of 3% for the product in question exceeds the limit arising from Arts.95 and 97, compliance with which the Commission has to ensure.

Consequently the appeal must be dismissed.'

(2)ZUCKERFABRIK SCHÖPPENSTEDT CASE

Aktien-Zuckerfabrik Schöppenstedt *v.* Council of the European Communities. Case 5/71, Judgment of 2 December 1971.

(Jur.XVII (1971), pp.984-985.)

Facts: On 1 July 1968 the national rules for the European sugarmarkets were replaced by Community rules. This caused a considerable change in sugar prices. By Regulation No.769/68 of 18 June 1968 (OJ 1968, L 143) the Council issued transitory measures for companies which had sugar in stock. As the changes on the German market were considered to be marginal, the Zuckerfabrik Schöppenstedt did not receive any compensation for the decrease in the price of the sugar it had in stock. It suffered damages of 38.852.78 Units of Account and sued the Council for compensation.

The Council submitted:

(1)that the claim was inadmissible as it would not lead to compensation for damage caused by the Community but, rather, would render the disputed Regulation inoperative or result in its replacement by another system; and:

(2)that, even if it were admissible, the claim should be rejected as no wrongful act had been committed.

The Court held:

....

'3.The claim for damages as provided by Articles 178 and 215 para 2 constitutes an independent appeal procedure which has a special function within the system of remedies and for which conditions for its application, tailored to its specific goal, have been imposed. This claim differs from the appeal for annulment in that its subject is not the rescission of specific measures but the compensation for damage caused by an institution in the discharge of its duties.

....

5.The sole objective of the principal claim is the award of compensation for damage, i.e. a payment which is intended to apply only to the particular plaintiff.

....

11.The non-contractual liability of the Community invoked in this case presupposes at least the unlawfulness of the act alleged to have caused the damage. In the case of a normative act which implies the existence of certain alternatives as regards economic policy, the Community can be held liable for damages to private persons (in view of Art.215, para 2 of the Treaty) only when a higher rule of law, provided for their protection is violated to a sufficiently qualified extent. In this action, therefore, the Court will have to investigate, first of all whether such a violation exists.'[1]

C. Appeals against penalties

EEC Council Regulation No.17/62, Article 15

para 2. 'The Commission may by means of a decision impose on enterprises and associations of enterprises fines from one thousand to one million units of account; this last figure may be increased to 10% of the turnover of the preceding business year of each of the enterprises having taken part in the infringement, where these enterprises, wilfully or through negligence:
a.have infringed the provisions of Article 85, paragraph 1, or of Article 86 of the Treaty, or
....
para 4. The decisions taken under paragraphs 1 and 2 shall have no penal character.'

Article 17.

'The Court of Justice shall have full jurisdiction within the meaning of Article 172 of the Treaty to adjudicate on proceedings instituted against the decisions by which the Commission has fixed a fine or a penalty; it may cancel, reduce or increase the fine or the penalty imposed.'

CASES

(1) BOEHRINGER CASE

Boehringer Mannheim GmbH *v.* Commission of the EC, Case 45/69, Judgment of 15 July 1970.
(Jur.XVI (1970), pp.769-813; Rec.XVI (1970), pp.769-813; Samml.XVI 1970, pp.769-813; 8 CMLRev. 1971, p.86. See also below, pp.115 and 153.)
Notes: Maas, *AA 1971, pp.510-519;* Markert, *EuR 1971, pp.54-60;* Mulder, *SEW 1971, pp.240-214;* Van der Sanden, *CDE 1971, pp.327-355.*

Facts: Plaintiff, a German manufacturer of chemical and pharmaceutical products, appealed against a decision of the Commission of the EC of 16 July 1969[2] by which a fine of 190.000 E.U.A. was imposed upon him for having been a party to an international gentlemen's agreement engaged in dividing the markets for, and fixing the prices of, quinine. It objected to this fine on a number of grounds.

The Court held:

....

[1]Translation by Europa Instituut. [2]*OJ 1969, L 192/5.*

'52.The appellant complains that the Commission has imposed a fine on it because of an already ended infringement. By failing to take this circumstance into account, at least for the purpose of fixing the amount of the fine, the defendant allegedly committed an abuse of power.

53.The sanctions provided by Article 15 of Regulation 17 do not have the character of coercive measures. Their goal is to stop illegal behaviour as well as to prevent its repetition. This objective could not be reached adequately if the application of a sanction would have to be limited to present infringements only. The power of the Commission to impose sanctions is not at all affected by the fact that the behaviour constituting the infringement and its possibly injurious effects have ceased to exist. For the purpose of fixing the amount of the fine, the seriousness of the infringement must be appreciated while particularly taking into account the nature of the restrictions imposed on the competition, the number and the importance of the concerned enterprises, the fraction of the market which they control within the Community as well as the market condition at the time when the infringement was committed.

54.The appellant complains that the Commission first fixed a lump sum as a fine for the agreement and that it subsequently apportioned this sum among the enterprises. This procedure allegedly was not compatible with the requirement that the fine be determined individually. Moreover, the appellant allegedly was treated prejudicially compared with the other enterprises, by reason of the disproportionate amount that was imposed on it.

55.To fix, in advance, a limit for the lump sum of the fine, determined in relation to the gravity of the danger that the agreement presented to the competition and the trade within the common market, is not incompatible with the individual determination of the sanction.

In point of fact, the position and the individual behaviour of each enterprise and of the importance of the role it played in the agreement can be taken into consideration at the time of the appraisal of the amount of the individual fine.

56.In the present case, the contested decision, notably in the paragraphs 2 and 4 of No.40, expressly considered the position and the role of the appellant in the framework of the agreement. The decision took notice of the strong influence that this enterprise exercised together with Nedchem during the preparation and effectuation of the agreement, and, above all, of its powerful position regarding the supply of raw materials. This last circumstance justifies, according to the Commission, the imposition on appellant of a relatively heavier fine than on the other enterprises; even taking into account that the return of appelant's quinine plantations in the Congo may have been small in 1963-1964, the fact that the appellant could count on important resources of its own for the future, in a period of growing scarcity of raw materials on the international market, was likely to furnish it with a strong influence on the other partners to the agreement who were in a weaker position regarding their supply.

57. This appreciation of the Commission is justified.

58. Lastly, it appears from the account given of the joint meetings held by the partners to the agreement on 25 September and 29 October 1962, that they were aware of the incompatibility of their actions with the prohibitions of Community law. The serious nature of the infringements and the fact that they were committed consciously therefore justifies a heavy fine.

59. The statements of the contested decision regarding the infringements attributable to the appellant are thus for the greater part well-founded. The exclusion of the fixing of sales quotas for the period running from November 1962 to February 1965 and of the sales prices for the period May 1964 to February 1965—which has not perceptibly reduced the seriousness of the restrictions on competition resulting from the agreement —justifies only a slight reduction of the fine. So there is reason to lower the fine to 180.000 units of account.

60. The appellant maintains that the fine of 80.000 dollars which has been imposed on it by a judicial authority in the USA, on account of the same facts, and which was already paid previous to the contested decision, should be deducted from the amount of the fine in dispute.

61. These sanctions have been imposed with regard to restrictions on competition which took place outside the Community. Consequently, there is no reason to take these sanctions into account in the present dispute.'[1]

. . . .

[1] Translation by Europa Instiuut.

Chapter Three

The application of Community law by national courts

I. THE OBLIGATION OF NATIONAL COURTS TO APPLY COMMUNITY LAW

LITERATURE: Rittersprach, *Das supranationale Recht und die nationalen Verfassungsgerichte, Festschrift für G.Müller, Tübingen, 1970,* p.301; Alder, *Koordination und Integration als Rechtsprinzipien,* Brugge, 1969, 344 pp.; Ganshof van der Meersch, Le droit communautaire et ses rapports avec les droits des Etats Membres, *Les Novelles, Droit des Communautés Européennes,* Brussels, 1969, pp.41-79; Garron, Reflexions sur la primauté du droit Communautaire, *RTDE 1969, pp. 28-48;* Hostert, Droit International et Droit Interne dans la Convention sur le droit des traités du 23 mai 1969, *AFDI 1969, pp.92-122;* Roemer, Betrachtungen zum Verhältnis Gemeinschaftsrecht—nationales Recht, *Juristische Studiengesellschaft Karlsruhe, 1969, Heft 91, 23 pp.;* Waelbroeck, *Traités internationaux et juridictions internes dans les pays du Marché Commun,* Paris-Bruxelles, 1969, 348 pp.; Zuleeg, *Das Recht der Europäischen Gemeinschaften in innerstaatlichem Bereich,* Kölner Schriften zum Europarecht, Band Carl Heymans Verlag (1969), 448 pp.; Gaudet, *Conflits du droit communautaire avec les droits nationaux,* Nancy 1967, 59 pp.; Monaco, *Diritto della Communita Europea e diritto interno,* Milano, 1967; Grabitz, *Gemeinschaftsrecht bricht nationales Recht,* Hamburg, 1966, 132 pp.; Hay, The Federal Relations of Community law to National law, *Federalism and Supranational Organisation, 1966, pp.152-202.*

A. The obligation in general

. . . .

B. The limitation to self-executing provisions

LITERATURE: Koller, *Die unmittelbare Anwendbarkeit völkerrechtlicher Verträge und des EWG-Vertrages im innerstaatlichen Bereich,* Bern Stämpfli 1971, 216 pp.; Bebr, Les dispositions de droit communautaire directement applicable, *CDE 1970, pp.3-49, ICLQ 1970, pp.257-298;* Daig, Die Rechtsprechung des E.G.H. zur unmittelbaren Wirkung von EWG-Bestimmungen auf die Rechtsbeziehungen zwischen Mitgliedstaaten und Gemeinschaftsbürger, *EuR 1970, pp.1-31;* Albert Bleckmann, *Begriff und Kriterien der innerstaatlichen Anwendbarkeit Völkerrechtlicher Verträge,* Versuch einer allgemeinen Theorie des self-executing Treaty auf rechtsvergleichender Grundlage, Revlin.1970, 333 pp; Pescatore, L'attitude des jurisdictions nationales à l'égard du problème des effets diverts du droit Communautaire, *RTDE 1970, pp.296-303;* Constantinesco, *Die unmittelbare Anwendbarkeit der Gemeinschaftsnormen und die Rechtsschutz im Recht der EWG,* Nomos, Baden/Baden 1969, 148 pp.; Mertens de Wilmars, De directe werking van het Europese Recht, *SEW 1969, pp.62-81.*

1.Treaty provisions

CASES

(1)EUNOMIA CASE

Eunomia Company *v.* Italian Ministry of Education, Case 18/71, Preliminary ruling of 26 October 1971 at the request of the President of the Court of Turin.
(Jur.XVII (1971), pp.815-816.)

Facts: According to an Italian law of 1939, artistic products were subjected to a progressive levy. On 10 December 1968 the Court of Justice (acting under Article 169 of the EEC Treaty), had decided that Italy violated Article 16 of the EEC Treaty by keeping this levy after January 1962 (Case 7/68, Jur.XVI, p.601). The Italian law was not withdrawn, however.

On 4 March 1970, Eunomia exported a picture to Germany. It had to pay an export levy of over 20 per cent. By request to the President of the Court of Turin, Eunomia claimed restitution of the levy paid.

The President of the Court asked a preliminary ruling on the question whether Article 16 was directly applicable since 1 January 1962, and on the question whether private parties had thus obtained rights against the Italian State which the courts should guarantee.

The Court held:

. . . .

'2.It appears from the Order referring the case that the judge doing so has to decide on an application for repayment of the export tax imposed on articles of artistic, historical, archaeological or ethnological value by Law No.1089 of 1 June 1939, which is charged on the occasion of export of a work of art to another Member State.

This tax, as was declared by this Court in its judgment of 10 December 1968 (Case 7/68)[1], is a tax having equivalent effect to a customs duty on exports, and falls under Article 16 of the Treaty.

. . . .

5.By Article 9 of the EEC Treaty, the Community is based on a customs union, which implies *inter alia* the prohibition as between Member States of customs duties and any taxes having equivalent effect. By Article 16 of the Treaty, member States shall, as between themselves, abolish customs duties and taxes having equivalent effect, at the latest by the end of the first stage.

6.Article 9 and 16, read in conjunction, contain a clear and precise prohibition, in

[1]See above, p.8.

relation to all taxes having equivalent effect to customs duties on export, and at the latest from the end of the first stage, against collecting such taxes, a prohibition whose effectiveness does not depend on any domestic legal measure nor on any intervention by the Community institutions. This prohibition is by its nature perfectly apt to produce effects directly on the legal relationships between the member States and their subjects.

7.Consequently, from the end of the first stage (i.e. from 1st January 1962), these Articles conferred on individuals rights which national courts must protect, and which must prevail over conflicting provisions of domestic law, even if the Member State has not taken steps at the proper time to repeal such provisions.'[1]

....

(2) GERMAN IMPORT OF DUTCH BARLEY CASE
Finanzgericht (Fiscal Court) Rheinland/Pfalz, Decision of 14 October 1970. CMLR 1971, pp.737, 738.

Facts: In 1962 the plaintiff had imported barley into Germany from the Netherlands.

The customs authorities preliminarily demanded (i) 25,766.70 DM levy and (ii) 935.40 DM sales equalisation tax. On the basis of a computation by the *Einfuhr- und Vorratstelle* (EVSt) the customs authorities,' by an advice dated 19 December 1962, changed the original levy demand and made a refund. The plaintiff appealed *inter alia* on the ground that for the period 1 August 1962 to 31 December 1962 the tax rates should be reduced by the amount of the tax, as only from that date onwards had account been taken of the fact that no other liabilities should arise for an importer apart from the levy.

It was argued that the failure to reduce the levy by the amount of the tax up to 31 December 1962 was contrary to the equalisation provisions. Furthermore, it was argued, the regulation concerning the threshold price was not in accordance with the principle of the German Constitution (Article 80) that any liability should be apparent from the statute itself.

The Finanzgericht held:

....

'The *Bundesfinanzhof*, in its judgment of 10 July 1968, expressed the view that the computation of the levy rates was merely a 'mathematical execution' of Community law on the basis of fixed individual items, namely:

the duty-free price, fixed by the Commission, and the threshold price, determined by decree of the Federal Minister of Food.

[1]Translation by Court of Justice.

Accordingly the essential items for the determination of the amount of the levy were known and thus the total amount 'could be regarded as adequately determined by law or on a legal basis'.

This view must be rejected. This court does not see how the *Bundesfinanzhof* could come to the conclusion that the levy rates had been adequately determined by law or on a legal basis.

Anyhow, in respect of one factor of the rates to be computed by the *EVSt*, namely, the duty-free price, it is not possible to maintain that, as the law then stood, that price had been *determined* by law or on a legal basis. The duty-free prices were fixed by a decision of the Commission (Articles 3 and 26 of Regulation 19).

However, such decisions, as opposed to regulations of the Council or the Commission, are not legislative acts of immediate applicability to the citizens of the member-States; they only affect those to whom they are directed (Articles 189(4) and 191 of the EEC Treaty).

A decision is directed to the member-State. It therefore requires incorporation into domestic law in order to acquire immediate legal effect as far as the citizens of that member-State are concerned. The publication of the duty-free prices, usually at a later date, in the Agricultural Supplement to the *Journal Officiel* of the EEC, does not affect their legal consequences. Such publication, in any event, concerned only the duty-free prices and did not contain the complete text of the decision, in accordance with the provisions of Article 190 of the EEC Treaty.

Contrary to the views of the *Finanzgericht* Baden-Württemberg, this court does not accept that the immediate rights and obligations of individual citizens can be founded upon secondary Community law, nor, consequently, upon decisions of the EEC Commission, even if they are of a 'self-executing' nature. In view of the clear wording of Articles 173(1) and 199(4) of the EEC Treaty—otherwise than in connection with individual provisions in the EEC Treaty itself—an interpretation as to whether or not such decisions are 'self-executing' is neither permissible nor necessary. It has already been decided by the European Court of Justice that the decision of the EEC Commission concerning cif prices (comparable to 'franco-frontier' prices) in connection with Article 10 of Regulation 19, does not immediately affect the citizens as individuals, and therefore does not accord to such citizens the right to bring an action under Article 173(2) of the EEC Treaty.

....

As the Court considers the above-mentioned provisions to be contrary to the Constitution, it is constrained under Article 100 of the Constitution to adjourn the claim and to request the decision of the Federal Constitutional Court.'[1]

[1]Translation by CMLR.

2.Community acts

CASES

(1)BELGIAN CORVELEYN CASE

Corveleyn *v.* Belgian State (minister of Justice), *Conseil d'Etat* (Council of State) (3rd ch.), Decision of 7 October 1968.

(JT 1969, p.694; CDE 1969, p.343, with conclusions auditeur general; RTDE 1969, p.821; RJDACE 1969, p.263; CMLR, 1970 pp.237-240)

Notes: Knaur, *Rev. crit. de droit int. privé*, *1970 pp.503-518;* Schrans, *7 CMLRev.1970, pp.237-240;* Gigon, *CDE 1969, pp.350-357;* Soldatos, *RJDACE 1969, pp.263ff;* Verhoeven, *JT 1969, pp.695-700.*

Facts: Mrs. Yvette Corveleyn, a person of French nationality, took up residence in Belgium on 5 September 1965. She duly complied with Belgian immigration laws, obtained a work permit, and was hired as a waitress in a bar. While she was living in France (1964), Mrs. Corveleyn had been criminally convicted by a French court because she had managed a house of ill-repute in that country. Her conduct in Belgium has, however, always been unobjectionable.

On 19 August 1966, the Belgian Minister of Justice served upon Mrs. Corveleyn a decision of expulsion from Belgium on the ground that 'her conduct (made) her presence within the Kingdom harmful' to the *ordre public* in Belgium.

This decision was based on Article 3 of an Act of 28 March 1952, with respect to *la police des étrangers.* Mrs. Corveleyn nevertheless requested the Belgian *Conseil d'Etat* (i.e. the highest administrative court, hereafter sometimes called 'the Court'), to annul the decision on the ground that it violated Article 3 of Directive No.64/221, dated 25 February 1964, of the EEC Council of Ministers, with respect to the coordination of measures applied to entry and residence of aliens, which may be justified on the grounds of public policy, public security or public health. Article 3 of this Directive provides that measures required by public policy or public security may be justified only on the basis of the individual conduct of the person concerned, and it goes on to say that the mere existence of a criminal conviction, is not in itself sufficient to justify these measures.

This Directive—which had to be implemented by the Member States within six months from its notification to them—plays an important role in the functioning of the Common Market. As is well known, Article 48, para 3, of the EEC Treaty, concerning the freedom of establishment and the free supply of services, provides that the Member States may depart from EEC liberalization measures on grounds relating to public polity, public security and public health. These concepts, however, may not be interpreted autonomously by the member States; their material contents have to be specified and co-ordinated by the EEC Council of Ministers.

Thus Article 3 of Directive No.64/221 imposes limits on the individual State's evaluation of measures justified by public policy or public security: some reasons (e.g. the mere existence of a criminal conviction) may not be invoked to justify any such measures.

In the present case, Mrs.Corveleyn contended that the Belgian Minister of Justice had violated this provision because:

—the reason invoked as to her individual conduct in Belgium was, in fact, not true, and

—no other reason could be invoked by the Minister, except the criminal conviction sustained in France, which reason, standing alone, would clearly be untenable under Article 3 of the Directive.

The Conseil d'Etat held:

....

'Since the petitioner had not obtained a permit allowing the acquisition of domicile in the Kingdom, either under a ministerial decision or by right pursuant to Art.39 of the Royal Decree of 21 December 1965, she could be expelled from the Kingdom by ministerial order.

As provided by Art.3 of the Directive of 25 February 1964, published in the Official Journal of the European Communities of 4 April 1964, concerning the coordination of special measures relating to the travel and residence of foreigners such special measures are justified on the grounds of public policy, public security and public health and must be based exclusively on the personal behaviour of the individual to whom they are directed.

The Article goes on to provide that the mere existence of a criminal conviction does not automatically justify such measures.

Art.3 is thus quite clear and specific; it falls to the Conseil d'Etat to ascertain whether the (defendant) was obliged to conform to the directive and whether it had applied the provisions thereof correctly.

By Art.189 EEC Treaty 'a directive shall be binding, as to the result to be achieved, upon each Member State to which it is addressed, but shall leave to the national authorities the choice of form and methods'.

To achieve the objective of Art.3 of the Directive of 25 February 1964, the government promulgated the Royal Decree of 21 December 1965 concerning the conditions of entry and residence on acquisition of domicile of foreigners, the preamble of which refers expressly to this directive.

....

Nothing in the legislation, nor in the administrative regulations prevents the Minister of Justice from acting in conformity with Article 3 of the directive. To do so, it is sufficient to abstain from expelling automatically a foreigner who has been criminally convicted.

Thus the measure challenged here has been taken in violation of Article 3 of the Directive of 25 February 1964. The Ministerial decree of 19 August 1966 is annulled.'

(2) GRAD CASE

Grad *v.* Finanzamt Traunstein, Case 9/70, Preliminary ruling of 6 October 1970, on the request of the *Finanzgericht* München.

(Jur.XVI (1970), pp.838-841; CMLR 1971, pp.22-25; EuR 1971, pp.31-38; RTDE 1970, pp.703-717.)

Notes: Brinkhorst, *AA 1971, pp.143-148 and 8 CMLRev.1971, pp.386-392;* Lauwaars, *SEW 1971, pp. 287-294;* Grabitz, *EuR 1971, p.1-22;* de Ripainsel-Landy, *CDE 1971, pp.453-468;* Meier, *AWD 1970, pp.474-475;* Wägenbauer, *AWD 1970, p.481.*

Facts: The EEC Council had issued directives on the harmonization of turnover taxes. The member States were to issue national laws introducing a system of value added tax before 1 January 1972.

As from the date on which a member State had introduced the required legislation it was no longer allowed to maintain or introduce any levies based on turnover tax on imports or exports between the member States.

The Federal Republic introduced the required legislation on 1 January 1968. On 1 January 1969, it introduced a *Strassengüterverkehrsteuer*, a tax of 1 *Pfennig* per ton-kilometer for long-distance transport on German roads.

Grad considered this tax as being contrary to the EEC directive and refused to pay.

The German Court asked three preliminary questions:

1. Can individuals before national courts invoke the directive of the Council and the decisions by which it was provided that this directive would be applicable to transport?
2. Could the Federal Republic introduce new turnover taxes after it issued the national tax provided for in the directive, but before 1 January 1972?
3. Is the *Strassengüterverkehrsteuer* a turnover tax?

As to the first question the Commission (intervening in the case) made the following list of arguments pleading *against* direct applicability.

(1) According to Article 189 of the Treaty, decisions directed to the member States are only binding upon the member States to which they are directed. Hence, they are only indirectly applicable to the citizen. It is only through an executory act of his own national authorities that he can be given rights and obligations, which he can invoke directly. To this end one can also point to the fact that Article 189 only declares regulations directly applicable.

(2) As for the secondary Community law the Treaty on purpose distinguishes between acts which are directly applicable and those which are not (regulations versus directives and decisions directed to States). This distinction which is carefully

made, would have no value at all, if the specific provisions of a decision directed to the member States were given direct application.

This would lead to legal insecurity.

(3) In certain sectors (e.g. agriculture, transport, trade policy) the Treaty leaves the choice as to the legal acts to be accomplished. In other sectors only a directive may be used (for instance the right of establishment, the services or the approximation of laws). It may be concluded therefrom that the member States have wished not to grant the Community any powers to establish directly applicable rules in these sectors.

(4) Finally, the Treaty does not prescribe that decisions must be published. Hence, it depends more or less on an accident or the private persons's address whether he may invoke provisions of the Community law, which are favourable for him, before the legal instances of his country. This leads to a certain degree of unequality before the law, for the judge may not be assumed *a priori* to have knowledge of non-published decisions.

The Commission also submitted the following list of arguments pleading in favour of direct applicability.

(1) According to the case of law of the Court of Justice concerning the directly binding Treaty provisions the fact that the member States are indicated as the addressees is not decisive. But it is decisive whether a provision lends itself to direct application on account of its nature. The consideration which the Court has so far advanced concerning the Treaty provisions, can also be applied to a decision directed to member States.

(2) It is true that Article 189 of the Treaty only declares a regulation directly applicable in each member State. But the description of a decision, given by Article 189, does not exclude at all that under certain conditions a decision directed to member States can be granted the same effect. One should distinguish between 'direct applicability' in the sense of Article 189 of the Treaty and provisions which 'can be directly applicable in the legal relations between the member States and their justiciables'. In the sense of Article 189 'direct applicability' notably means that no positive act of national law is needed to give a certain community legal act effect. The question whether in the sense of the Court's case law certain provisions as to their nature can have direct effect to private persons, depends on the contrary whether—as far as obligations to act are concerned—direct claims are created for a private person despite the absence of a national execution law.

(3) The danger of legal insecurity should not be over-estimated. Problems can only arise when decisions prescribe the member States an action in a certain sense and the term set expires without the decision being followed. For security's sake terms of sufficient length could be provided for, while the member States too make every

effort to issue the necessary execution provisions in due time. If one adds that according to the Court's case law the provisions must be explicit and unconditional, it appears that the question of the direct applicability only has to arise with very few decisions.

(4) The fact that certain provisions in decisions directed to member States are granted a directly binding character, does not mean that the system of community legal acts of secondary nature, such as provided for in Article 189 of the Treaty, is abandoned. On the contrary the direct applicability of certain provisions entails the individual rights of the private persons enjoying increased legal protection—the system of Article 189 has indeed been maintained as such—.

(5) Except in rare exceptional cases the Community's institutions publish the decisions they direct to member States *ad informandum* in the Official Journal. Hence the argument that such publication of the decisions directed to member States is not prescribed, proves of little weight as far as the Community's organs do more than they are obliged to do in virtue of Article 191 of the Treaty by equally publishing decisions directed to the member States.

(6) The Court's case law seems to give no arguments against, but in favour of the direct applicability of decisions. In its judgment of 18 February 1970, given in the case 38/69, the Court of Justice has expressed its standpoint with regard to the 'Acceleration' Decision' of the Council of 26 July 1966[1] as follows:

'whereas that decision, although as to its form only directed to the member States has as its aim to have effect on the whole Common Market and forms the condition or preparation for the establishment—in virtue of Article 9, para 1, and as far as notably the relations with third countries are concerned in virtue of the Council's Regulation nr.950/68/EEC of 28 June 1968, on the Common Customs Tariff[2]—of provisions directly binding in the member States.'[3]

This reasoning might justify the conclusion that the Court of Justice is willing to recognize the 'Acceleration' Decision direct applicably in the same way as it has already done with regard to the provisions concerning the regulation of customs matters 'although it is, as to its form, only directed to the member States'.

In the light of all these arguments and notably pointing to the aspect of the legal protection given to the private person, the Commission thinks that there is no reason to deny provisions of Community law direct application, only because they are part of a decision directed to member States.

As to this question, the Court held:

. . . .

[1] *OJ 1966, p.2971.* [2] *OJ 1968, L172/1.* [3] *Jur.XVI (1970), p.58.*

'2.With its first question the *Finanzgericht* asks the Court for a decision as to whether Article 4(2) of the Decision in conjunction with Article 1 of the Directive produces a direct effect on the legal relations between the member States and individuals and whether these provisions create rights for individuals to which the national courts must give effect.

3.The question concerns the total effect of provisions contained in a decision or a directive. According to Article 189 of the EEC Treaty a decision is binding in its entirety upon those whom it designates. Furthermore, according to this Article a directive is binding, in respect of the aim to be achieved, on every member State to which it is directed although it leaves the choice of forms and methods to the internal national authorities.

4.The German Government in its submission maintains that Article 189 by distinguishing between the effects of regulations on the one hand and of decisions and directives on the other hand thus precludes the possibility of decisions and directives producing the effects mentioned in the question; it claims that such effects are on the contrary reserved to regulations.

5.It is true that by Article 189 regulations are directly applicable and may therefore certainly produce direct effects by virtue of their nature as law. However, it does not follow from this that other categories of legal measures mentioned in that Articles could never produce similar effects. The provisions that decisions are binding in their entirety on those to whom they are addressed especially enables the question to be posed as to whether the obligation created by the decisions can only be invoked by the organs of the Community as against the addressee or whether such a right in a given case is attributed to all those who have an interest in the fulfilment of this obligation. It would be incompatible with the binding effect attributed to decisions by Article 189 to exclude in principle the possibility that persons affected might invoke the obligation imposed by a decision. Particularly in cases where, for example, the Community organs impose an obligation on a member State or all the member States by decision to undertake certain conduct, the useful effect of such a measure would be weakened if the nationals of this State could not invoke it in the courts and the national courts could not take it into consideration as part of Community law. Although the effects of a decision may be different from those of a provision contained in a regulation this difference does not prevent the end-result, namely the right of the individual to invoke the measure in the courts, from being the same in a given case as that in the case of a directly applicable provision of a regulation.

6.Article 177, whereby the national courts are empowered to submit to the Court all questions regarding the validity and interpretation of all measures of the organs without distinction, also pre-supposes that individuals may invoke such measures in the national courts.

Therefore, in each particular case, one must examine whether the provisions in question, by its legal nature, lay-out and wording, is capable of creating direct effects on the legal relations between the addressee of the measure and third parties.

7.The Council's Decision of 13 May 1965 addressed to all the member States is based in particular on Article 75 of the Treaty which empowers the Council to make 'common rules', 'licence conditions' and 'all other appropriate provisions' to implement a common transport policy. The Council therefore has a very wide scope in the choice of the measures to be instituted.

8.Thus this provision imposes two obligations on the member States: first, to apply the common turnover tax system to freight transport in rail, road and inland water traffic not later than from a certain date, and then, to permit this system to replace the specific taxes within the meaning of paragraph (2) not later than upon its entry into force. This second obligation obviously includes the prohibition on introducing or re-introducing such taxes whereby it is intended to prevent the common turnover tax system from coinciding in the field of transport with similar additional tax systems.

9.According to the documents submitted by the Finanzgericht the question relates, in particular to the second obligation.

The second obligation is by its nature binding and general, although the provision leaves the determination of the date on which it becomes effective open. It expressly prohibits the member States from cumulating the common turnover tax system with specific taxes which are imposed instead of turnover taxes. This obligation is unconditional and sufficiently clear and precise to be capable of creating direct effect in the legal relations between the member States and individuals.

10.The date on which this obligation becomes effective was laid down by the Council's Directives on the harmonisation of the legal provisions relating to turnover tax; it is determined therein by the latest date by which the member States must introduce the common added value tax system. The fact that this date was determined by a directive does not deprive this provision of any of its binding force. Thus the obligation created by Article 4(2) of the Decision of 13 May 1965 was completed by the First Directive. Therefore this provision imposes obligations on the member States, in particular the obligation from a certain date no longer to cumulate the common added value tax system with the specific taxes mentioned, which are capable of producing direct effects in the legal relations between the member States and individuals and of creating the right for the latter to invoke these obligations in the courts.'[1]

....

The Court answered the second question in the affirmative and the third in the negative.

[1]Translation by CMLR.

(3) SACE CASE

SACE *v.* Italian Ministry of Finance, Case 33/70 Preliminary ruling of 17 December 1970 on the request of the Brescia Tribunal.
(Jur.XVI (1970), p.1221-1231; CMLR 1971, pp.123-137; RTDE 1971, pp.182-191.)
Notes: Meier, *AWD 1971, pp.234-235;* Wägenbauer, *AWD 1971, pp.101-105.*

Facts: To cover the administrative costs of import clearing the Italian government subjected all imports to a levy of 0,5 per cent of their value. The Commission had considered this levy to have an effect equivalent to customs duties and ordered its abolishment by Directive 68/31 of 22 December 1967.[1]

Italy failed to comply with this directive, which moved the Commission to the application of Article 169 against Italy for violation of article 13 para 2 of the EEC Treaty. This procedure led to case 8/70, in which the Court of Justice decided that the Italian levy was in violation with the Treaty.[2]

SACE had paid over 50.000 lire of this import levy and had required repayment of that amount on 1 July 1970.

The Brescia Tribunal asked for a preliminary ruling on the question whether as a result of the adoption of Directive 68/31 of 22 December 1967 the provisions of Article 13(2) of the Treaty, or at least, of the directive itself were directly effective in the internal legal system in Italy.

If the first question was answered in the affirmative the Court was also asked whether from 1 July 1968 rights were created for individuals which the national courts had to take into account.

The Court held:

....

'10. The combined effect of Articles 9 and 13(2) implies, at the latest from the end of the transitional period, with regard to all charges with an equivalent effect to customs duties on imports, a clear and precise prohibition on the imposition of these charges, which is not accompanied by any reservation on the part of the States to make its entry into force subject to a positive measure of internal law or an intervention of the institutions of the Community. This prohibition is of its own nature perfectly capable of producing direct effects on the legal relations between the member States and their nationals. Therefore, from the end of the transitional period, these provisions generate for individuals, as far as charges to which they relate are concerned, rights to which the national courts must give effect.

11. Article 13(2) gave the Commission power, before the end of the transitional period, to provide for the abolition of taxes with equivalent effect designated by the

[1] *OJ 1968, No.L12/8.* [2] Decision of 18 November 1970, *Jur.XVI (1970), pp.961-975.*

Commission and the elimination of which the Commission, by means of directives, had ordered 'during' this period. Exercising this power the Commission, as a result of the 'acceleration decision' 66/532, fixed, with Directive 68/31, 1 July 1968 as the date by which the abovementioned charge had to be completely abolished.

12.It follows from this that the question posed by the President of the Brescia Tribunale, with regard to the direct effect of the obligation relating to the abolition of the Italian charge for administrative services, refers, in reality, to the combined provisions of Articles 9 and 13(2) of the Treaty. Decision 66/532 and Directive 68/31.

13.The effect of Directive 68/31 must be appraised in the light of the provisions as a whole. For this purpose, it is necessary to consider not only the form of the measure in issue but also its substance and its function in the system of the Treaty.

14.The fixing by the Commission, under Decision 532/66, of a date prior to the end of the transitional period did not modify in any way whatsoever the nature of the obligation imposed on the member States by Article 9 and 13(2). This obligation is therefore capable of producing direct effects, as it would have done at the end of the transitional period.

....

16.This interpretation is all the more valid since in its judgment of 18 November 1970[1] this Court held that Italy had failed to fulfil the obligations imposed on it by the Treaty by continuing to impose the charge in question after 1 July 1968.'[2]

....

(4)SLAUGHTERED COW CASE

Orsolina Leonesio v. Italian Ministry of Agriculture and Forestry, Case 93/71, Preliminary ruling of 17 May 1972 on the request of the *Pretore* of Lonato.
(Jur.; Rec. XVIII/3, pp.293-298.)

Facts: In Regulation 1975/69 of 27 June, 1968 the Council provided that farmers, having at least two dairy-cows qualified for a slaughter-premium, half of which would be paid by the European Agricultural Guidance and Guarantee Fund.

In a further Regulation, No. 2195/69, the Commission established that the premium would be paid within two months of the delivery of the certificate of slaughter. The member States were empowered to issue further rules.

The Italian Government issued directives but decided that their execution should be postponed until the necessary budgetary provisions had been made.

During 1970 Mrs.Leonesio slaughtered five dairy-cows and claimed a premium of 625.000 lire.

The *Pretore* requested a preliminary ruling on the questions whether the Regulations

[1]EC Commission v. Italy (8/70). [2]Translation by CMLR.

1975/69 and 2195/69 were directly applicable in the Italian legal order and, if so, whether they created a claim which individuals may enforce against the State and whether national legislation may postpone payment, under the claim.

The Court held:

....

'3.According to Article 189(2) of the Treaty regulations have 'general application' and are 'directly applicable' in every State. They therefore have direct effect on account of their nature and of the function in the system of Community sources of law and as such can give rise to private rights which national courts are bound to safeguard. The present claims which can be enforced against the State arise when the conditions provided for in a regulation are fulfilled without a possibility to subject their execution at the national level to provisions regarding application other than those which may be laid down in the regulation itself. The questions put must be answered in the light of these considerations.

....

9.The Italian government pleads that the regulations in question do not give rise to a right of payment of the premium so long as the national legislature has not granted the necessary credits for this.

10.According to Article 5, para (1) of the Treaty member States shall take all appropriate measures, whether general or particular, to ensure fulfilment of the obligations arising out of this Treaty or resulting from action taken by the institutions of the Community. If the objection of the Italian Republic were to be recognised, the farmers of that State would be placed in a less favourable position than those in the other states; this would involve disregard of the basic role that regulations must be uniformly applied throughout the whole Community. Furthermore, the Regulations No. 1975/69 and 2195/69, enumerating exhaustively the conditions on which the creation of the individual rights concerned depend, do not mention considerations of a budgetary character.

In order to have the same force for the nationals of all member States, Community regulations are integrated in the legal system applicable in the national territory, which must permit the direct operation provided for in Article 189 so that private individuals can invoke them without national provisions or procedures being used against them; the budgetary provisions of a member State can neither stand in the way of the direct application of a Community provision nor, consequently, in the way of the realisation of individual rights which are conferred on private individuals by such a provision.'

Note: The priority of regulations over national law (previous as well as posterior) was confirmed by the Court in Case 43/71 (Politi) of 14 December 1971, consideration No.9, Jur.XVII (1971), p.1049.

II. COURT SYSTEMS IN THE MEMBER STATES

LITERATURE: Auby et Fromont, *Les recours contre les actes administratifs dans les pays de le C.E.E.*, Dalloz, 1971, 473 pp.; *idem*, Les recours juridictionnels contre les actes administratifs spécialement économiques dans le droit des Etats membres de la C.E.E., *série Concurrence-Rapprochement des législations, 1971, no. 12, 63 pp.*

....

III. NATIONAL CONSTITUTIONS AND THE APPLICATION OF COMMUNITY LAW

LITERATURE: Lecourt, *Le juge devant le Marché Commun*, Genève 1970; Mertens de Wilmars, 'Les enseignements communautaires des jurisprudences nationals', *RTDE 1970, pp.454-469* and *RW 1970, Col.1905-1916;* Pescatore, 'L'application directe des traités européens par les juridictions nationales: la jurisprudence nationale', *RTDE 1969, pp.697-723* and *Riv.Dir.Eur.1970, pp.3-36* and *EuR 1970, pp.56-79;* Lagrange ,'Les obstacles constitutionnels à l'intégration européenne', *RTDE 1969, pp.240-254;* Waelbroeck, *Traités internationaux et juridictions internes dans les pays du Marché Commun*, Bruxelles-Paris 1969, 348 pp.; Hay, 'Supremacy of Community Law in National Courts', *AJCL 1968, pp.524-551;* Wengler, Réflexions sur l'application du droit international public par les tribunaux internes, *RGDIP 1968, pp.921-990.*

A. Belgium

LITERATURE: Ganshof van der Meersch, *De Belgische Rechter tegenover het Internationaal Recht en het Gemeenschapsrecht*, Brussels, 1969, 73 pp.; *JT 1969, pp.537-551; RBDI 1970, pp.409-461; Ibid*, Le droit communautaire et ses rapports avec les droits des Etats membres, *Les Novelles, Droit des Communautés Européennes*, Brussels 1969, pp. 41-79; Delva, 'Toetsing van de interne overheidsdaad aan het Verdrag', *Tijdschrift Bestuurswetenschappen en Publiekrecht, 1970, p. 397-411.*

During the Belgian constitutional revision in 1967-1971 a new provision, Article 25 *bis*, was added to the Belgian constitution, which provides:

'L'exercise de pouvoirs déterminés peut être attribué par un traité ou par une loi à des institutions de droit international public'.[1]

The insertion of this provision was deemed necessary to take into account the development of the international legal order.

The participation of Belgium in international organisations such as the N.A.T.O. and the European Communities had created doubts as to the compatibility with Article 25 of the Constitution, which stipulates that all powers emanate from the nation and are exercised in the way provided for by the Constitution. Article 25 *bis* has removed these doubts.

[1]Approved by the Belgian Senate on 7 June 1970 and published on 18 August 1970. See Louis, 'L'article 25 *bis* de la Constitution belge', *RMC 1970, pp.410-416.*

CASE

(1) BELGIAN FROMAGERIE LE SKI CASE (FINAL INSTANCE)

Belgian State (represented by the Minister of Economic Affairs) *v.* S.A. Fromagerie Franco-Suisse 'Le Ski'. *Cour de Cassation* (first chamber), Decision of 27 May 1971. (JT 1971, pp.460-474; RTDE 1971, pp.494-501; CMLR 1972, pp.372-373.)

Notes: Mertens de Wilmars, *SEW 1972, pp.44-51;* Plouvier, *RMC 1972, pp.171-185;* Bebr, *EuR 1971, pp.263-267;* Pescatore, *CDE 1971, pp.564-586;* Salmon, *JT 1971, pp.509-520;* Senelle, *RW, 5 December 1971.*

Facts: After the Court of Appeal, in the Belgian Fromagerie Le Ski case (Second instance see above, pp. 15-17) had declared that the S.A. Fromagerie Franco-Suisse 'Le Ski' was in principle entitled to claim restitution of the duties paid pursuant to the Royal Decrees of 3 November 1958, notwithstanding the law of 19 March 1965 which had stipulated that the amounts paid could not be recovered, the Belgian State instituted an appeal for cassation with the *Cour de Cassation.*

It contested the decision of the Court of Appeal on a number of grounds, claiming *inter alia* that under Belgian law only the legislature could test the conformity of laws to the constitution or to treaties binding the Belgian State.

The Court of Appeal had therefore wrongly refused to apply the law of 19 March 1968 which was of a later date than the law ratifying the EEC Treaty.

Furthermore by enacting the law of 19 March 1968 the Belgian legislature had clearly implied its intention that this law should be applied irrespective even of article 12 EEC.

In the submission of the government this provision did not preclude the Belgian legislature from deciding for internal purposes whether duties paid should be capable of restitution.

The Cour de Cassation held:

'According to Article 12 of the Treaty setting up the European Economic Community, the member States must refrain from introducing, as between themselves, any new customs duties on imports or exports or any charges having equivalent effect, and from increasing those which they already apply in their trade with each other;

The special duties on imports, of which the defendant claims restitution, were levied by the appellant pursuant to Royal Decrees and departmental orders that are all of a later date than 1 January 1958, the day on which the Treaty entered into force;

These Royal Decrees were repealed by Article 13 of the Royal Decree of 28 December 1961 and by Article 1 of the Royal Decree of 23 October 1965;

The law of 19 March 1968 nevertheless approved, with retroactive effect, the orders subsequent to 1 January 1958, under which the special duties have been levied—

duties of which the defendant claims restitution. The only Article of this law provides that the amounts paid pursuant to these orders constitute 'final payment', and that 'this payment is irrevocable and cannot give rise to dispute before any authority whatsoever';

The orders, which established, after 1 January 1958, special duties on imports of certain milk products, were contrary to Article 12 of the Treaty;

In as much as it consolidates the effects of these orders, the law of 19 March 1968 is also contrary to this provision;

Even when the consent to a treaty, required by Article 68, paragraph 2 of the Constitution, is given in the form of a law, the legislature does not exercise a normative function;

The conflict which exists between a rule of law established by an international treaty and a rule of law established by a subsequent statute, is not a conflict between two statutes;

The rule, according to which a law repeals the earlier law in so far as the two conflict, is not applicable in the case of a treaty conflicting with a law;

When the conflict is one between a rule of domestic law and a rule of international law having direct effects within the domestic legal order, the rule established by the treaty must prevail; its pre-eminence follows from the very nature of international treaty law;

This is all the more so, when the conflict is one, as in the present case, between a rule of domestic law and a rule of Community law;

In point of fact, the treaties which have created Community law set up a new legal order, in whose favour the member States have restricted the exercise of their sovereign powers in the fields defined by these treaties;

Article 12 of the Treaty establishing the European Economic Community produces direct effects and creates individual rights, which the national courts must safeguard;

It follows from the preceding considerations that the court had the duty to reject the application of the provisions of domestic law that are contrary to this provision of the Treaty;

Since it had noted that the rules of Community law and the rules of domestic law were incompatible in the case at issue, the judgment on appeal here could decide— without violation of the provisions of law indicated in the grounds for annulment— that the effects of the law of 19 March 1968, were 'stayed in as much as this law was in conflict with a directly applicable provision of international treaty law';

In this respect the grounds of appeal fail for lack of a legal basis.'[1]

....

---

[1]Translation by Europa Instituut.

The appeal is rejected.

In his conclusions the *Procureur-Général* Ganshof van der Meersch made the following observations on the relationship between international and national law:

....

'The doctrine of the pre-eminence of the rule of international law over the rule of domestic law, as formulated in the judgment (of the Court of Appeal), is correct. It is applied here only in as much as the rule of international treaty law is concerned.
It is only within these limits that the question was posed to the court and settled by it. Hence, it is only within these limits that it must be examined.

....

Now, the States are under a duty to see to it that a rule of domestic law, incompatible with a rule of international treaty law which is in conformity with the obligations they have assumed, can not be validly opposed to the latter. This obligation, which is sanctioned by the responsibility under international law, binds the legislator. It also rests on the court. In spite of the statutory independence of the latter, 'the judicial decisions which have an effect contrary to international law, do not release the States from their responsibility towards foreign countries'.
The International Law Commission of the United Nations included in its 'Draft declaration on the rights and duties of States' an Article affirming that every State 'has the duty of complying', in its relations with other States, 'with international law and especially with the principle that international law overrides the sovereignty of the States' (Art.14). Such an affirmation would necessarily be of a declaratory character.
The obligation of the States not to create a rule of domestic law incompatible with a rule of international law must have the superiority of the contractual rule of international law over as its corollary the rule of domestic law. If the rule of international law were not to prevail, international law would be doomed, threatened constantly with failing to achieve or maintain its general nature.
Professor Virally expressed the evidence of the superiority of the rule of international law over the rule of national law in a striking formula: 'every legal order confers on the addressees of its norms legal rights and duties which they would not be capable of claiming without that order'; it 'imposes obligations on them that are binding'. By this very act, every legal order affirms its superiority to its subjects. 'International law is inconceivable other than superior to the States, its subjects. To deny its superiority is to deny its existence' (in Mélanges offerts à Henri Rolin (1964), p.497).
The submission of the State—and therefore of its law—to international law, in its interstate relations, is based in the international legal order. This submission implies the priority of the rule of international law over the rule of domestic law.

The superiority of the treaty is justified as it is an act expressing a rule of international law of a contractual nature; the State which violates its obligations assumes in principle responsibility for it.

The Court (of *Cassation*), until now, has not expressly pronounced its opinion on the principle of the pre-eminence of the rule of international law. Today, the question is posed to it formally.

....

An express provision in the Constitution affirming this primacy is not indispensable in a constitutional system such as the Belgian one, which, like the one of Luxembourg, is not a comprehensive text but is situated halfway between the systems with a written and with an unwritten constitution. The adaptability of this system has allowed—as Professor Mast has written—a smooth evolution, avoiding the numerous formal amendments of countries with a rigid constitution.

The Constitution is, in point of fact, silent in respect to the relations between a treaty and a domestic law. No provision gives the latter pre-eminence over a rule of international law. Besides, the Constitution generally contains, apart from some rare exceptions, only principles and no comprehensive and exact rules. This system, which until now was the system of the Belgian constitution favours through the 'blank spaces' (vague norms), left in the text, which are subsequently filled in by a comparative study of principles, the evolution of our constitutional law and its expression through the precedents of case law.

One can prove the absence of any incompatibility neither of the text nor of the constitutional system with the primacy of international law. It is, above all, in the very nature of a rule of international law, as the *Cour supérieure de Justice* of the Grand Duchy of Luxembourg said, that a court finds the justification for its primacy.

If the Constitution should tomorrow follow the principle expressed in foreign constitutions and incorporate the supremacy of duly approved and ratified treaties or conventions over laws, such a provision would be, I believe, of a declaratory nature.

....

The ever growing number of normative treaties, the extension of the matters that these treaties comprise and, as my predecessor, Procureur Général, Mr.Hayoit de Termicourt already said in a remark which shows its full validity in the case submitted to you, 'nowadays the difficulty for the legislature itself to perceive every contradiction between a new law and existing treaties' does not allow you to abstain from clearly taking a stand on the solution that these conflicts require—conflicts that until now did not receive decisive echoes in the precedents and that a 'conciliatory interpretation' could not resolve.

....

This consideration, however, calls for a correction: not *every* international treaty takes precedence over the domestic law; thus a treaty that would impose only the duty to legislate according to principles determined in the treaty on the contracting parties, would certainly not create a conflict, not even to that extent. But, on the other hand, any rule of international law directly effective in the domestic legal order, must prevail over the norm of domestic law.

The directly effective provision of international law solves the conflict for the national court. It will be applied by this court notwithstanding any national law.

....

Hence, if the rule as set forth by the Court of Appeal within the framework of international treaty law, is correct, subject to the restriction just made, it follows that the Court would not be able to rely only on the doctrine of classical international law; but the legal justification of the decision of the judge is not exhausted with that doctrine.

The Treaty establishing the Economic Community—and also those establishing the two other European Communities, it must be added presents—compared to classical international treaties—pecularities which force us to consider specifically the problem of the relations between Community law and the law of each nation.

....

Today, for the first time, the question of the pre-eminence of the Community law is squarely posed to the Court and you also have to determine the legality of the effects of a directly applicable provision of the Treaty; it is therefore fitting to recall how this pre-eminence was justified by the Court of Justice, while keeping in mind that its decision, including this one, save for the competence exercised pursuant to Article 177 of the Treaty, is not binding on you.

....

The pre-eminence of the rules of Community law has a double legal justification. On the one hand, by their consent to the transfer of their rights and duties under the Treaty, to the legal order of the Community, the States have definitively restricted 'their sovereign rights'; more accurately one should say 'the exercise of their sovereign powers'.

The structure of the Community implies some surrender of sovereignty and Community law is a specific law which sanctions these instances of surrender. The objective of integration of the treaties of Paris and Rome materializes through the attribution of powers to the Community institutions that have the goal and effect to fix a corresponding restriction of the powers of the member States. In this manner a duty arises for them to refrain from legislating in fields governed by the Treaty and to implement the Treaty in the cases where they must complete the Community legislation.

On the other hand, Community law is a specific and autonomous law which imposes itself on the jurisdiction of the Member States and does not allow the domestic law of any Member State to oppose it. The very nature of the legal order established by the treaties of Rome supplies this precedence with a foundation of its own, independent of the constitutional provisions of the States. This special character of Community law results from the objectives of the Treaty, which are the establishment of a new legal order of which the subjects are not only the States but also the nationals of these States.

It results also from the fact that the Treaty created institutions with powers of their own at their disposal and notably the power to create new sources of law. By their very structures these institutions are witnesses to the will of the authors of the Treaty to by-pass the national spheres in order to impose delegated duties directly on private persons or to give them the direct benefit of certain rights.'[1]

. . . .

Note: A few years earlier a lower judge, the *Juge de Paix* of Antwerp (*2e Canton*), in a decision of 24 December 1968[2] had come to the conclusion that Treaty law enjoyed priority over national law, whether of an earlier or of a later date. This court had requested a preliminary ruling of the Court of Justice (Consolidated Cases 2 and 3/69) concerning the concept of measures having equivalent effect to customs duties. See *CMLR 1969, p.315.*

The *Juge de Paix* of Berchem in a decision of 23 May, 1967[3], was more restrictive than the Antwerp court in a case based on identical facts.

B. Germany

LITERATURE: Rambow, L'exécution des directives de la CEE en République fédérale d'Allemagne, *CDE 1970, pp.379-411;* Emricht, *Das Verhältnis des Rechts der europäischen Gemeinschaften zum Recht der Bundesrepublik Deutschland,* Marburg, 1969, 148 pp.; Rahn, Der Bundesfinanzhof und das Gemeinschaftsrecht der EWG, *AWD (1969), pp.341-345;* Arnold, *Das Rangverhältnis zwischen dem Recht der europäischen Gemeinschaften und dem innerdeutschen Recht,* thesis Würzburg, 1968, 226 pp.; Basse, *Das Verhältnis zwischen der Gerichtsbarkeit des Gerichtshofes der europäischen Gemeinschaften und der deutschen Zivilgerichtsbarkeit,* Berlin 1967, 464 pp.

1.General aspects

Constitution Article 25

'The general rules of public international law are an integral part of federal law. They should take precedence over the laws and shall directly create rights and duties for the inhabitants of the federal territory'.

[1]*JT 1971, pp.461-471, RTDE 1971, pp.423-457;* translation by Europa Instituut; see also Mosler, L'application du droit international public par les tribunaux nationaux, *RCADI 1957, I, p.628.* [2]*JT 1969, p.281; RW 1968-1969, Col.1654; RTDE 1969, pp.324-337; CDE 1969, pp.683-70.* [3]*RW 1968-1969, Col.1142; CDE 1970, p.197.*

CASES

(1) GERMAN CASE ON APPLICATION OF INTERNATIONAL LAW
Bundesverfassungsgericht (Federal Constitutional Court), Decision of 14 May 1968,
AWD 1968, p.305.

Facts: If it is doubtful, in a lawsuit, whether a rule of international law is part of the
federal law and whether it directly creates rights and duties for individuals (Article 25
of the German constitution), the court has to obtain a decision from the *Bundesverfassungsgericht* (Article 100, para 2, *GG*). With respect to this provision of the
constitution.

The Bundesverfassungsgericht held:
'Submission of the question to the *Bundesverfassungsgericht* pursuant to Article 100,
para 2, of the constitution, is already required in the case the court concerned, considering the question whether and to what extent a general rule of international law
applies, comes across feelings of doubt that must be taken seriously, and not only in
case the court itself has doubts.

....

By means of the incorporation—accomplished by Article 25 of the constitution of the
general rules of international law into the federal law, with priority over the ordinary
laws, the constitution compels federal law to conform with the general provisions of
international law. The meaning of the direct applicability of the general rules of
international law lies in thrusting aside conflicting domestic law or accomplishing its
application in accordance with international law. As the general rules of the law of
nations develop steadily, the occasions of possible conflict between general international law and domestic law cannot be forseen.

The process of transformation of the domestic law by the incorporated international—
hence federal—law takes place outside the formal legislative process provided for by
the Constitution. The general rules of international law predominantly are universally
applicable customary law of nations, complemented by acknowledged general principles of law (*B.Verf.GE*.15, 25 (32 ff., 34 ff); 16, 27, (33)). Only in some instances they
are evident, whereas in many cases their existence and scope must be determined first.
The founders of the constitution have put up with the dangers that result from the
incorporation of international law into the federal law with precedence over the ordinary laws for the authority of the legislature and for legal security—both are part of
the basis of the structure of a State governed by law and order—in so far as these
dangers are in the nature of things. The procedure of Article 100, para 2 of the Constitution, aims chiefly at the strictest possible limitation of the dangers that result
from the incorporation of international law for the authority of the legislature and for

legal security. In case of doubt regarding existence and scope of a general rule of international law, only the *Bundesverfassungsgericht* should decide, but with generally binding effect and with force of law.

Apart from when the case is clear, only the *Bundesverfassungsgericht* should be competent to determine the existence or non-existence and the scope of a general rule of international law.

An interpretation of Article 100, para 2 of the Constitution according to which the duty to refer would depend on the subjective opinion of the court concerned in case of objectively doubtful general rules of international law, would not do justice to this goal of Article 100, para 2 of the Constitution.'[1]

Note: For another decision of the *Bundesverfassungsgericht* (Federal Constitutional Court), see below, p.70, German Lütticke Case, Constitutional Appeal.

(2)GERMAN MOLKEREI-ZENTRALE CASE (FINAL JUDGMENT)

Firm of Molkerei-Zentrale Westfalen/Lippe GmbH Trockenmilchwerk v. Hauptzollamt Paderborn, *Bundesfinanzhof* (Federal Finance Court), Decision of 11 July 1968, No.VII 156/65.

(Sammlung der Entscheidungen 92, p.405; CMLR 1969 pp.312-314; EuR 1968, pp.401-403; AWD 1968, p.356; CDE 1970, p.216.)

Notes: Brändel, *EuR 1969, pp.52-55;* Hopt, *6 CMLRev.1968, pp.415-419;* Meier, *AWD 1968, pp.357-358.*

Facts: Plaintiff imported dairy products from Belgium into Germany. At the border a 4 per cent compensation tax was levied.

Plaintiff alleged that this tax violated Article 95 of the EEC Treaty and was therefore invalid. According to the Second Lütticke Case (Jud.Rem.pp.111, 112), Art.95 could be directly invoked by citizens of the Communities. The *Bundesfinanzhof* seriously doubted whether this was the intention of the ruling in the Lütticke case and asked for a further preliminary ruling on Articles 95 and 97.[2] On 3 April 1968, this preliminary ruling was given (Jud.Rem.pp.112, 113).

In the meantime (up to 31 March 1968) 340480 claims had been made for repayment of compensatory taxes; 25912 cases had been brought before Financial Courts; 67 Revisions were pending before the *Bundesfinanzhof*. On the basis of the preliminary ruling of the Court of Justice, the Federal Minister of Finance has issued a statement that repayments would not be possible since the Court of Justice had denied the direct effect of Article 97 of the EEC Treaty.[3]

[1]Translation by Europa Instituut. [2]Decision of 18 July 1967, *AWD 1967, p.319; NJW 1968, p.367; Entscheidungen des Bundesfinanzhofs 89,p.52.* [3]*AWD 1968, pp.241, 242.*

The *Bundesfinanzhof* had to decide what effect should be given to the preliminary ruling of the Court of Justice.

The Bundesfinanzhof held:

....

'If the imposition of internal duties on products imported from other member States is contested, then as long as the conditions of Article 97 of the Treaty are not satisfied, so as to preclude any reliance on the immediate rights conferred on individuals by Article 95, the national court has to decide whether the provision of national law in issue contravenes the prohibition against discrimination contained in Article 95. In so far as the court finds that there is a contravention of that rule of Community law it must take account of the precedence of Community law. That is the only way in which the immediate effectiveness accorded to Article 95 by the European Court can be interpreted, and a corresponding judicial protection be given to the individual subjects of member States of the Community. The limitation on the revenue jurisdiction of member States established at the outset by Article 95 *et.seq.* and the consequent precedence of Community law, to the extent at any rate that simple provisions of national law conflict with it, are based on the transfer of sovereignty to the European Economic Community under the *Zustimmungsgesetz* of 27 July 1957.

If a rate of taxation contravenes Article 95, the relevant provision of national law is not void in the sense that no tax may be levied under it at all. That view is contradicted by the fact that such a rate of taxation contravenes a legal rule only in relation to the member States of the Community and not in relation to third countries. In the case of imports from member States, therefore, a rate of taxation is inapplicable only to the extent that it contravenes Article 95. In the same way, as long as no other rule of law applies, the determination of a rate of taxation is only illegal to the extent that it is based on the application of the part of the tax rate which contravenes Article 95. It is generally the case with compensatory taxes that only a part of the rate contravenes Article 95 because even those comparable domestic products which are exempt from tax are affected by the turnover tax charge on the raw materials and capital equipment used in their manufacture, and that turnover tax charge on the preliminary stages of manufacture may be compensated for in the rate of compensatory tax.

The relevant court must therefore recognise the validity of the determination of a tax rate up to the amount which would result from the application of a tax rate in a conformity with Article 95.

....

When the court examines the compatibility of rates of compensation tax with Article 95, therefore, as long as there has been no substantial change between the date of the import and the coming into effect of the Umsatzsteuer Änderungs-Gesetz No.17 in the relevant economic relationships or in the turnover tax charge on similar or comparable domestic products, a contravention of Article 95 may be ruled out to the extent that the rate in force at the relevant date does not exceed the rate which was in force at the date of the publication of the Umsatzsteuer Änderungs-Gesetz No.17, and was established by that Act as an average rate with effect from the following day. For the purpose of the present case that means that the relevant rate of 4 per cent must be regarded as contravening Article 95 of the EEC Treaty only to the extent that it exceeds the rate which was reduced to 3 per cent in 1965 and was established as an average rate at that level by the Umsatzsteuer Änderungs-Gesetz No.17 in other words, to the extent of 1 per cent.'[1]

Note: The direct effect of Article 95 of the EEC Treaty within the German legal order remained difficult to accept for the German financial authorities. For official standpoints of the German Minister of Finance and of the Financial Courts, see *AWD 1969, pp.155-157;* for further cases before the *Bundesfinanzgericht*, see Hopt, *8 CMLRev.1971, pp.97-103.* See also *AWD 1970, pp.135, 136; CMLR 1969, pp.221-243* and *261-265; CMLR 1971, pp.87-91*, and for an earlier case *CMLR 1968, pp.62-68.* The *Bundesverfassungsgericht* (Federal Constitutional Court) discussed the question in its decision of 9 June 1971, 2 BvR 225/69, *AWD 1971, pp.418-420*, and finally settled the dispute. See also Meier, Zur Geltung von Gemeinschaftsnormen im innerstaatlichen Bereich, *AWD 1968, pp.205-212*, who gives a full review of developments before the final judgment in the German Mölkerei-Zentrale Case. See also Meier, *AWD 1968 pp.167 ff and in AWD 1969, pp.72, 242 and 300.*

(3) GERMAN NEUMANN CASE (FINAL JUDGMENT)

Neumann *v.* Hauptzollamt Hof/Saale, *Bundesfinanzhof* (Federal Court of Finance), Decision of 10 July 1968, No.VII 198/63.

(Sammlung der Entscheidungen 93, p.102; AWD 1968, pp.397-399; EuR 1969, pp.255-262; CMLR 1969, pp.289-292; NJW 1969, p.388; ZZV 1969, pp.16-19.)

Notes: Meier, *NJW 1969, p.388;* Pescatore, *Rec.D.1969, p.179;* Zuleeg, *EuR 1969, pp.262-268.*

Facts: Neumann imported chickens from Poland and was required to pay a levy under Regulations Nos.22 and 135/62. The question arose whether the German Ratification Law of the EEC Treaty was valid under the German constitution and whether the above regulations had been validly made under EEC law. By its decision of 25 April, 1967, the *Bundesfinanzhof* decided the first question in the affirmative and asked for a preliminary ruling on the second one (Jud.Rem., pp.147-149). On 13 December 1967, the Court of Justice gave the requested preliminary ruling (Jud.Rem.pp.107, 108). In the present case the *Bundesfinanzhof* had to decide what consequences should be given to the preliminary ruling.

[1]Translation by CMLR, footnotes omitted.

The Bundesfinanzhof held:

. . . .

A

'By virtue of Article 189(2) of the EEC Treaty, legal rules made by the organs of the Community are directly applicable and generally binding in the member States of the Community. Their reception into the legal systems of member States, unlike the case of the provisions of the usual international law treaties, is not based on a transformation of the particular rules by means of specific acts of ratification. Rather, the original member States created a new and autonomous source of sovereign power within a limited sphere of action by means of the EEC Treaty, and the law derived from that source obtains validity within member States from the fact that they have made their jurisdictions subject to that sovereign authority.

The existence and the sovereign powers of the European Community are based solely on the external powers of the member States, which include the capacity to create international institutions with their own sovereign powers. For that reason they depend only on the validity under international law of the Act constituting the Community, that is, on the valid ratification of the EEC Treaty by the original member States. Accordingly, Community legislation implements itself independently of and apart from the legal and constitutional systems of the individual States. They are affected on the other hand by the granting of immediate effectiveness within member States to laws passed by the Community. The consequent subordination of member States' jurisdictions and the rights of legal subjects residing therein to a wider outside sovereign power operating side by side with the national sovereign power, limits their internal jurisdiction and therefore implies a change in the constitutions of the individual States. But that can only be achieved by an Act of the national legislature and not by means of an international treaty.

According to the view taken by the Court, therefore, European Community law on the one hand and the national law of the German Federal Republic on the other constitute two separate legal systems independent of each other, the first being based on the EEC Treaty, the second on the *Grundgesetz* as the national constitution. For that reason the validity of Community law may only be tested by the EEC Treaty and that of national law may only be tested by the relevant national constitution. On the other hand, the validity of European law within the internal jurisdiction of member States presupposes that the relevant national legislature has effectively made that jurisdiction subject to the legislative power of the European Community. If that has been done in the case of the German Federal Republic, then Community law has the same binding force as national law within the sphere to which the internal legal system applies.

The rules of Community law, which operate within the systems of individual member States, are therefore co-ordinated with European law so far as their creation is concerned and with national law so far as concerns their applicability.

That is why the jurisdiction to interpret the effects of Community law within their internal jurisdictions, belongs basically to member States, although the European Court is competent to give preliminary rulings under the provisions of Article 177 of the Treaty. For the validity and content of a rule of law depend on the legislative act, and in the case of Community law legislation takes place within the European legal system. Since, as explained above, all questions concerning the valid implementation or the interpretation of rules of Community law must be decided exclusively on the basis of European law, it is logical that the task of deciding on those questions should be assigned to the jurisdiction of the European Court. Seen in that light, the competence of the European Court and the binding force of its judgments relate to the question whether a rule of Community law has been validly brought into effect according to the European legal system and how it should be interpreted.

It is the task of national courts on the other hand to decide whether a rule of European law, which is valid as such, has legal effects within the relevant internal jurisdiction, and if so what effects. That is when the question arises whether the national legislature has effectively made the internal jurisdiction of the State subject to the sovereignty of the European Community, and also whether or not the application of the rule of European law conflicts with the provisions of national law in a particular case.

The last question depends on whether and to what extent European law can prevail over national law in cases of conflict. The European Court has continuously recognised the consequent limits on its jurisdiction, and has frequently explained that the decision whether the Treaty is applicable according to the basic principles of the law of the individual State concerned is a matter for national courts.

There is nothing contradictory in the Court's speaking in its judgment in Costa v. Enel (6/64) about the precedence of Community law over national law. For it only dealt with the internal application of the European law in the context of the admissibility of the question referred to it by the national court, a matter which it had to decide. The Court did not take up the question of precedence in the judgment, and in fact stated expressly that it did not have to decide the question of the compatibility of a provison of national law with the Treaty.

The judgment of the European Court in Fa.Max Neumann v. Hauptzollamt Hof/ Saale is a binding decision against all the objections raised by the appellant to the validity of Regulation 135 as an act of Community law. This Court is therefore precluded for the purposes of the present case from considering the validity of legislation passed by the organs of the Community and implemented outside the national legal system. That applies to the appellant's arguments that the EEC Treaty gives the Community no jurisdiction to pass agricultural levy regulations and that the Council's Regulation 22 is no valid basis for the regulation of the Commission applied by the Customs Office. The contention that there is a breach of general principles of European law is in the same category. Furthermore, the questioning of the validity of Regulation 135 according to the rules of the German Constitution is also excluded for the reason that, as shown above, the organs of the EEC exercise their sovereign powers outside the sphere of application of any individual Member State's constitution.

B

As far as matters within the competence of the Court are concerned, it remains to be decided whether the national legislature has effectively made the internal domain subject to the EEC Treaty, and whether, as has been argued, there are rules of national constitutional law which prevent the application of Regulation 135 to the present case.'[1]
....

(4) GERMAN YOGA CASE

Bundesgerichtshof (Federal Supreme Court), Decision of 27 February 1969.
(AWD 1969, pp.230-232; NJW 1969, p.978; WuW 1969, pp.504-508; CMLR 1969, pp.134-137; GP 1970, p.9).
Notes: Belke, *AWD 1969, pp.214-220;* Ulmer, *BB 1969, p.692.*

Facts: An Italian firm had registered its trade mark Yoga and had granted to a German firm an exclusive right to sell Yoga products in German. Disputes concerning the agreement were to be decided by an arbitration tribunal.

After two years a dispute arose between the parties and the German firm obtained a decision from the arbitration-tribunal condemning the Italian firm to a payment of 1.250.000 DM. The Italian firm refused to pay. In the litigation on the *exequatur* of the arbitration-decision, the question of a violation of the German public order was decisive.

The Bundesgerichtshof held:

....

'Under Article 1041 (1) (ii) of the Code of Civil Procedure the court must determine not whether the arbitration award conflicts with public policy but whether its recognition (by the national court) would conflict with public policy.

....(1) Although the provisions of the EEC Treaty are part of so-called 'Community law', with the entry into force of the EEC Treaty they have been adopted into the laws of the member States and must be applied by their courts. Therefore, provided

[1] Translation by CMLR, footnotes omitted.

that they concern the basis of the Common Market and have not merely been enacted out of considerations of expediency, they form part of the doctrine of 'public policy' in force in the Federal Republic....

The unambiguous wording of Article 85 of the EEC Treaty (Paragraph (1): 'incompatible with the Common Market and... prohibited'; Paragraph (2): 'void') clearly shows that these rules form a basic and compulsory provision of the EEC competition law. In view of the clear wording of these provisions and their treatment by the European Court up to the present, contrary to the opinion of Professor Steindorff, there is no need to refer to the European Court under Article 177 (3) of the EEC Treaty for a preliminary ruling on the question as to whether these provisions are to be interpreted merely as a *lex quasi imperfecta* the implementation of which is made dependent on considerations of expediency.

The agreement of the parties of 8 August 1963, being an agreement which contained an exclusive sales right for the plaintiff company with absolute territorial protection in the Federal German Republic, was, as the appellate court also held in theory, void under Article 85(1) and (2) of the EEC Treaty. The appellate court came to this conclusion, after following the detailed statement of the views of the *Bundeskartellamt* of 9 October 1967, by considering the case in the light of the previous decisions of the European Court on similar agreements. Its detailed findings reveal no error of law and, in particular, do not deviate from the interpretation which the European Court has given to the provisions of Article 85 of the Treaty in its previous decisions. On this point too there is, therefore, no need to submit a question to the European Court for a preliminary ruling under Article 177(3) of the Treaty....

Accordingly, if the agreement of the parties of 8 August 1963 was—with the exception of the arbitration clause—void in its entirety for the infringement of Article 85(1) of the EEC Treaty, the arbitration award of 27 May 1966 cannot be recognised since its recognition would also conflict with that Article of the Treaty (Article 1041(1) (ii) of the Code of Civil Procedure).'[1]

(5) GERMAN LÜTTICKE CASE

Bundesverfassungsgericht (Federal Constitutional Court), Decision of 9 June 1971, AWD 1971, pp.418-420.

Facts: Plaintiff raised a Constitutional Complaint (*Verfassungsbeschwerde*) against the judgment of the Bundesfinanzhof of 15 January 1969 (AWD 1969, p.154) which was delivered subsequent to the decision of the Court of Justice in the Second Lütticke (Jud.Rem.p.111) and Molkereizentrale (Jud.Rem.p.112) cases. In accordance with these latter decisions the Bundesfinanzhof had reduced the compensatory turn-

[1]Translation by CMLR, footnotes omitted.

over tax on imported milkpowder by 1 percent to conform to the 3 pecrcent tax permitted under Article 95.

Lütticke submitted that this decision violated the German Constitution on the grounds *inter alia* that the BFH had acted contrary to the principle of the separation of powers, in that the BFH itself, instead of the legislator, had decided the permissible level of the tax. This complaint caused the Constitutional Court to explain its position on the relationship between the Community legal order and national law.

The Bundesverfassungsgericht held:

'No constitutional objections exist against the precedence that the Bundesfinanzhof has given Article 95 of the EEC Treaty over incompatible German tax law, on the basis of the preliminary decision of the European Court of Justice (of 16 June 1966) which was applied for in accordance with Article 177 of the Treaty. For in accordance with Article 24, para 1, of the Constitution, a separate legal order of the EEC has originated through the ratification of the EEC Treaty, which has effects on the domestic legal order and which must be applied by the German courts.

The decision of the European Court of Justice interpreting Article 95 of the Treaty, laid down in the framework of its competence according to Article 177 EEC Treaty, was binding on the Bundesfinanzhof. Article 24, para 1, of the Constitution, holds—when properly interpreted—not only that the delegation of sovereign rights to international institutions is possible, but also that sovereign acts of its organs, as—in this case—the judgment of the Eruopean Court of Justice, must be recognized by the originally exclusive holder of sovereignty.

Starting from this legal position, the German courts must apply, since the moment the Common Market became effective, also those rules of law that, it is true, are to be appropriated to a separate, foreign, sovereign power, but still unfold direct effect in the domestic field and overrule and set aside incompatible national law on the basis of their interpretation by the European Court of Justice; for only in this way the subjective rights accorded to the citizens of the Common Market can be realised.

According to the rules laid down in the Constitution for the relation between legislative and judicial power it belongs to the tasks of the Judiciary to verify the validity each applicable norm. The Court may not apply a provision which conflicts with a superior rule in the case it has to decide. This rule does not apply to the extend the incompatibility of formal sub-constitutional law in relation to the Constitution has been reserved to the Federal Constitutional Court in accordance with art.100 para.1 of the Constitution.

The Federal Constitutional Court is not competent to decide the question whether a simple norm of national law is incompatible with a provision of superior European Community law, and whether therefore its validity must be denied. The solution of this conflict of norms is therefore left to the competent courts as part of their power to review and reject.

Within this competence the Federal Court of Finance could in so far deny recognition of para.7, section 4 UStG 1951 applicable in the case at hand, with Art.95 EEC. In doing so it only gave a correct application of national law in an individual case, which was required to garantee the direct effect of Art.95 EEC to individual citizens and its precedence over conflicting national law.

The Federal Court of Finance has not gone beyond this competence:

When lowering the applicable percentage of the compensetory turn-over-tax of 4 to 3 per cent it has strictly fololowed the calculations of the Commission of the EEC and the decision of the legislator made in application thereof in Art.6 USÄndG for a later time periode.'

2.Constitutionality of the Community Treaties

LITERATURE: Günter Gorny, *Verbindlichkeit der Bundesgrundrechte bei der Anwendung vom Gemeinschaftsrecht durch deutsche Staatsorganen*, Berlin 1969; Schwaiger, Zum Grundrechts-schutz gegenüber den Europäischen Gemeinschaften, *NJW (1970), pp.975-980;* Constantinesco, L'introduction et le contrôle de la constitutionalité des traités européens et le droit allemand, *RBDI 1969, pp.425-459;* Kleinmann, Verfassungsbeschwerde gegen deutsche Gesetze, die euro-päisches Gemeinschaftsrecht transformieren?, *NJW (1969), pp.355-358;* Oppermann, *Deutsche und europäische Verfassungsrechtsprechung. Vergleichende Gedanken zur Judikatur des BVerfG. und des Gerichtshofes der Europäischen Gemeinschaften*, Der Staat, Berlin 1969, pp.445-466.

(1)SECOND GERMAN EXPORTBOND CASE (FIRST DECISION)

Internationale Handelsgesellschaft mbH *v*. Einfuhr und Vorratsstelle für Getreide und Futtermittel, *Verwaltungsgericht* Frankfurt a/M, Decision of 18 March 1970, Case II/2 E 228/69. CMLR 1970, pp.294-313.

Facts: The *Handelsgesellschaft* obtained an export licence for 20.000 tons of corn-flour, valid until 31 December 1967. On the ground of Article 12, para 1(3) of Council Regulation 120/67/EEC of 13 June 1967.[1] The obtaining of the licence depended on a deposit of 0.50 Units of Account per ton, as a guarantee that the export would be realized. When it did not export the full amount of corn-flour a notice was served upon it, dated 8 April 1969, for forfeiture of the deposit of 17.026,47 DM. It maintained before the *Verwaltungsgericht* that such forfeiture was unconstitutional. From 1966 onwards the *Verwaltungsgericht* Frankfurt am Main had declared certain similar regulations invalid without asking on each occasion for a preliminary ruling.[2]

[1]*OJ 1967, p.2269.* [2]For the basic judgement of the Verwaltungsgericht Frankfurt a/M. on this question see the First German Exportbond Case, *Jud. Rem.*, pp.205, 206. For an enumeration of the other cases see 1972 CMLR., pp.178, 179 no.16-23.

The Verwaltungsgericht held:

....

'...This Chamber, in deciding the position, conceives at the outset that Regulations 120/67 and 473/67 are not German statutes but special European Community provisions, being part neither of public international law nor of the national law of a member State.

However, by ratifying the EEC Treaty the Federal Republic has not renounced its rights, by means of Article 24(1) of the Constitution, to protect elementary constitutional rights within the framework of a European Community. It must be assumed that the German legislator agreed to enter the EEC only on condition that the law governing the relations between the Community States is equivalent in value to German constitutional law, and thus the essential structural principles of national law are protected in Community law. Under Article 24(1) of the Constitution all statutes are bound to observe the requirements of the Constitution.

They cannot effect a type of constitutional amendment through the device of European Community law. Failure to observe these structural principles of the German Constitution within the framework of European Community law is technically a breach of the EEC Treaty. It cannot have any validity within the sphere of national law, as the first elementary principle of supranational treaty law depends, according to the above principles, on the fundamental principles of the German Constitution. Thus it is incorrect for the respondent authority to argue, as it has done in this case, that the principle of reasonableness exists only in German law and not in the law of the EEC Treaty. Quite apart from the fact that the principle of reasonableness exists in public international law as an emanation of the general principle prohibiting abuse of law, the EEC institutions are obliged to recognise that reasonableness is an essential part not only of the law of the Federal Republic but also of the Community.

....

On studying these cases which are conceivable in theory and have in fact occurred, the Chamber has reached the conclusion that the export deposit regulations infringe the freedom of exporters to develop their business and sell their products....

Duty to export and the obligation to pay a deposit infringe fundamental rights. The well-being of the Community cannot justify such infringements....

It is a fundamental principle of German legal theory that the compulsory payment of money or a penalty, which is a category into which a deposit must in the legal sense be put, cannot be imposed without fault on the part of the individual. This principle cannot be satisfied simply because of defects in the Authority's organization. The fact that this type of deposit regulation is unconstitutional because it infringes the freedom of the individual to carry on and develop his business and the principle of reasonableness has been made clear by the Federal Constitutional Court in its decision on the constitutional validity of the said Penalties Act....

The Chamber has reached a firm conclusion that the Federal Republic in accepting Regulations 120/67 and 473/67 within the framework of European Community legislation was not prepared to tolerate such invasion and infringement of its fundamental rights and that it did not abdicate its vigilance over such constitutional principles.'[1]

....

The Court stayed proceedings and referred the following questions to the Court of Justice:

1. Whether the obligation to export laid down in Article 12(3) of EEC Council Regulation 120/67 dated 13 June 1967, the requirement of a deposit and the power to order forfeiture of such deposit if the articles are not exported within the period of the licence, are lawful.

2. If the answer to question 1 is yes, whether Article 9 of EEC Commission Regulation 473/67 dated 21 August 1967, in its application to Regulation 120/67, is lawful in that it excludes the power to order forfeiture of the deposit only in cases of *force majeure*.

Note: For the reply of the Court of Justice to the question of the *Verwaltungsgericht*, see Chapter Five, p.150.

(2) SECOND GERMAN EXPORTBOND CASE (SECOND DECISION)

Internationale Handelsgesellschaft mbH *v*. Einfuhr- und Vorratsstelle für Getreide und Füttermittel, *Verwaltungsgericht* (Administrative Court) Frankfurt a.M., Decision of 24 November 1971.

(CMLR 1972, pp.177-212.)

Facts: By its first decision in the Second German Exportbond case, (see above) the *Verwaltungsgericht* Frankfurt a.M. had asked for a preliminary ruling. Similar preliminary rulings had been requested by the *Verwaltungsgerichtshof* of Hessen when dealing, on appeal, with cases in which the *Verwaltungsgericht* Frankfurt had refused to ask for preliminary rulings. The requested rulings were delivered by the Court of Justice on December 17, 1970 (see e.g. case 11/70, below p.150).

Having received a ruling that the disputed regulations were valid the *Verwaltungsgericht* had thus to decide on the forfeiture of the exportbonds.

The Verwaltungsgericht held:

....

[1]Translation by CMLR.

This Chamber cannot agree with the decision of the European Court; it considers the Community provisions cited to be unconstitutional.

....

Thus if the decision of the European Court is followed the forfeiture decision would be lawful, and the plaintiff company's application would have to be dismissed, since in the view of this Chamber a case of *force majeure* must be ruled out, although the company might possibly succeed on the principle of non-liability (*Nichtvertreten-müssen*) in the event of the legality of the security system.

On the other hand, according to the view held by this Court, the claim must succeed in any event. Since even after the preliminary ruling the opinion of the European Court cannot be brought into harmony with that of this Chamber, this Chamber submits the case to the *Bundesverfassungsgericht* under Article 100(1) of the Constitution. The question of the validity of the law in issue is in fact relevant to the decision.

....

The question whether the *Bundesverfassungsgericht* (German Constitutional Court) can review the provisions of Community law is closely connected with the question of whether and to what extent Community law can be scrutinised against the fundamental principles of the Constitution.

If, in fact, it was established that Community law took precedence over the national constitution, there would certainly be reason to assume that Community law could not be reviewed by a national organ, the *Bundesverfassungsgericht*, but solely by the appropriate organs of the Community. Various answers are found in decided cases and among writers on the subject to the question of whether the supra-national law of the European Communities can be compared with and scrutinised against the fundamental principles of the Constitution, *i.e.*, the national constitution of a member-State. In its above-mentioned decisions the European Court considers that the uniform application of Community law would be impaired if provisions or principles of national law could be invoked when deciding on the validity of measures of the Community organs; that the validity of these measures can only be tested within the framework of Community law, as a national legal provision, however formulated, cannot take precedence over the law created by the EEC Treaty, and thus derived from an autonomous source of law, because of its independent status, if it is not to be deprived of its character as Community law and if the legal basis of the Community itself is not to be jeopardised. Zweigert, Wohlfahrt and Constantinescu come to the same conclusion, albeit for other reasons. Whereas Zweigert and Wohlfahrt see in the transfer of sovereign rights under Article 24 of the Constitution a definitive transfer of certain national legislative powers to the Community, with the result that Community law takes precedence over the national constitution. Constantinescu bases his view on the fact that within the Community only Italy and Germany have a constitutional check on statutes. He maintains that if it were conceded that these States could test Community law against their constitutions they would be privileged as against the other member-States of the Community. Badura, too, considers that Community law takes precedence over national constitutional or statute law, without however annulling it. He maintains that the national legislature cannot annul or amend Community law and the Community legislative organs cannot annul or amend national law, whereas Rupp comes to the conclusion that Community institutions and Community organisations are justified solely by the aim of a national and political unification of Europe, so that it is tolerable that a temporary decline in national democracy and constitutionality is suffered as the price for the construction of a political union of Europe.

(11)On the other hand, the VGH Kassel, Carstens, von Mangoldt-Klein, Maunz-Dürig and Hamann-Lenz consider that Community law can at least be scrutinised against the fundamental provisions of the Constitution which the Federal legislature has no power to abrogate or restrict. They maintain that these provisions are not only the general human rights and basic rights (Articles 1 to 19 of the Constitution), the division of the Federation into *Länder* (Article 20 (1), the democratic and social welfare system of the Federation and the *Länder* (Articles 20 and 28) and the participation of the *Länder* in the legislative process (Article 70), but all the principles of a constitutional state. They conclude that since according to Articles 19 (2) and 79 (3) the German legislature is bound by these superior provisions in relation to all legislation, it can neither enact laws that conflict with these principles nor in this respect invoke the superior provisions for the transfer of sovereign powers to international institutions permitted by Article 24. They maintain that accordingly under Article 24 the legislature can only transfer to the Community the legislative powers attributed to it by the Constitution and restricted by Articles 19 (2) and 79(3). They contend that if any other view prevailed the result would be that the Federal legislature could evade its subjection to the provisions of the Constitution by transferring the relevant legislative powers to a superior Community which could then enact the unlawful provision forbidden to the Federal legislature by the Constitution, and that this unconstitutional provision would then have validity as unconstitutional national law and would have to be observed. Agreeing with those who hold this view, Professor Wengler therefore sees in the infringement of the fundamental principles of the Constitution in the framework of Community law a breach of the EEC Treaty.

(12)This Chamber agrees with those who wish to test Community law against the fundamental principles of the Constitution, since a critical appraisal of the views set out above shows that the view that Community law takes precedence *cannot be based on any legal foundation*....

(13)This chamber believes that it has found the real reason for the contradictory views in the various, purely politically conditioned attitudes to the Community. Some (the European Court, Grosfeld, Zweigert, Wohlfahrt, Constantinescu, Rupp and Badura) see in too rigid an adherence to the traditional legal structures and claims to sovereignty a considerable obstacle to the necessary progress within the Community, which was conceived by its founders as the preliminary stage of a European federal state and regarded as a method for achieving the national and political unification of Europe. Others (VGH Kassel, von Mangoldt-Klein, Maunz-Dürig, Hamann-Lenz and Carstens) do not wish to renounce completely the safeguards that accrue to citizens from the existing 'traditional' institutions, unless new written constitutional guarantees are provided.

.... The supreme power contained in and bound by the Constitution must not yield to a constitutional change effected from the outside by the Community, for which the democratic authorisation for the future has not been ensured. Hamann/Lenz summarise the whole problem, albeit coarsely, but in the opinion of the Chamber, fundamentally correctly, thus: 'Anyone who tears the rigid norm-structure of constitutional law from its hinges with the integration lever of Article 24 (1) of the Constitution and sacrifices it on the altar of a Eurocratic economic union will have to bear the responsibility in the end when United Europe has been achieved but the guaranteed form of democratic, constitiutonal decision-making has been gambled away.' The decision of the European Court of 15 December 1970, which suppresses the individual interests of the market citizens of the member States in favour of a system of flat-rate charges, just as in the case of the forfeiture of security, shows precisely that the national fundamental principles must be observed so long as there is no written constitutional law of the Community.'[1]

Note: By an order of 14 July 1971 the *Verwaltungsgericht* had submitted the case to the *Bundesverfass:ungsgericht*.[2] Because of a formal defect that order was annulled on 12 October 1971. The same questions were submitted once again in the present case.

C. France

LITERATURE: Bigay, L'application des règlements communautaires en droit pénal français, *RTDE 1971, pp.53-62;* Lange, Die Anwendung des EWG Rechts durch die französischen Gerichte, *DÖV 1971, pp.588-590;* Tallon, Kovar et Lagarde, L'exécution des directives de la CEE en France, *CDE 1970, pp.274-313;* Constantinesco, Effets et rangs des traités et du droit communautaire en droit français, *Riv.Dir.eur.1968, pp.259-301;* Prats, Incidences des dispositions du traité instituant la CEE sur le droit administratif français, *RTDE 1968, pp.19-50.*

[1]Translation by CMLR, footnotes omitted. [2]*AWD 1971, pp.541-546.*

1.General aspects

CASES

(1)SAARKNAPPSCHAFT CASE

Saarknappschaft *v.* Freund und Martin, *Cour d'Appel* (Court of Appeal) de Colmar, Decision of 15 November 1967.

(GP 24-26 April 1968, p.3; RGDIP 1968, p. 860; CMLR 1969 pp. 82-84).

Facts: Saarknappschaft, a social security board in Saarland in Germany, appealed against a judgment of the *Tribunal de Grande Instance*, Saverne, of 22 December 1964, dismissing its claim against the defendants of 3.885.17 French francs which Saarknappschaft had paid to the victims of a road accident for which the defendants had been declared responsible. The lower court had held that Article 52, para 1, of EEC Regulation No.3 of the Council of Ministers relating to the social security of migrant workers —which provides for subrogation to the rights of beneficiaries, and invoked in the present case by Saarknappschaft—did not come into force until the bilateral agreements provided for by Article 52, para 2, had been concluded between the member States concerned. In the meantime, on 11 March, 1965, the Court of Justice of the EC had declared that Article 52, para 1, was applicable before the conclusion of the bilateral agreements.

Therefore, Saarknappschaft asked the *Cour d'Appel* to allow the appeal and quash the judgment of the lower court.

The Cour d'Appel held:

....

'The combination of Article 177 with Article 219 of the same Treaty, which provides that 'Member States undertake not to submit a dispute concerning the interpretation or application of this Treaty to any method of settlement other than those provided for in this Treaty', excludes, within the State, the interpretation by a governmental authority to the extent that this interpretation would serve as a basis, explicitly or implicitly, for a jurisdictional decision. Therefore the defendants cannot rely in the present case, as they attempt to do, on the opinion given by the Ministry of External Affairs and their contention to this effects must be rejected.

Finally, since the task of the Court of Justice is in particular to state the law in a case concerning the interpretation of the provisions of the Treaty or of acts of institutions of the Community, decisions given by the Court under Articles 177 and 219 of the Treaty are integrated into the law of the Community and *ipso facto* enjoy the supremacy of the Treaty over internal legislation. The decisions of the Court are thus imposed on national jurisdictions to the same extent as Community law. The respect for decisions of the Court of Justice is directly and intimately bound up with the respect for the Treaty itself, the supremacy of which cannot be disputed, and results, in France at least, from Article 55 of the Constitution, which provides that 'Treaties or agreements duly ratified or approved have, from the date of their publication, an authority superior to that of statutes (*lois*), provided in each case that there is reciprocity'.

For these reasons therefore the plaintiff board's claim must succeed and the judgment of the lower court must be quashed.

The case is remitted to the lower court for its judgment as to the amount of the claim. The defendants shall pay the costs of the appeal.'[1]

(2) FRENCH RAMEL CASE

Administration des Contributions indirectes et Comité Interprofessionnel des vins doux naturels *v.* P. Ramel. *Cour de Cassation* (*Chambre Criminelle*) (Court of Cassation), Decision of 22 October 1970.

(GP, 9-11 December 1970, No.334-336; RTDE 1970, p.750; JT 1971, pp.25-26; CDE 1971, p.356; Rec.D.1971, pp.221-224; JCP 1971 II, p.16671; CMLR 1971, pp.315-324.)

Notes: Rolin, *JT 1971, p.26;* P.L., *JCP 1971 II, p.16671;* Rideau, *Rec.D.1971, p.221;* Tallon and Gaudemet-Tallon, *CDE 1971,* pp.360-366; See also Kovar and Tallon, *CMLRev.1971, pp.404-406.*

Facts: The defendant, a French merchant and importer of wines, had imported a certain quantity of Italian wines in April and May 1966. Upon examination by the French tax authorities it appeared that these wines did not conform to the requirements of the internal French legislation on the matter, which fixed a certain alcohol- and sugar percentage for tax purposes (Article 4 of the Wine Code).

When prosecuted by the plaintiff for fraudually selling wine of an excessive alcohol- and sugar percentage, the *Tribunal Correctionnel* at Bourg en Bresse declared the defendant Ramel not guilty. This judgment was confirmed by the *Cour d'Appel* of Lyon. The plaintiff asked for a review in cassation.

Before the *Cour de Cassation* the defendant objected that the French legislation was inapplicable as being contrary to the provisions of the Common Market Organization for Wines of the EEC-Regulation No.24 and a Council Decision implementing the Regulation, both of 4 April 1962. According to Article 2 of the Decision, France and Italy were to admit a quota of 150.000 hectoliters of quality wines to all member States.

Article 3 adds that wines from Italy are admitted within this quota provided that they are accompanied by a valid certificate of origin. It was not disputed that the wines imported by Ramel satisfied the Italian legal requirements.

The *Cour de Cassation* had to determine whether the municipal or the Community law provisions had to be applied.

[1]Translation by CMLR.

The Cour de Cassation held:

....

'Under Article 55 of the Constitution of 4 October 1958, treaties and agreements regularly ratified and approved have, as soon as they are published, a higher authority than municipal laws, provided that the other party to the agreement or treaty also implements them.

Furthermore, under Article 520 *et seq.* of the General Taxation Code, and Article 2 of Decree 1001 of 4 October 1963, imported alcohol, wine, perry and mead are subject to all the provisions laid down by municipal law and must therefore comply with French regulations.

In view of these laws and regulations, it was in strict pursuance of Article 55 of the Constitution that the Appeal Judges considered that they could not apply to imported wines the provisions of Article 4 of the Wine Code, or inflict on Ramel the penalties laid down by Article 3 of the Law of 1 August 1905 and Articles 443, 444 and 445 of the General Taxation Code. The reason was that the principle of territoriality of taxation laws could not overrule international law whose authority must prevail by virtue of constitutional law.

The wines involved in the present case were imported from Italy within the quota opened by the decision of 4 April 1962 and of Regulation 24, which decision and regulation are published international instruments having acquired the force of international treaties.'[1]

....

The court dismissed the appeal.

Note: By a decision of 7 January 1972, the *Cour de Cassation* (Ch.Crim.) (No.90.217/71—B. et R.A.) similarly quashed a judgment of the *Cour d'Appel* of Aix en Provence in the Case of Guerrini which had imposed a fine under a French law held to be contrary to the Community regulations establishing the Common Market organisation for eggs.

It concluded that since the regulation was directly applicable as of the date it provided for, the charged violation of the French decree lacked any legal foundation.

See also the implicit priority granted to Community law by the *Cour de Cassation* (Ch.Crim.) on November 1970, in the Case of Von Saldern et al, *RTDE 1971, pp. 504-509.*

[1]Translation by CMLR.

2.Constitutionality Control

CASE

(1)FRENCH BUDGETARY POWERS CASE
Conseil Constitutionnel (Constitutional Council), Declaration (or Decision) of 19 June 1970, Nr.70-39 DC.
(JO 1970, 21 June, p.5806; CMLR 1971, pp.70-74; EuR 1971, pp.60-62; RTDE 1971, pp.210-212.)
Notes: Goose, EuR 1971, pp.62-68; Kovar and Tallon, 8 CMLRev.1971, pp.402-404; Ruzié, JCP No. 2354.

Facts: This was the first time that a procedure under Article 54[1] of the Constitution of the Fifth Republic was instituted. (See for the structure of Constitutional review in France, Jud.Rem.p.128). The present case arose as a result of a parliamentary initiative by the representative Foyer, who had placed a draft of a constitutional law before the National Assembly. He was of the opinion that the Treaty of 22 April 1970 amending certain budgetary provisions of the Treaties establishing the European Communities[2] and the Decision of the Council of the European Communities of 21 April 1970, relating to the establishment of the Communities' own resources[3], were incompatible with the French Constitution and could therefore not be approved by the French parliament and ratified by the French Government. Under these circumstances the Prime Minister deemed it desirable to invoke a declaration by the Constitutional Court.

The Conseil Constitutionnel held:
'The need for an amendment of the Constitution prior to authorisation to ratify or approve an international undertaking, laid down in Article 54 of the Constitution, is subject therein to a declaration by the Constitutional Council, at the initiative of the President of the Republic, the Prime Minister or the President of one or other of the Assemblies, that the said international undertaking contains a clause which is contrary to the Constitution.
It is therefore for the Constitutional Council, in the present instance, as in all cases of this nature, to declare whether the international undertakings brought before it for examination under Article 54 do or do not contain clauses contrary to the Constitution.
As regards the Treaty signed at Luxembourg on 22 April 1970 amending certain

[1]This provision reads: 'If the Constitutional Council, the matter having been referred to it by the President of the Republic, by the Premier, or by the President of one or the other assembly, shall declare that an international commitment contains a clause contrary to the Constitution, the authorization to ratify or approve this commitment may be given only after amendment of the Constitution'. [2]*OJ (1971), L 2/1.* [3]*OJ (1970), L 94/19.*

budgetary provisions of the Treaties instituting the European Communities and of the Treaty instituting a single Council and a single Commission of the European Communities.

This Treaty contains only provisions relating to the internal working of the Communities modifying the distribution of powers between their various organs and it does not affect the balance of relations between the European Communities on the one hand and the member States on the other.

Furthermore, the undertakings contained in the provisions subjected to the scrutiny of the Constitutional Council do not come into force until after deposit of the last instrument of ratification and they therefore have the nature of reciprocal undertakings.

Consequently they cannot be contrary to any provision of the Constitution.

As regards the decision of the Council of het European Communities of 21 April 1970 relating to the replacement of financial contributions of the member States by the Communities' own resources.

It follows from the provisions of the Paris Treaty of 18 April 1951 instituting the European Coal and Steel Community and of the Rome Treaties of 25 March 1957 instituting the European Economic Community and the European Atomic Energy Community respectively, that the development of the European Communities involves, in particular, for the financing of their budget, subject to the procedures laid down in the stipulations of the above-mentioned Treaties, the gradual passing from a system of member State contributions to a system of own resources. The said Treaties were duly ratified and published and consequently fall within the field of application of Article 55 of the Constitution.

The decision of 21 April 1970, which recommends the replacement of the member States' financial contributions by the Communities' own resources, has the character of a measure applying the Treaty provisions mentioned above, seeing that it was made in the circumstances laid down in particular in Article 201 of the Treaty instituting the EEC and in Article 173 of the Treaty instituting the European Atomic Energy Community, that is to say in conformity with the respective constitutional rules of the member States. The application of these rules requires that the adoption of the provisions laid down in that decision and which, on certain points, bear upon matters of a legislative nature, such as are listed in Article 34 of the Constitution, shall be subjected under Article 53 to the passing of a statute. The above-mentioned condition of reciprocity is met.

Consequently, and subject to its approval by statute, the said decision is not in conflict with the Constitution.

Besides, the decision of 21 April 1970 is situated within a complex of implementation measures linked to the establishment of a common policy. It could not therefore have, on its own, policy-making status.

In the present case it cannot, either through its nature or through its importance, affect the essential conditions for exercise of national sovereignty.

The constitutional Council for these reasons, hereby declares:

1. The Treaty amending certain budgetary provisions of the Treaties instituting the European Communities and of the Treaty instituting a single Council and a single Commission of the European Communities, signed at Luxembourg on 22 April 1970, and the decision of 21 April 1970, relating to the replacement of the member States' financial contributions by the Communities' own resources do not contain any clause contrary to the Constitution.'[1]

D. Italy

LITERATURE: Panico, L'Art.11 della Costituzione Italiana come fondamento della rilevanza interna della sfera di competenze delle Communitá Europe, *Riv.Dir.Eur.1969, pp.123-149.*

1.General aspects

CASE

(1)ITALIAN SICILIAN REGION CASE

State Commissioner (Commissario dello Stato) for Sicily *v.* President of the Region Sicily. *Corte Costituzionale* (Constitutional Court), Decision of 7 July 1969, No.120/ 1969.

(Foro It.1969, Col.2069; RTDE 1970, pp.550-552; CMLR 1970, pp.35-42).

Notes: Pappalardo, *EuR 1970, pp.341 ff.;* Pizzorusso, *Foro It.1969 I, Col.2070;* Catalano, *id., Col.3023.*

Facts: The State Commissioner for Sicily (the representative of the central government in the region) disputed the constitutionality of a regional Sicilian law before the Constitutional Court on the ground of violation of procedural rules. He claimed that the draft of this law, which introduced state aids in support of the price level of citrus fruit, had not been notified to the EEC prior to its enactment as required by Artcile 93, para 3, of the EEC Treaty.

The Constitutional Court had to decide whether the regional law was under these circumstances constitutional.

The Corte Costituzionale held:

....

'The provisions of the EEC Treaty (which became executory in Italy under the pro-

[1]Translation by CMLR.

visions of Law No.1203 of 14 October 1957), which are aimed at ensuring freedom of circulation of goods and parity of access to markets to all member States, impose upon each of such States obligations and duties which are partially derived from the provisions of the Treaty itself and partially from rules issued by the Community bodies in the shape of 'regulations' (which are 'compulsory in all their provisions and which are directly applicable' in each member State (see Article 189(2) of the EEC Treaty)).

It follows that there can be no doubt—and this is not denied by the Sicilian Government—that the said obligations and duties which are derived from the Treaty provisions and from Community regulations are binding upon the exercise of the legislative function of regions having a special character.

The reasons why this is so—and which pertain to the sovereign positions of the State *vis-à-vis* those regions which enjoy autonomous powers 'within the political unity of the Italian State' (Article 1 of the Special Charter for Sicily), which State is 'one and indivisible' (see Article 5 of the Italian Constitution) and which enjoys international recognition—have been expounded at a great length by this Court in its judgment in State Commissioner for the Sicilian Region *v*. Regional Government of Sicily (9 April 1963).

Amongst the obligations that arise from the EEC Treaty there is indeed that contained in Article 93(3) to which we have already adverted and which imposes upon member States the obligation to notify 'plans to grant or alter grants of aid'. These subsidies or aids include all those interventions which public bodies may effect to modify the establishment of prices within the competitive sphere: a sphere which the Treaty intends substantially to protect whilst at the same time recognising the possibility of acknowledging such interventions in the social interest provided this is done in conditions of parity for all member States. And therefore, normally, under the control and with the authority of the Community bodies.

We do not think it is pertinent to consider for the purposes of our judgment which subsidies the Treaty acknowledges as compatible either directly or upon authorisation. Suffice it to say for the purpose of these proceedings that any subsidy which results in 'interventions upon the market' in matters of fruit and vegetables is considered as compatible only after authorisation by the Community bodies and as such it is minutely regulated by two 'regulations', Nos. 23 of 1965 and 159 of 1966, this latter regulation dedicating to the subject-matter the whole of its second part.

....

It is argued on behalf of the Sicilian Government that the Italian State was bound to follow and did indeed follow such a procedure because it applied for and obtained— to support the operation—the financial intervention of the special fund set aside by the Community itself; whereas the Sicilian region has acted of its own initiative through its own bodies and with its own moneys and asks for no refund and therefore is not bound by such procedures. But this argument cannot be accepted because the framework of the Treaty, which is aimed at ensuring freedom and parity of access and of conditions to all the member States upon the national markets of each, allows no discrimination to be made in any price subsidies—whether they be effected with or without financial contribution by the Community bodies—because they nevertheless represent activities aimed at modifying freedom of competition and are subject there-fore to a prior investigation on the merits as to their advisability before any authorisa-tion is granted.'[1]

....

For these reasons the law was declared unconstitutional.

2.Constitutionality of the Community Treaties

CASE

(1) First Italian Costa-enel Case (final judgment)
Costa *v*. ENEL, *Giudice Conciliatore* (Justice of the Peace) of Milan, Decision of 2 January 1967.
(CDE 1969, pp.336-338).
Notes: Ferrari Bravo, *CDE 1969, pp.338-342.*

Facts: This is the final judgment in the First Case in which the Justice of the Peace of Milan asked the Constitutional Court to render an opinion on the constitutionality of the Italian Nationalization Law; *inter alia*, whether this law conflicted with Article 11 of the Constitution. The *Corte Costituzionale*, in a much publisized opinion of 7 March 1964, held that the above law could not be considered to be unconstitutional (Jud.Rem., p. 167). It may be recalled that an underlying feature was the question whether a municipal act enacted after the EEC Treaty came into force, could derogate from that Treaty. The *Corte Costituzionale* confirmed that this could be the case.

In the Second Italian Costa *v*. ENEL Case (Jud.Rem., p.168), a preliminary ruling was requested from the Court of Justice in Luxembourg, which came to a contrary conclusion with respect to the relationship between Community law and national law (Jud.Rem., p.106).

The present Justice of the Peace *was not bound*—at least from a formal point of view—by the holding of the Luxembourg Court, but *was bound* by the ruling of the *Corte Costituzionale* of 7 March 1964. Nevertheless the Justice of the Peace discussed once more the relationship of Community law to national law in Italy.

[1] Translation by CMLR.

The Giudice Conciliatore held:

'The question of the constitutional illegitimacy of the law establishing ENEL and, consequently, of its executive orders is at present barred beyond remedy by the judgment of 24 February—7 March 1964, No.14 of the Constitutional Court.

This is true, be it on account of the force *'erga omnes'* (= of general effect; authors) of the said judgment, or be it on account of the force of final decision which it is entitled to most specifically in the present proceedings in the course of which it has been pronounced. Therefore, this force of final decision that the above-mentioned judgment of the Constitutional Court has, can not be neglected, not even for the purpose of considering the question concerning the influence of the EEC Treaty (rendered enforceable by the Law of 14 October 1957, No.1203) on the law establishing ENEL. It appears, moreover, that Mr.Costa himself did not express a different opinion in his pleas.

Even if the case is such, and given the fact that the said judgment denied law No.1203 of 1957 a status higher than that of the other ordinary laws, excluding its constitutional nature and proclaiming that 'the authority of subsequent laws, in accordance with the principles of the succession of laws in time' must be guarded firmly, the court, called upon to apply the law of 6 December 1962, No.1643, could not decide that it is outranked by the law of 14 October 1957, No.1203, which precedes it, without violation of the principle of final decision and articles 2909 of the Civil Code, and 15 of the provisions concerning the law in general. And this is true, whatever the criticisms and the doctrinal discussions concerning the above-mentioned judgment of the Constitutional Court; after all, criticisms and discussions cannot detract from its obligatory status.

It follows that Mr.Costa's claim must be rejected, when we regard the historical-legal act of the transfer in toto to ENEL, by force of law, of the business capital of Edison-Volta, as an established fact, with the result that Article 2558 of the Civil Code applies in this case. Besides, even if no appeal were taken to the preclusion that results from the force of final decision, these conclusions could not be different. In fact, if one is of the opinion that law No.1203 of 1957 has constitutional status, then any decision concerning its violation and the consequences thereof, could only come under the jurisdiction of the Constitutional Court. However, since the Constitutional Court already expressed its opinion, it is useless to invoke its jurisdiction again.

If one is of the opinion, on the contrary, that law No.1203 of 1957, although lacking constitutional status, takes precedence of subsequent laws, for other reasons, then an ordinary court could solve the conflicts that would arise between the two laws (and hence refuse to apply the subsequent law); however, such a court could do this only within the limits, on the one side, and to the extent, on the other side, necessary to reach this goal and within the scope of its competence as meant in the Treaty rules, as they have been intepreted by the Court of Justice—be it at the request of the afore-said court, or on any other occasion.

Now, among the provisions of the Treaty that Mr.Costa invokes as violated by the law that set up ENEL, the only rule that—in the abstract—could authorize such a decision would be Article 102. That one, in point of fact, is the only Article that would be capable of affecting in the aggregate the principles of the law setting up ENEL.

The preferential application of the other articles invoked by Mr.Costa cannot be consented to, for the transfer of the business capital to ENEL retains its effectiveness, even if that is under restrictions that concern neither Mr.Costa nor the present matter.

However, the Court of Justice, has already expressed its opinion in its judgement of 15 July 1964, on the application of the aforesaid Article 102. This judgment, although pronounced in the course of another procedure (but concerning the same parties), excludes the necessity of a new request for interpretation.

In its judgment, the Court of Justice, although affirming that no subsequent national enactment can have priority over the Community rules, distinguished between two categories of Community rules.

On the one hand, the rules that—as they create subjective, private rights—realize the protection of these by way of application of these rules by the national court; on the other hand, the rules that escape direct application by the national court, since they do not create subjective, private rights. Violation of these rules is countered with sanctions only on the Community level.

If this distinction is applied to the present case, we see that precisely this judgment of the Court of Justice classified Article 102 among the rules that escape application by the national court, because they do not create subjective rights. It follows that the court in the present matter does not have the power—nor the duty—to avail itself of Article 102 in order to deny a law of the State its force.'[1]

Consequently, the claim of Mr.Costa must be rejected.

E. Luxembourg

....

F. Netherlands

....

[1]Translation by Europa Instituut.

IV. LEGAL ASPECTS OF THE ACCESSION OF NEW MEMBER STATES

LITERATURE: *Legal Problems of an Enlarged Community* (Ed. by Bathurst, Simmonds, Hunnings, Welch) London, 1972; *Die Erweiterung der Europäischen Gemeinschaften* (Conference), Kölner Schriften zum Europarecht, Band 15, Carl Heymanns Verlag KG, 1972; Report on this Conference by Millarg, *EuR 1972, pp.179-187.* Hunnings, Constitutional Implications of joining the Common Market, *6 CML Rev.1968, pp.50-66.*

A. The Accession Documents

LITERATURE: Kapteyn and VerLoren van Themaat, De uitbreiding van de Europese Gemeenschappen, *SEW 1972, pp.323-359;* Nass, Der Beitrittsvertrag—Erste Bemerkungen zur Erweiterung der Gemeinschaft, *EuR 1972, pp.103-124;* Le Tallec, Les instruments de l'adhésion de l'Angleterre, du Danemark, de la Norvège et de l'Irlande aux Communautés, *RMC 1972, pp. 229-236.*

If the various ratification documents are duly completed in time by all parties, the European Communities will have four new member States as of 1 January 1973: Denmark, Ireland, Norway and the United Kingdom.

The accession procedures under the Treaty of Paris differ from those under the Treaty of Rome. Article 98 ECSC provides for a unilateral procedure: a unanimous decision on the accession and its term, by the Council after an opinion has been given by the High Authority. Accession shall take effect on the day the instrument of accession is received by the French Government. Articles 237 EEC and 205 Euratom, on the other hand, stipulate that the condition of admission and the adjustments to the Treaties shall be laid down in an agreement between the member States and the applicant State or States.

Having regard to these differences, a Treaty concerning the Accession to the EEC and Euratom was signed and a Decision was taken by the Council for Accession to the ECSC on 22 January 1972, each instrument containing no more than three articles. The substantive provisions are laid down in a joint annex entitled 'Act concerning the Conditions of Accession and the Adjustment to the Treaties' (Accession Act).

The Final Act enumerating all accession documents, including Annexes, Protocols, Joint and Unilateral Declarations was signed not only by the present members and applicant States, but also by the President of the Council (on behalf of the Communities). The Accession Documents have been published in eight official languages in the Official Journal of the European Communities 1972, No.L 73. Summaries of the negotiation procedures, the course of the negotiations and their outcome have been published on consecutive issues of the CMLRev. for 1971 and 1972 and in the 5th General Report on the Activities of the European Communities. Prior to the signing of the Accession Documents the Commission issued a formal opinion.

1.Opinion of the Commission
'The Commission of the European Communities, having regard to Article 98 of the Treaty establishing the European Coal and Steel Community, Article 237 of the Treaty establishing the European Economic Community and Article 205 of the Treaty establishing the European Atomic Energy Community;

whereas the Kingdom of Denmark, Ireland, the Kingdom of Norway and the United Kingdom of Great Britain and Northern Ireland have applied to become members of these Communities;

whereas in its Opinions of 29 September 1967 and 1 October 1969 the Commission has already been able to express its views on certain essential aspects of the problems arising in connection with these applications;

whereas the terms for the admission of these States and the adjustments to the establishing Treaties necessitated by their accession have been negotiated in a Conference between the Communities and the applicant States, and whereas singleness of Community representation was ensured with due regard for the institutional dialogue provided for by the Treaties;

whereas on the completion of these negotiations, it is apparent that the provisions so agreed are fair and proper, and whereas, this being so, the Community's enlargement, while preserving its internal cohesion and dynamism, will enable it to take a fuller part in the development of international relations;

whereas in joining the Communities the applicant States accept without reserve the Treaties and their political objectives, all decisions taken since their entry into force, and the choices made in the field of the development and reinforcement of the Communities;

whereas in particular the essential feature of the legal system set up by the Treaties establishing the Communities is that certain of the provisions of the latter and certain Acts of the Community institutions are directly applicable, that Community law takes precedence over any national provisions conflicting with it, and that procedures exist for ensuring the uniform interpretation of this law, and whereas accession to the Communities entails recognition of the binding force of these rules, observance of which is indispensable to guarantee the effectiveness and unity of Community law.

Gives its opinion in favour of the accession to the European Communities of the Kingdom of Denmark, Ireland, the Kingdom of Norway and the United Kingdom of Great Britain and Northern Ireland.'[1]

[1] *Fifth General Report on the Activities of the Communities, 1971, para.95; OJ 1972, No.L73/3.*

2.Treaty of Accession

Article 1

'1. The Kingdom of Denmark, Ireland, the Kingdom of Norway and the United Kingdom of Great Britain and Northern Ireland hereby become members of the European Economic Community and of the European Atomic Energy Community and Parties to the Treaties establishing these Communities as amended or supplemented.

2. The conditions of admission and the adjustments to the Treaties establishing the European Economic Community and the European Atomic Energy Community necessitated thereby are set out in the Act annexed to this Treaty. The provisions of that Act concerning the European Economic Community and the European Atomic Energy Community shall form an integral part of this Treaty.

3. The provisons concerning the rights and obligations of the Member States and the powers and jurisdiction of the institutions of the Communities as set out in the Treaties referred to in paragraph 1 shall apply in respect of this Treaty.'

Article 2

'This Treaty will be ratified by the High Contracting Parties in accordance with their respective constitutional requirements. The instruments of ratification will be deposited with the Government of the Italian Republic by 31 December 1972 at the latest.

This Treaty will enter into force on 1 January 1973, provided that all the instruments of ratification have been deposited before that date and that all the instruments of accession to the European Coal and Steel Community are deposited on that date.

If, however, the States referred to in Article 1 (1) have not all deposited their instruments of ratification and accession in due time, the Treaty shall enter into force for those States which have deposited their instruments. In this case, the Council of the European Communities, acting unanimously, shall decide immediately upon such resulting adjustments as have become indispensable, to Article 3 of this Treaty, and to Articles 14, 16, 17, 19, 20, 23, 129, 142, 143, 155 and 160 of the Act concerning the Conditions of Accession and the Adjustments to the Treaties, to the provisions of Annex I to that Act concerning the composition and functioning of various committees, and to Articles 5 and 8 of the Protocol on the Statute of the European Investment Bank; acting unanimously, it may also declare that those provisions of the aforementioned Act which refer expressly to a State which has not deposited its instruments of ratification and accession have lapsed, or it may adjust them.'

Article 3

'This Treaty, drawn up in a single original in the Danish, Dutch, English, French, German, Irish, Italian and Norwegian languages, all eight texts being equally authentic, will be deposited in the archives of the Government of the Italian Republic, which will transmit a certified copy to each of the Governments of the other signatory States.'

In WITNESS WHEREOF, the undersigned Plenipotentiaries have affixed their signature below this Treaty.

DONE at Brussels on this twenty-second day of January in the year one thousand nine hundred and seventy-two.[1]

[1]Her Majesty's Stationary Office, Cmnd 4862-I.

3. Accession Act

Article 1 of the Accession Act contains some definitions; Articles 2, 3, 4 and 5 stipulate the specific obligations of the new member States:

Article 2

'From the date of accession, the provisions of the original Treaties and the acts adopted by the institutions of the Communities shall be binding on the new Member States and shall apply in those States under the conditions laid down in those Treaties and in this Act.'

Article 3

'1. The new Member States accede by this Act to the decisions and agreements adopted by the Representatives of the Governments of the Member States meeting in Council. They undertake to accede from the date of accession to all other agreements concluded by the original Member States relating to the functioning of the Communities or connected with their activities.

2. The new Member States undertake to accede to the conventions provided for in Article 220 of the EEC Treaty, and to the protocols on the interpretation of those conventions by the Court of Justice, signed by the original Member States, and to this end they undertake to enter into negotiations with the original Member States in order to make the necessary adjustments thereto.

3. The new Member States are in the same situation as the original Member States in respect of declarations or resolutions of, or other positions taken up by, the Council and in respect of those concerning the European Communities adopted by common agreement of the Member States; they will accordingly observe the principles and guidelines deriving from those declarations, resolutions or other positions and will take such measures as may be necessary to ensure their implementation.'

Article 4

'1. The agreements or conventions entered into by any of the Communities with one or more third States, with an international organisation or with a national of a third State, shall, under the conditions laid down in the original Treaties and in this Act, be binding on the new Member States.

2. The new Member States undertake to accede, under the conditions laid down in this Act, to agreements or conventions concluded by the original Member States and any of the Communities, acting jointly, and to agreements concluded by the original Member States which are related to those agreements or conventions. The Community and the original Member States shall assist the new Member States in this respect.

3. The new Member States accede by this Act and under the conditions laid down therein to the internal agreements concluded by the original Member States for the purpose of implementing the agreements or conventions referred to in paragraph 2.

4. The new Member States shall take appropriate measures, where necessary, to adjust their positions in relation to international organisations and international agreements to which one of the Communities or to which other Member States are also parties, to the rights and obligations arising from their accession to the Communities.'

Article 5

'Article 234 of the EEC Treaty and Articles 105 and 106 of the Euratom Treaty shall apply, for the new

Member States, to agreements or conventions concluded before accession.'¹

In the legal order of the Communities the Accession Documents will have the same status as the Treaties of Paris and Rome.

Consequently, revision of their provisions will, in principle, only be possible in accordance with Articles 96 ECSC, 236 EEC and 204 Euratom Treaties. This principle is confirmed by Article 6 of the Accession Act:

Article 6

'The provisions of this Act may not, unless otherwise provided herein be suspended, amended or repealed other than by means of the procedure laid down in the original Treaties enabling those Treaties to be revised.'¹

An important exception to this principle is provided by Article 2 para 3 of the Treaty of Accession, whereby the Council has been empowered to make some adjustments to the Treaty and the Act in the event that the Treaty is not ratified by all the new member States.

A second exception concerns amendments to acts of the institutions of the Communities (regulations, directives and decisions). A number of amendments have been effected by the Act itself under Article 29 and Annex I; in the case of many other amendments the Act has merely indicated the guidelines for those adaptions which are required to be drawn up by the proper authorities, i.e. either by the Council or the Commission, according to which of these two institutions adopted the original act (see Article 30 and Annex II; also Article 153). Should the principle of Article 6 of the Act apply also to these latter amendments, they would acquire Treaty status and could therefore never be revised other than by means of the revisions-procedures laid down for the Treaties themselves. In order to prevent secondary Community law thus becoming 'frozen', Article 8 of the Act was inserted:

Article 8

'Provisions of this Act the purpose or effect of which is to repeal or amend acts adopted by the institutions of the Communities, otherwise than as a transitional measure, shall have the same status in law as the provisions which they repeal or amend and shall be subject to the same rules as those provisions.'¹

On the other hand Article 8 excludes amendments effected by means of a transitional measure. Clearly the Communities and the acceeding states intend to prevent agreed

¹Her Majesty's Stationary Office, Cmnd. 4862-I.

transitional measures, containing mutual political and economic concessions, from being revised by a principle act of the institutions. To such measures, Article 6 continues to apply.

Nevertheless this guarantee does not lead to the result that, during the transitional period, which terminates at the end of 1977, the underlying Community acts to which the transitional provisions relate may not under any circumstances be revised by the institutions. Article 7 has been inserted to deal with such a situation:

Article 7

'Acts adopted by the institutions of the Communities to which the transitional provisions laid down in this Act relate shall retain their status in law; in particular, the procedures for amending those acts shall continue to apply.'[1]

The result of this provision is that, provided the system of the act or acts, to which the transitional provisions relate, is maintained, the latter cannot be suspended; but such provisions can be rendered inoperative by a simple decision of the institutions, if the system itself is revised. Thus in such a case the transitional provisions may be modified by a Community act. As an example, Article 62(2) of the Act may be mentioned. Should e.g. the system of the Common Market Organisation for cereals be modified fundamentally, the Council 'may make the necessary adaptation to the provisions (of the transitional measures on the free movement of goods), if made necessary as a result of a change in Community'.

The other provisions of the Accession Act relate mainly to the necessary adjustments to the existing Treaties, to the necessary adaptions to the acts of the institutions and to the transitional measures.

B. Community Law and the New Members

1.Denmark

LITERATURE: Due and Gulmann, Constitutional Implications of the Danish Accession to the European Communities, 9 *CMLRev.1972, pp.*256-270. Sørensen, Die Anwendung des Rechts der Europäischen Gemeinschaften in Dänemark, in: *Die Erweiterung der Europäischen Gemeinschaften*, Kölner Schriften zum Europarecht, Band 15, 1972, pp.1-25.

Constitution Article 19

(1) 'The King shall act on behalf of the Realm in international affairs. Provided that without the consent of the Folketing the King shall not undertake any act whereby the territory of the Realm will be increased or

[1]Her Majesty's Stationary office, Cmnd. 4862-1.

decreased, nor shall he enter into any obligation which for fulfilment requires the concurrence of the Folketing, or which otherwise is of major importance; nor shall the King, except with the consent of the Folketing, terminate any international treaty entered into with the consent of the Folketing.

....

(3) The Folketing shall appoint from among its Members a Foreign Affairs Committee, which the Government shall consult prior to the making of any decision of major importance to foreign policy. Rules applying to the Foreign Affairs Committee shall be laid down by Statute.

Constitution Article 20

(1) Powers vested in the authorities of the Realm under this Constitution Act may, to such extent as shall be provided by Statute, be delegated to international authorities set up by mutual agreement with other states for the promotion of international rules of law and co-operation.

(2) For the passing of a Bill dealing with the above a majority of five-sixths of the Members of the Folketing shall be required.

If this majority is not obtained, whereas the majority required for the passing of ordinary Bills is obtained, and if the Government maintains it, the Bill shall be submitted to the Electorate for approval or rejection in accordance with the rules for Referenda laid down in section 42.'[1]

'The Danish Constitution seems to presuppose that even where a treaty has been duly ratified, it does not, normally, automatically become a part of municipal Danish law.

Incorporating the particular rule of international law into Danish law may be achieved in different ways. As examples may be mentioned the adoption of an act by the Folketing, or the issuance of some other legal ordinance with a view to implementing the national rule of law required by the substance of the treaty. This involves, in other words, a transcription or transformation of the rule of international law.

A treaty will, however, become part of Danish law, if Danish legislation contains a provision authorising the Government to conclude a treaty and subsequently implement it as part of national law. In such cases no transcription is called for.

The Danish Constitution, however, views certain treaties as so significant and of such consequence for the structure of the Danish Constitution as to necessitate stricter requirements, in form as well as in substance, for the making of a treaty.

The provisions on this subject are incorporated in Article 20 of the Constitution which to a certain limited extent authorises the Government to delegate powers vested in the authorities of the Realm to international organs, set up by mutual agreement with other states for the promotion of international rules of law and co-operation.

The Constitution provides that a delegation of this kind shall be made by enactment. In this type of situation it has, however, been found appropriate to deviate

[1]Peaslee, *Constitutions of Nations, 1968, Vol. III, pp.255-256.*

from the normal legislative procedure, simply because the effects of an act of this nature upon the Danish community could be of far-reaching importance.

The procedure laid down by article 20 of the Constitution has not previously been used in Denmark, this being the first time Denmark is faced with the problem of joining a supranational organisation. Admittedly, Denmark has already joined other international organisations, such as EFTA, but although they are of a far-reaching nature they are, in the strict legal sense, merely organizations, whose decisions have no immediate and direct effect upon the Danish community.

To join such international organisations all that is required is the consent of the Folketing, given by an ordinary majority, to the Government's ratification of the treaties at hand.'[1]

2.Ireland

LITERATURE: John Temple Lang, The Republic of Ireland and the EEC, The Constitutional Position, in *Legal Problems of an Enlarged Community, 1972, pp.13-27; idem*, Legal and Constitutional Implications for Ireland of Adhesion to the EEC Treaty, *9 CMLRev.1972, pp.167-178; European Communities*, April 1967 (Pr.9283-301 pp.), a White Paper supplementing two similar White Papers of 1961 and 1962, issued by the Government and describing the Common Market system; *The Irish Legal System and the Common Market*, 7 October 1967, a lecture by the Minister for Justice to the Galway branch of the Graduates Association of the National University of Ireland; Statement by the Taoiseach introducing the Dáil Motion relating to the reactivation of Ireland's application for membership of the EEC, 25 July 1967; John Temple Lang, The Application of Community Law in the Republic of Ireland in: *Die Erweiterung der Europäischen Gemeinschaften*, Kölner Schriften zum Europarecht, Band 15, 1972, pp.47-65.

Constitution Article 6

'(1) All powers of government, legislative, executive and judicial, derive, under God, from the people, whose right it is to designate the rulers of the State and, in final appeal, to decide all questions of national policy, according to the requirements of the common good.

(2) These powers of government are exercisable only by or on the authority of the organs of State established by this Constitution.'

Constitution Article 15

....

'(2) 1. The sole and exclusive power of making laws for the State is hereby vested in the Oireachtas: no other legislative authority has power to make laws for the State.

Constitution Article 29

'(1) Ireland affirms its devotion to the ideal of peace and friendly co-operation amongst nations founded on international justice and morality.

[1] Isi Foighel, *7 EFTA Bulletin, September- October, 1971, p.11.*

(2) Ireland affirms its adherence to the principle of the pacific settlement of international disputes by international arbitration or judicial determination.

(3) Ireland accepts the generally recognised principles of international law as its rule of conduct in its relations with other States.

(4) 1. The executive power of the State in or in connection with its external relations shall in accordance with Article 28 of this Constitution be exercised by or on the authority of the Government.

2. For the purpose of the exercise of any executive function of the State in or in connection with its external relations, the Government may to such extent and subject to such conditions, if any, as may be determined by law, avail of or adopt any organ, instrument, or method of procedure used or adopted for the like purpose by the members of any group or league of nations with which the State is or becomes associated for the purpose of international co-operation in matters of common concern.

(5) 1. Every international agreement to which the State becomes a party shall be laid before Dáil Eireann.

2. The State shall not be bound by any international agreement involving a charge upon public funds unless the terms of the agreement shall have been approved by Dáil Eireann.

3. This section shall not apply to agreements or conventions of a technical and administrative character.

(6) No international agreement shall be part of the domestic law of the State save as may be determined by the Oireachtas.'[1]

An amendment in the form of an addition to Article 29 of the Constitution was adopted by the legislature and approved by the People of the Republic of Ireland in a referendum on 12 May 1972 ('The Third Amendment'). It reads as follows:

'The State may become a member of the European Coal and Steel Community (established by Treaty signed at Paris on the 18th day of April, 1951), the European Economic Community (established by Treaty signed at Rome on the 25th day of March, 1957) and the European Atomic Energy Community (established by Treaty signed at Rome on the 25th day of March 1957). No provision of this Constitution invalidates laws enacted, acts done or measures adopted by the State necessitated by the obligations of membership of the Communities or prevents laws enacted, acts done or measures adopted by the Communities, or institutions thereof, from having the force of law in the State'.

. . . .

'The amendment avoids listing the provisions of the Constitution which are inconsistent with the present powers of the Community institutions. This makes for brevity, and avoids including a fairly long list of clauses in the amendment. It ensures that no problem can arise as a result of the accidental omission of some clause in the Constitution which it had not been foreseen would be incompatible with some provision of Community law. It ensures that no difficulty can arise if one of the existing Communities obtains powers, such as power to impose taxes, which would be inconsistent with provisions of the Irish Constitution which have not so far been relevant. Omission of any list of constitutional provisions affected also enabled the Irish Government to avoid having to argue whether the Community Treaties are inconsistent with Article 5 of the Constitution: 'Ireland is a sovereign, independent,

[1]Peaslee, *Constitutions of Nations, 1968, Vol.III, pp.482-483.*

democratic state'. The better legal view is that the Treaties are consistent with this Article, but the question is, obviously, politically controversial.

The all-embracing terms of the amendment go further than is necessary to confer on the Community institutions the legislative, executive and judicial powers which the Treaties enable them to exercise. The amendment probably unnecessarily ensures that any Community legislation which in its content (as distinct from its source) is incompatible with, *e.g.* the fundamental human rights provisions of the Irish Constitution (Arts.40-44), will nevertheless be beyond challenge on constitutional grounds in the Irish courts. On this interpretation, the only limitations under Irish law will be those laid down by the Treaties themselves. The Communities have no powers outside the economic, nuclear energy and coal-and-steel spheres governed by the three Treaties, except in so far as other powers may have been given by the Treaties, either directly in, *e.g.* the social sphere or indirectly under Article 235 of the EEC Treaty (which allows the Council to adopt unanimously any measure to further the objectives of the Treaty, even if there is no express power under the Treaty to adopt the measure in question). Of course, the Community institutions must not infringe Community law in such a way as to invalidate their own acts under Article 173 of the EEC Treaty, and apparently will be required by the Community Court to comply with principles of fundamental human rights which the court will take into consideration.

The amendment has therefore eliminated any chance of conflict between the Constitution of Ireland and Community law. The amendment did not attempt to deal with the question of inconsistency between other rules of Irish law and Community law....

The Irish legislature will have power to bring the Community Treaties into force in Irish domestic law by means of an ordinary Act. This is necessary because Article 29.6 of the Constitution lays down that: 'No international agreement shall be part of the domestic law of the State save as may be determined (by the legislature)'. It seems likely that the entire text of the three Treaties, in an official translation, will be enacted as Irish domestic law in a Schedule to this Act. This Act will make the executive, legislative and judicial powers of the Community institutions exercisable in Irish law, and will bring into force in Irish law all Regulations and other directly applicable Community law already adopted, subject to any changes due to the terms of Ireland's entry into the Communities. Other Irish measures will carry out Ireland's obligations under the directives adopted up to that date. The terms of Ireland's accession to the Treaties lay down a timetable by which the various implementing measures will have to be carried out.

Formally, the enactment or reception into Irish law of all directly applicable rules of Community law, plus the implementing of the directives which will become binding on Ireland, would be sufficient to comply with Ireland's obligations under Community law. However, very serious practical difficulties would arise if the Irish domestic laws which are inconsistent with the directly applicable rules of Community law were not expressly repealed. In that event, Irish lawyers would be faced with two large, complex, technical and relatively unfamiliar bodies of law, written in different terminology and different styles of legislative draftsmanship and in no way related to one another, and known to be mutually inconsistent in many respect. In such circumstances it would be quite impossible for the legal profession, and perhaps even for the Irish courts, to say clearly which rules of Irish law had been repealed and which rules remained in force. Express repeal of all rules of Irish law inconsistent with the directly applicable rules of Community law is therefore an urgent practical necessity.

Supremacy of Community law

Under Article 29.6 of the Irish Constitution, the reception of Community law into Irish law can be effected only by an Act of the Irish legislature.

The proposed amendment to the Constitution validates any Community measure which would be otherwise inconsistent with the Constitution, but it does not confer any special status in any other respect on either Community measures or national measures adopted to implement Community obligations. It follows that, even as amended, the Irish Constitution will not give an express answer to the question: if the Irish legislature in the future passed an Act inconsistent with the Act enacting the Treaty, which Act would prevail? No doubt the Irish courts would try to interpret the two Acts so as to reconcile them. The question may be academic, since the Irish legislature would amend any later Act which was unintentionally in breach of the Treaty, and because a deliberate breach of the Treaty would be a repudiation of Ireland's commitments in the EEC. Since the corresponding question has been discussed in relation to the other applicant countries and the Six original member States, however, it calls for analysis.

Although the view that the Irish legislature cannot enact a law in breach of a treaty binding in the State appears superficially incompatible with Article 29.6, it would produce a reasonable result. Irish citizens would be protected from legislation by the executive by means of international treaties (Article 29.6), but once the legislature had implemented a treaty (or, in the case of the second and third arguments outlined above, a treaty of the type in question) the legislature would have no power to break it.

Several types of conflict are theoretically possible.

All previous Irish laws which are inconsistent with the Community Treaties or with directly applicable Community rules will be repealed automatically by the Act bringing the Treaties and these Community rules into force in Ireland.

If Irish delegated legislation, enacted after the Treaties and the directly applicable Community rules adopted before January 1, 1973, have been brought into force in

Ireland, is inconsistent with either of them, Community law will prevail, because it will have the force of an Act of the Irish legislature.

If Irish delegated legislation was inconsistent with a Community Regulation adopted *after* the Treaties had been brought into force in Ireland, both measures would derive their force in Irish law from powers given by Irish Acts. Clearly the Community measure would ultimately have to override the Irish rule, whatever the dates on which they were respectively adopted. A clause to this effect in the Act enacting the Treaties might be useful to make the position clear.

The question of a later Act clearly inconsistent with the Community Treaties (or with directly applicable Community law) is more difficult (assuming there is no relevant constitutional rule on the lines discussed above). As far as the Treaties are concerned, Article 5 of the EEC Treaty requires each member State to take all necessary steps to see that its obligations are carried out, and this could be held to imply a rule of interpretation that the Treaty would override later inconsistent national legislation. Similarly, Articles 5 and 189 of the EEC Treaty (which will of course be in force in Irish law) might be held to imply a rule of interpretation to the effect that directly applicable Community law would override later national laws in case of conflict. The present writer has suggested that the Act enacting the Treaties should contain a clause to the following effect:

'Where this Act (the Treaty-enacting Act) or any directly applicable Community measure is inconsistent with any future Act (whether passed before or after the Community measure), this Act and the Community measure shall prevail unless the future Act expressly, but not merely by implication, provides otherwise.'

This proposed rule of interpretation of statutes would override the normal rule that later inconsistent legislation overrides earlier, and that Acts override measures adopted under the authority of an Act. Although Irish law contains the principle that the legislature cannot (subject to any rule there may be about treaties once enacted) tie the hands of its successors, it is submitted that there is no rule of Irish constitutional law which would invalidate a clause on the lines set out.

No doubt, even in the absence of such a clause, the Irish courts would try to interpret any Irish legislation in such a way as to make it consistent with Community law.

If Irish subordinate legislation adopted after the Treaty-enacting Act was inconsistent with that Act, or with Community regulations carried into Irish law by that Act, the subordinate legislation would be invalid to the extent of the inconsistency. This would be the result even without a clause of the kind set out above. This is because the Community law carried into Irish law by the Treaty-enacting Act would itself have the force of an Act, and therefore would override later subordinate legislation .

The last possibility is that Community regulations might be inconsistent with an Irish Act, both being adopted after the Treaty-enacting Act. In the absence of a clause of the kind outlined, such a conflict would be difficult to resolve in Irish law. Formally, the Community regulation would have been adopted, as far as Irish domestic law is concerned, under the authority of an Act, and so another Act would prevail over a Community regulation. Article 189 of the EEC Treaty might well be interpreted so as to give the Community regulation priority over an earlier Irish Act, but it would be difficult in Irish law to argue that an Act passed after the relevant Community regulation would not override it in case of inconsistency. The Community solution (which is, of course, that Community law should prevail) could be brought about only by a clause as outlined above or a constitutional principle of the type discussed in the last section of this article, above.'[1]

3.Norway

LITERATURE: Fleischer, Le Droit des Communautés Européennes et le Droit norvégien, *RMC 1972, pp.33-47;* Opsahl, Constitutional Implications in Norway of Accession to the European Communities, *9 CMLRev.1972, pp.271-292;* Gundersen, Die Anwendung des Rechts der europäischen Gemeinschaften in Norwegen in: *Die Erweiterung der Europäischen Gemeinschaften,* Kölner Schriften zum Europarecht, Band 15, 1972, pp.65-93. *Betenkninger fra professorene Frede Castberg, Johs. Andenaes og Torkel Opsahl om de konstitusjonelle spørsmål i tilknytning til Norges forhold til de europeiske fellesskap* (St.dok.nr.10 (1966-67), 32 pp.), reports by Professors Castberg, Andenaes and Opsahl on the constitutional law questions relating to Norwegian membership of the Communities.

Constitution Article 26

'The King shall have the right to assemble troops, to commence war in the defence of the Kingdom and to make peace, to conclude and denounce treaties, to send and to receive diplomatic envoys.

Treaties on matters of special importance, and, in any case, treaties the implementation of which, according to the Constitution, necessitates a new law or a decision on the part of the Storting, shall not be binding until the Storting has given its consent thereunto.'

Constitution Article 75

'The duties and prerogatives of the Storting are:

...

(g) to have communicated to it the treaties and agreements which the King, on behalf of the State, has concluded with foreign powers; the provisions contained, in paragraph (f) concerning such matters as are to be kept secret, shall apply equally to secret clauses which, however, must not be at variance with the public ones';

....

[1]John Temple Lang, *9 CMLRev. 1972, pp.168-175.*

Constitution Article 93

In order to secure international peace and security or in order to promote international law and order and co-operation between nations, the Storting may, by a three-fourths majority, consent that an international organization of which Norway is or becomes a member, shall have the right, within a functionally limited field, to exercise powers which in accordance with this Constitution are normally vested in the Norwegian authorities, exclusive of the power to alter this Constitution. For such consent as provided above at least two-thirds of the members of the Storting—the same quorum as is required for changes in or amendments to this Constitution—shall be present.

   The provisions of the preceding paragraph do not apply in cases of membership in an international organization, the decisions of which are not binding on Norway except as obligations under international law.'[1]

'One may say that there are three types of international agreements as far as the Constitution of Norway is concerned:

   1.Agreements which are entered into through a decision by the King in Council, without the consent of Parliament.

   ii.Agreements which are entered into through a decision by the King in Council, but which are subject to prior consent by Parliament according to art.26, para 2.

   iii.Agreements which are made by ministries or by other executive authorities (inter-departmental agreements), and which do not fall under either art.26, para 2 or art.28 of the Constitution.

   To these may be added a fourth type, namely agreements subject to the special procedure of article 93 of the Constitution, calling for the consent of the Parliament by a 3/4 majority. This article covers the entry into the European Economic Community or similar entities; whose organs shall have powers to make regulations or decisions directly applicable in member States.

....According to the view of most writers Norway adheres to the so-called dualistic doctrine, that international law and municipal law must be viewed as two separate systems. In other words, Norway does not apply the maxim 'international law is part of the law of the land'. A Norwegian court will be bound to give effect to the legislation of the Parliament even if such legislation should be contrary to the obligations undertaken in an international agreement.

   This view is, in part, borne out by a decision of the Supreme Court (see the 'Norsk Retstidende' (1957), p. 942). Here an Act of Parliament on enemy property was challenged on the ground that it violated international law. The Supreme Court did not take any definite position as to what were the existing international rules on this subject and whether the Act was in fact compatible therewith, but upheld the confiscation in question on the sole ground that it was in conformity with the provisions enacted

[1]Peaslee, Constitutions of Nations, 1968, Vol. III, pp. 692.

by the Parliament. The general and long-standing practice of the Government is also to implement treaties in Norwegian law through ordinary legislation.

It should be noted, however, that a conflict between the internal legislation of Norway and her international obligations is regarded as a rather remote contingency by most writers.

No such case, in which the conflict was clearly established, has ever been put before the Supreme Court. Some writers have lately, in opposition to the usually accepted dualistic and so-called traditionalist doctrine, advanced the view that international law should prevail (both on a *de lege ferenda* and a *de lege lata basis*).

In practice most possible conflicts between the two systems will be solved by other methods, which favour the solutions prescribed by international law. A general doctrine accepted by all writers and also by court practice is that Norwegian law is presumed to conform to international law. Unless there is a clear indication to the contrary, in the text or in the intentions of the legislature, the provisions of an Act of Parliament will be interpreted so as to avoid any conflict with the international obligations of the state. In some cases a treaty may even occupy a position similar to that of the *travaux préparatoires* in relation to subsequent legislation. And the Parliament must, as a rule, be presumed to have intended to respect the provisions of any treaty which is binding upon Norway.

The acceptance by Norway of membership in the European Communities, with the relevant treaty obligations, would fall under art.93 of the Constitution, which was adopted on 8 March 1962. This article covers the transfer of powers to an international organization to issue acts or decisions which are directly applicable in member States (as is the case in the European Communities). If the international organ is only competent to issue directives binding for the State, and not for the individual, the organization does not fall under the special rules of art.93, and participation by Norway can take place on the basis of other and earlier rules of the Constitution. The main difference in practice would, it seems, lie in whether a 3/4 majority (art.93) or only a simple majority is required in the Parliament (art.26).

Some writers maintain that art.93 must be subject to a literal and narrow interpretation. According to the wording of art.93 the Parliament's decision will only confer powers upon Community organs with respect to future regulations. Consequently, the decision by the Parliament under art.93 must be supplemented by ordinary legislation, incorporating earlier regulations of the Community as well as the self-executing provisions of the Treaties in Norwegian law. According to other writers the decision by a 3/4 majority must be sufficient even here, and art.93 should be subject to an *a fortiori* interpretation with regard to such regulations and provisions. However, in order to avoid any possible contestation as to the validity of Community law, the Government will probably propose that an ordinary Act on incorporation should be passed by the Parliament in addition to the decision under art.93.'[1]

4.United Kingdom

LITERATURE: Mitchell, Kuipers and Gall, Constitutional Aspects of the Treaty and Legislation relating to British Membership, *9 CML Rev.1972, pp.134-150*; Trinidade, Parliamentary Sovereignty and the Primacy of European Community Law, *Mod. Law Rev.*1972, pp.375-403; Williams, The Constitution of the United Kingdom, Cambr.Law J.1972, pp.266-293; Petersmann, *Die Suprematie des Europäischen Gemeinschaftsrechts und die Supramatic des Britischen Parlaments*, thesis Hamburg, 1972; Simmonds, Community Law and National Law in: *die Erweiterung der Europäischen Gemeinschaften*, Kölner Schriften zum Europarecht, Band 15, *1972, pp.25-47;* Mitchell, British Law and British Membership, *EuR 1971, pp.97-119; idem*, L'Adhésion du Royaume-Uni aux Communautés, *CDE 1970, pp.251-274;* De Smith, The Constitution and the Common Market, a tentative appraisal, *Mod.Law Rev.1971, pp.597-614;* Martin, The Accession of the United Kingdom to the European Communities, jurisdictional problems, *6 CMLRev.1968, pp.7-49; Legal and Constitutional Implications of United Kingdom Membership of the European Communities, May 1967* (Cmnd.3301-15 pp.), a White Paper presented by the Lord Chancellor; *Membership of the European Communities*, 2 May 1967 (Cmnd. 3269-6 pp.), a statement made by the Prime Minister to the House of Commons on the Government's intention to apply for membership of the European Communities.

'In the United Kingdom, because the conclusion and ratification of an international treaty is within the prerogative of the Crown, a constitutional doctrine has been evolved in consequence of which a treaty only forms part of English Law if an enabling Act of Parliament is passed.

The basic rule that obligations do not directly *per se* affect the subjects of the Crown derives from historical circumstances in the seventeenth century and has no ideological roots. Its object has been, of course, to prevent the Crown from legislating without the consent of Parliament and the rule has been held to be applicable to all international treaties which affect private rights or liabilities, or which result in a charge on public funds, or require a modification of common law or of statute for their enforcement in the courts.

This dualist approach to conventional international legal obligations is supplemented by a doctrine of 'incorporation' or 'adoption' in regard to customary rules of international law; such customary rules are considered as part of the law of the land, and enforced as such, only in so far as is not inconsistent with Acts of Parliament or prior judicial decisions of final authority. Nevertheless the formal 'incorporation' of a Treaty by Act of Parliament does not of itself establish an hierarchical order as between treaty law and national law. This is because, in strict constitutional theory and under certain conditions, a statute may bind the courts even if it is in conflict with subsequent treaty law. In addition treaty law may have to give way, in the event of conflict, to decided precedents.

[1]Carl August Fleischer, *8 EFTA Bulletin (November 1971), pp. 11-13.*

Normally, however, British practice recognises that States have a duty to bring their national laws into conformity with their treaty obligations, and to maintain a consistent conformity at all times. British courts will, when called upon to ascertain the meaning of an Act of Parliament, presume that the intention of the legislature was not to violate treaty obligations or generally accepted principles of international law.
....

It is very important here to stress that the law of the Communities, deriving from the Treaty of Rome, the legal acts of Community institutions, and the jurisprudence of the European Court of Justice and of national courts, is essentially a *lex specialis*. It must be carefully distinguished from international law and will certainly pose problems as to its application and implementation within the United Kingdom that are quite unlike those deriving from traditional obligations. As Mr.Lecourt recently said, 'Qui participe à la Communauté épouse son droit'.

The Law of the Communities breaks away from traditional ideas of reciprocal rights and duties as between contracting State parties to an international agreement. Instead, an autonomous, inherently supreme, legal order has been created for the implementation of the objectives of the Treaty of Rome—and this legal order is intended to penetrate very deeply into the national legal systems of member States. It is not possible here to examine particular problems of penetration and of reconciliation that will arise in the United Kingdom, but I would agree with a leading commentator, Professor J.D.B.Mitchell, that Parliament should be able to transfer certain of its legislative powers to Community institutions as required by the Treaty of Rome and that British Courts ought to be able to rise to the responsibility that will be imposed upon them of understanding and accepting the implications, as well as the rules, of a thoroughly novel legal order.'[1]

a. European Communities Act[2]

Part I—General Provisions

Short title and interpretation

'1.—(1) This Act may be cited as the European Communities Act 1972.'
....

General implementation of Treaties

2.—(1) All such rights, powers, *liabilities, obligations* and restrictions from time to time created or arising by or under the Treaties, and all such remedies and procedures from time to time provided for by or under the Treaties as in accordance with the Treaties are without further enactment to be given legal effect or used in the United Kingdom shall be recognised and available in law, and be enforced, allowed and followed ac-

[1]K.R.Simmonds, 9 EFTA Bulletin (December 1971), pp.11, 12. [2]From Sweet and Maxwell's European Community Treaties, 1972, pp.309 et seq.

cordingly; and the expression 'enforceable Community right' and similar expressions shall be read as referring to one to which this subsection applies.

(2) Subject to Schedule 2 to this Act at any time after its passing Her Majesty may by Order in Council, and any designated Minister or department may by regulations, make provision—

(a) for the purpose of implementing any Community obligation of the United Kingdom, or enabling any such obligation to be implemented, or of enabling any rights enjoyed or to be enjoyed by the United Kingdom under or by virtue of the Treaties to be exercised; or

(b) for the purpose of dealing with matters arising out of or related to any such obligation or rights or the coming into force, or the operation from time to time, of subsection (1) above;

and in the exercise of any statutory power or duty, including any power to give directions or to legislate by means of orders, rules, regulations or other subordinate instrument, the person entrusted with the power or duty may have regard to the objects of the Communities and to any such obligation or rights as aforesaid.

In this subsection 'designated Minister or department' means such Minister of the Crown or government department as may from time to time be designated by Order in Council in relation to any matter or for any purpose, but subject to such restrictions or conditions (if any) as may be specified by the Order in Council.

....

(4) The provision that may be made under subsection (2) above includes, subject to Schedule 2 to this Act, any such provision (of any such extent) as might be made by Act of Parliament, and any enactment passed or to be passed, other than one contained in this Part of this Act, shall be construed and have effect subject to the foregoing provisions of this section; but, except as may be provided by any Act passed after this Act, Schedule 2 shall have effect in connection with the powers conferred by this and the following sections of this Act to make Orders in Council and regulations.

Decisions on, and proof of, Treaties and Community instruments, etc.

3.—(1) For the purposes of all legal proceedings any question as to the meaning or effect of any of the Treaties, or as to the validity, meaning or effect of any Community instrument, shall be treated as a question of law (and, if not referred to the European Court, be for determination as such in accordance with the principles laid down by any relevant decision of the European Court).

(2) Judicial notice shall be taken of the Treaties, of the Official Journal of the Communities and of any decision of, or expression of opinion by, the European Court on any such question as aforesaid; and the Official Journal shall be admissible as evidence of any instrument or other act thereby communicated of any of the Communities or of any Community institution.

(3) Evidence of any instrument issued by a Community institution, including any judgment or order of the European Court, or of any document in the custody of a Community institution, or any entry in or extract from such a document, may be given in any legal proceedings by production of a copy certified as a true copy by an official of that institution; and any document purporting to be such a copy shall be received in evidence without proof of the official position or handwriting of the person signing the certificate.

(4) Evidence of any Community instrument may also be given in any legal proceedings—

(a) by production of a copy purporting to be printed by the Queen's Printer;

(b) where the instrument is in the custody of a government department (including a department of the Government of Northern Ireland), by production of a copy certified on behalf of the department to be a true copy by an officer of the department generally or specially authorised so to do;

and any document purporting to be such a copy as is mentioned in paragraph *(b)* above of an instrument in the custody of a department shall be received in evidence without proof of the official position or handwriting of the person signing the certificate, or of his authority to do so, or of the document being in the custody of the department.

(5) In any legal proceedings in Scotland evidence of any matter given in a manner authorised by this section shall be sufficient evidence of it.

Part II—Amendment of Law

....

SCHEDULES

Schedule 1—Definitions Relating to Communities

....

Schedule 2—Provisions as to Subordinate Legislation

1.—(1) The powers conferred by section 2 (2) of this Act to make provision for the purposes mentioned in section 2 (2) *(a)* and *(b)* shall not include power—

(*a*) to make any provision imposing or increasing taxation; or

(*b*) to make any provision taking effect from a date earlier than that of the making of the instrument containing the provision; or

(*c*) to confer any power to legislate by means of orders, rules, regulations or other subordinate instrument, other than rules of procedure for any court or tribunal; or

(*d*) to create any new criminal offence punishable with imprisonment for more than two years or punishable on summary conviction with imprisonment for more than three months or with a fine of more than £400 (if not calculated on a daily basis) or with a fine of more than £5 a day.

(2) Sub-paragraph (1) *(c)* above shall not be taken to preclude the modification of a power to legislate conferred otherwise than under section 2 (2), or the extension of any such power to purpose of the like nature as those for which it was conferred; and a power to give directions as to matters of administration is not to be regarded as a power to legislate within the meaning of sub-paragraph (1) *(c)*.

2.—(1) Subject to paragraph 3 below, where a provision contained in any section of this Act confers power to make regulations (otherwise than by modification or extension of an existing power), the power shall be exercisable by statutory instrument.

(2) Any statutory instrument containing an Order in Council or regulations made in the exercise of a power so conferred, if made without a draft having been approved by resolution of each House of Parliament, shall be subject to annulment in pursuance of a resolution of either House.

3. Nothing in paragraph 2 above shall apply to any Order in Council made by the Governor of Northern Ireland or to any regulations made by a Minister or department of the Government of Northern Ireland; but where a provision contained in any section of this Act confers power to make such an Order in Council or regulations, then any Order in Council or regulations made in the exercise of that power, if made without a draft having been approved by resolution of each House of the Parliament of Northern Ireland, shall be subject to negative resolution within the meaning of section 41 (6) of the Interpretation Act (Northern Ireland) 1954 as if the Order or regulations were a statutory instrument within the meaning of that Act.

b. Explanatory and Financial Memorandum of the European Communities Bill[1]

The Bill[2] makes the legislative changes which will enable the United Kingdom to comply with the obligations entailed by membership of the ECSC, the EEC and the EAEC, and to exercise the rights of membership. These obligations and rights derive from the Treaty concerning the accession of the United Kingdom to the EEC and to

[1] 25 January 1972. [2] Before parliamentary approval a British Act is called 'Bill'.

the EAEC and the Decision of the Council of the European Communities concerning the accession of the United Kingdom to the ECSC (Cmnd.4862-I and II).

The basic requirements of Community membership are dealt with in Part I, with Schedules 1 and 2. The main purposes of Part I are:

   (a) to give the force of law in the United Kingdom to present and future Community Law which under the Community Treaties is directly applicable in Member States;

   (b) to provide for subordinate legislation in connection with the implementation of Community obligations or the exercise of rights under the Treaty;

   (c) to provide for the United Kingdom share of the budget of the Communities and for other payments and receipts arising under the Treaties.

. . . .

Part I—General Provisions

Clause 1 introduces the principal definitions, and in particular those of 'the Treaties'. The Treaties will include the Treaty and Decision relating to the accession of the United Kingdom to the Communities, the six principal pre-accession Treaties listed in Part I of Schedule 1 (i.e. the ECSC-, EEC-, and Euratom Treaties, the Convention on Common Institutions, the Merger Treaty, the Treaty amending certain Budgetary Provisions, note Authors) and treaties entered into by one of the Communities (before January 1972).

They will also include other ancillary treaties to which the United Kingdom becomes a party—but any such treaty entered into by the United Kingdom after 22nd January 1972, otherwise than by acceding to it on terms settled by that date, is included only if a draft Order in Council declaring it to be included has been approved by resolution of each House of Parliament.

Clause 2 makes general provision for rights and obligations arising under the Treaties. It gives the force of law in the United Kingdom to present and future Community law which, under the Treaties, is to be given legal effect without further enactment (subsection (1)). Subsection (2) provides that Orders in Council and regulations may be made for the purpose of implementing a Community obligation, exercising a right under the Treaties or dealing with related matters, subject to the restrictions in Schedule 2, which also makes provision for the parliamentary procedure to apply to such Orders in Council and regulations. There is provision for payments to the Communities and Member States and for other expenditure and receipts under the Treaties. There is provision for legislation by the Parliament of Northern Ireland and by the legislatures of the Channel Islands, the Isle of Man and Gibraltar in implementation of obligations under the Treaties.

Clause 3 deals with the treatment and proof of the Treaties and Community instruments in legal proceedings in the United Kingdom, and makes it clear that questions of their validity, meaning and effect are to be determined in accordance with the jurisprudence of the European Court.

....

c. Further Commentary

'Direct effect is given to Community rules, both as that effect is now understood and as it may evolve. Properly understood, clause 3(2), in combination with this direct effect, can overcome the supposed difficulties springing from the British doctrine of the sovereignty of Parliament and dualist views.

Yet, the question remains will they be so in practice. The dualist view presented technical problems of incorporation of Community law without transforming its character. This danger has been avoided. The specific nature of that law is emphasized by the words 'as in accordance with the Treaties' in clause 2(1). This body of law is separated off from general international law. The Treaties themselves are not enacted by the Bill when it becomes law. Their principles are taken to have been approved by Parliament on 22 October, 1971. All that the Bill, when enacted, will do is to derive necessary consequences. The traditional way of scheduling the Treaties to an Act has been avoided and would have been impracticable.

....

The problems of dealing with existing Community law, and of creating a satisfactory system of processing mediately effective Community law as we have demonstrated—found relatively easy solutions. The hard problem was that of installing the supremacy of Community law as against future British statutes.

....

Pursuing the lines of honesty and legal elegance which mark the drafting of the Bill, this problem is faced by clause 2(4). There are three elements in this clause. The first ends with the word 'Parliament'. It expressly overcomes the problem of the repeal or amendment of Acts of Parliament, past or future, by delegated legislation made by the procedures described. It allows that process. The third element, which starts with the word 'but', ensures that the limitations on this power contained in Schedule 2 endure unless and until repealed by a future statute. Thus the limitations receive a degree of entrenchment. The second elements connects the two. It reads 'and any enactment passed or to be passed other than one contained in this part of this Act, shall be construed to have effect subject to the foregoing provisions of this section'. This looks to the past and the future. The future is most important in the context of the sovereignty of Parliament. Harking back to section 4 of the Statute of Westminster, the binding effect of which even on the Westminster Parliament has (as will appear) now been accepted, it enjoins courts, in their behaviour, in their interpretation of future legislation to give full effect to the concept of 'enforceable Community right' which, as defined in clause 2(1) contains that element of supremacy. It does not say that Parliament cannot enact legislation which is in conflict with Community obligations. It denies effectiveness to such legislation by controlling the way in which the institutions concerned with the application of legislation, *i.e.* the courts, must both construe and give effect to it. Equally, since all life is not litigation, the effect of such legislation is subjected equally to clause 2(1). In their dealings any legal person is bound only to give effect to a statute consistently with that. The future statute is not invalidated, its consequences are limited.

....

For the reasons just given, a frontal attack was excluded on the grounds that such an attack might well lack juridical efficacy and that it would open up all the false arguments that can be based upon that elusive word 'sovereignty'. Finally the argument is not about legal theory but about how to secure within the Community the smooth working of a system in order that the desired economic and social results can be achieved by individuals too.

....

Thus the combination of clauses 2(1) and 2(4) achieve the essential results and Part I of the Bill is excluded from any possibility of amendment under the procedures contained within it. To depart from the position there set out would, in effect, require renunciation of the Treaty.'[1]

[1]Mitchell, Kuipers and Gall, 9 CMLRev. 1972, pp.141-144.

Chapter Four

Division of competences between national courts and Court of Justice

I. INTERACTION COMMUNITY LAW AND NATIONAL LAW: THE DIVISION OF COMPETENCES

LITERATURE: Kolber, Grundsatzfragen der Auslegung des Gemeinsamen Zolltarifs, *AWD 1971, pp.374-382;* Louis, Compétences des Etats dans la mise en oeuvre des règlements, *CDE 1971, pp. 627-641;* Torley Duwel, Incorporatie van communautaire verordeningen in de nationale vervoerswetgevingen, *NJB 1971, pp.457 ff.;* Das Zusammenwirken der europäischen Rechtsordnung mit den nationalen Rechtsordnungen, in: Gemeinschaftsrecht und Nationale Rechte, Kölner Schriften zum Europarecht, Band 13, Carl Heymans Verlag, 1971; Pescatore, Das Zusammenwirken der Gemeinschaftsordnung mit den nationalen Rechtsordnungen, *EuR, 1970, pp.307-324;* Mestmäcker, *Die Vermittlung von europäischem und nationalem Recht im System unverfälschten Wettbewerbs,* Ghelen 1969; Bülck (Ed), *Zur Stellung der Mitgliedstaaten im Europarecht,* in: Schriftenreihe der Hochschule Speyer, Band 32 Berlin 1967.

In the previous Chapter the over-all relationship between Community Law and National Law was discussed from the vantage points of both the Community and the national legal structures.

The Court of Justice has gradually developed the arguments for the necessity of applying Community law uniformly with priority over national legislation. In recent case law the Court has even spoken of 'the principle of the supremacy of Community rules', in cases where conflicts between Community law and national law arise (see Case 14/68, Walt Wilhelm and others, reported below p.111).

Closely connected with the relationship between the two legal systems as such, is the question of the division of competences between Community and national authorities. This question is a complicated one as the competences attributed to the institutions vary considerably from field to field and cannot be covered by one general formula. In the present subchapter three problem areas will be dealt with where Community and national competences may conflict.

A. Where Community legislation and national legislation covering the same field co-exist as complete and separate systems, the question arises to what extent and under which circumstances they may be cumulatively applied. A typical example of such a problem is the cartel legislation of the Community—limited to agreements which 'may affect trade between Member States'—which may coincide with national cartel legislation (see EEC Article 87).

B. Where competences have been attributed to the institutions of the Communities, the member States in general have retained the competence to implement the products of such competences by national acts or regulations. Such implementation may leave an extensive or restrictive discretion to the national authorities, and is in some instances even limited to a purely technical execution. The question then arises to what extent the exercise of the powers which have been retained is affected by the powers which have been transferred. *E.g.* in the field of custom legislation, the Community regulations have transferred to the Community the nature, scope and condition of the manner in which the functions of the customs services of member States are exercised, even though the latter have retained their administrative activities.

As is clear from the case law reported below, the adoption of a Community regulation has deprived the member States of the power to enact 'autonomous provisions' in the same field. That power can subsist only under the provisions of the regulation itself and within the limits specified therein.

C. As a result of Community and national legislation being interwoven in many areas and the combined actions of Community and national authorities it is sometimes difficult to place the responsibility for a particular public act on the one or on the other. Where both administrations have acted there may be room for concurrent tort or delict actions against each of them, such actions being instituted before different courts (respectively the European and the municipal courts) and based on different legal systems.

A. Cumulative application of Community and National Legislations

CASES

(1) WALT WILHELM CASE
Walt Wilhelm and others *v.* Bundeskartellamt, Case 14/68, Decision of 13 February 1969.
(Jur.XV (1969), pp.1-29; CMLR 1969, pp.100-121; 6 CMLRev.1969, pp. 488-490.)
Notes: Pescatore: *Rec.D.1969, p.183;* Schumacher, *AWD 1969, pp.35-89;* VerLoren van Themaat, *AA 1969, pp.316-321;* Mok, *SEW 1970, pp.167-182.*

Facts: Walt Wilhelm and others were fined by the *Bundeskartellamt* (Federal Cartel Office) for violation of the German Law on Restraint of Competition by their cartel concerning aniline.

The EEC Commission had initiated proceedings against Walt Wilhelm and others under Article 85 of the EEC Treaty. In this appeal against the German fines, Walt Wilhelm submitted that the *Bundeskartellamt* could not maintain proceedings for an offence which was at the same time the subject of parallel proceedings by the EEC Commission. The German Court (*Kammergericht Berlin*) asked for a preliminary ruling on the question of cumulation of proceedings.

The Court held:

....

'Community law and national law consider competition in different lights, whereas Article 85 regards restrictive agreements in the light of the obstacles which may result for trade between the Member States, the national laws, inspired by considerations peculiar to each, consider the agreements only in that context.

It is true that by reason of the interdependence of the economic phenomenae and legal situations under consideration, the distinction between the Community and national aspects could not serve in all cases as a determinant criterion for the delimitation of jurisdiction. However, it implies that one and the same agreement may, in principle, be the object of two sets of parallel proceedings, one before the Community authorities under Article 85 of the EEC Treaty, the other before the national authorities in application of internal law. Besides, this concept is confirmed by the provision of Article 87(2) (e), which authorises the Council to define the relations between the national laws and the Community rules on competition, whence it follows that in principle the national authorities in competition matters may take proceedings also with regard to situations liable to be the object of a decision of the Commission.

However, by virtue of the respect of the general finality of the Treaty, such parallel application of the national system should only be allowed in so far as it does not impinge upon the uniform application, throughout the Common Market, of the Community rules on restrictive business agreements and of the full effect of the acts decreed in application of those rules. Any other solution would be incompatible with the objectives of the Treaty and the character of its rules on competition.

....

The EEC Treaty instituted its own legal order, integrated into the legal systems of the member States and which has priority before their courts. It would be contrary to the nature of such a system to accept that the member States may take or maintain in force measures liable to compromise the useful effect of the Treaty. The imperative force of the Treaty and of the acts issued in implementation of it could not vary from State to State by the effect of internal acts, without the functioning of the Community system being obstructed and the attainment of the aims of the Treaty being placed in peril.

Consequently, conflicts between the Community rule and the national rules on competition should be resolved by the application of the principle of the primacy of the Community Rule.

It follows from the foregoing that in the case where national decisions regarding an agreement would be incompatible with a decision adopted by the Commission at the end of the proceedings initiated by it, the national authorities are required to respect its effects.

In the case in which, during national proceedings, it appears possible that the decision whereby the Commission will put an end to proceedings in progress concerning the same agreement may conflict with the effects of the decision of the national authorities, it is for the latter to take the appropriate measures.

Consequently, and so long as no regulation adopted under Article 87(2)(e) of the Treaty has provided otherwise, the national authorities may intervene against an agreement, in application of their internal law, even when the examination of the position of that agreement with regard to the Community rules is pending before the Commission, subject, however, to the provison that such application of the national law may not prejudice the full and uniform application of the Community law or the effect of acts in implementation of it.

....

The possibility of a cumulation of sanctions would not be of a nature to exclude the admissibility of two parallel proceedings pursuing different ends.

....The admissibility of such dual proceedings results in fact from the peculiar system of division of jurisdiction between the Community and the Member States in competition matters.'[1]

....

(2) GERMAN WALT WILHELM CASE

Walt Wilhelm and others *v.* Bundeskartellamt. *Bundesgerichtshof* (Federal Civil Court), Decision of 17 December 1970 (No. KRB 1/70).
(AWD 1971, pp.82, 83; BB 1971, pp.190-193; Betrieb 1971, pp.280-281; NJW 1971, pp.521-525; WuW 1971, p.187; Wettbewerb im Recht und Praxis 1971, pp.128-132; Juristenzeitung 1971, pp. 391-394.)

Facts: After having obtained the above-mentioned preliminary ruling, the German Court (*Kammergericht Berlin*) annulled the fines. The *Bundeskartellamt* appealed to the *Bundesgerichtshof*.

The Bundesgerichtshof held:

'According to the preliminary ruling of the Court of Justice of the European Communities (Decision of 13 February 1969 in Case 14/68 Samml. Vol. XV p.1) made under

[1]Translation by CMLR.

Article 177(1) and (2) of the EEC Treaty at the request of the *Kammergericht* there is no question of Community law preventing the German courts from giving a decision in this case.

. . . .

Moreover, consideration should be given to the question of whether the case is barred under German constitutional law and German procedural law.

. . . .

According to current case law, however, the prohibition of cumulative prosecution does not apply in relation to foreign jurisdiction. The Senate has doubts, however, about regarding the Court of Justice of the European Communities as a foreign court in the sense of that case law. The organs of the European Communities exercise 'supranational', public authority conferred on them by the EEC Treaty. They have sovereign rights which they use for the benefit of the member States which founded them.

. . . .

Nevertheless, the Community and the member States are closely bound together in the exercise of their sovereign powers. The provisions of Community law are part of the internal legal order of the Federal Republic of Germany. Procedurally, the application of community law is not fundamentally separated from the application of German law, but they will partially be treated as a unit.

. . . .

However, the prohibition of cumulative prosecution cannot be resorted to in the present case. The peculiarity of the procedural position is that the Commission of the Communities can, under EEC Regulation No.17, Article 15, impose fines for breach of Community law while on the other hand the German cartel authorities may not mpose fines for contraventi on of Article 85 para 1 of the EEC Treaty on the basis of provision of Community law. They can only proceed against a breach of internal German cartel law. Accordingly both of these proceedings for imposing fines are conducted from quite different legal standpoints.

. . . .

It would, of course, be intolerable and incompatible with the fundamentals of legal order if a German organ of State were to impose a fine without at the same time taking into consideration the fact that the person in question had already been fined for the same act by a Community organ. The idea of justice which is at the basis of the principle of legal order requires that in such a case—in accordance with the basic principle of Article 60(3) *St.GB*—the earlier but parallel proceedings should, vis-à-vis their effect on the person in question, be taken into account in the imposition of later fines even if there are other points of law to be taken into consideration.'[1]

---

[1]Translation by Europa Instituut.

(3) DOUBLE-PENALTY DECISION

Decision IV/26.945 of the Commission of 25 November 1971, *OJ 1971, no.L 282/46* on the accumulation of fines payable by Boehringer for its participation in the Quinine-Cartel.

Facts: By a decision of the Commission of 16 July 1969, Boehringer had been ordered to pay a fine of 190.000 Units of Account. In case 45/69 of 15 July 1970 the Court of Justice reduced this amount to 180.000 Units of Account (see below, p.153).

On 3 July 1969, the US-District Court, Southern District of New York had fined Boehringer $ 80.000 for its participation in the Quinine-cartel, which also violated US anti-trust law. Boehringer requested the Commission to lower the European fine by taking the one paid in the US into account.

The Commission decided:

Admissibility of double penalties according to EEC antitrust law

....

9.The Commission starts from the premise that the Court, in its judgment of 15 July 1970, denied credit for the penalty imposed in the USA only with regard to the case under consideration, that it therefore did not take a final decision on the claim, which was not expounded as to the merits in the lawsuit.

10.The claim of 3 September 1969 must be dismissed on the following grounds: the claim's object is to make the penalty imposed in the USA creditable towards the penalty inflicted by the Commission. The EEC Treaty and the implementing regulations do not provide such an obligation to credit. In the Commission's view neither the legal systems of the member States contain a common principle of law, obliging it to take a penalty imposed by a court of a third State into account when establishing a penalty pursuant to Community law.

11.The Court affirmed, in its judgment 14/68 (Walt Wilhelm, see above p.111) the obligation of the Community and the member States to take an earlier incurred penalty into account when fixing penalties because of the same fact. The Court deduced this obligation from a general principle of fairness, pointing to Art.90, para.2 of the ECSC Treaty. This decision of the Court, however, is limited to penalties pursuant to Community law and those which are imposed according to the national laws of the member States. In this connection it is of importance that the territorial sphere of application of the EEC law on competition of the national anti-trust laws of the member States overlap, and that the relevant economic occurrences and legal situations may be intertwined closely. Through the obligation of both the member States and the Community institutions to take an earlier penalty into account, the concept of fairness requiring avoidance of double punishment, is effectuated.

12. These conditions do not exist in the relation of penalties pursuant to Community law and the law of third States. The legal systems of the member States do not share the principle that in case of penalties according to Community law, penalties imposed by third States must be credited. In the penal law of only two member States a court is obliged to take a penalty executed abroad into account.[1] In the other member States a conviction abroad bars prosecution. In three member States (France, Belgium, Luxembourg) a penalty, imposed and executed abroad, does not bar the initiation of a domestic criminal procedure, when the penal offence has also been committed within the State. The principle 'non bis in idem' does not hold true in these member States, in the case of competence to prosecute on the basis of the territorial principle.[2] In such a case the court is not obliged to take the penalty imposed abroad into account.

13. The principle 'non bis in idem'—in the shape of a bar to prosecution or in the shape of an obligation of the domestic court to take a penalty, imposed and executed abroad, into account—furthermore intervenes only when it concerns 'the same offence' or 'the same infraction'. This condition is not fulfilled either. The American court penalized certain of the petitioner's acts—as a participant in the International Quinine Cartel—which reduced competition in the USA. The Commission, on the other hand, penalized acts of those involved in the International Quinine Cartel which reduced competition in the Common Market. These acts, were indeed done partly to implement the export agreement that the participants had entered into. To answer the question whether 'the same offence' is concerned, one should—in anti-trust law—not consider the agreement or the decision by which the participants bind themselves to competition-reducing behavior, but the acts done to effectuate the obligation and the resulting damage to protected interests. The acts, which the participants in the International Quinine Cartel performed in pursuance of the export-agreement of April 1962—the sale of quinine and quinidine at jointly fixed exportprices—in the USA on the one hand and in the member States on the other, are consequently not to be considered the same offence.

14. The same offence is furthermore not involved as the Commission in its decision directed itself above all to the reduction of competition within the Common Market which had been agreed upon by the participants on the basis of the gentlemen's agreements of 7 April 1962. These gentlemen's agreements provided the participants in particular with protection of their national markets, and interdicted the French partners to produce synthetic quinidine.

---

[1] Sect. 60, para. 3 of the German Penal Code; Arts. 11 and 138 of the Italian Penal Code. [2] France: Code of Criminal Procedure, Title X, 'Of felonies and misdemeanors committed abroad', Art. 692; Belgium: Code of Criminal Procedure, Chapter II: 'Of the employment of the public action on account of felonies or misdemeanors committed outside the territory of the Kingdom', Art. 13; Luxembourg: Code of Criminal Procedure, Art. 5.

The Commission considered the export agreement only with regard to the application of the jointly fixed exportprices in Italy and in Belgium/Luxembourg.

From the information concerning the trial held in the USA appears moreover, that for the American court the gravamen lay in facts, of which the Commission did not regard as proved that they violated Art.85 of the EEC Treaty—as is demonstrated by the decision of 16 July 1969.

B. Community competences and residual national competences

CASES

(1)TURKEY TAIL CASE

Hauptzollamt Hamburg-Oberelbe v. Firma Paul G.Bollmann, Case 40/69, Preliminary ruling on the request of the *Bundesfinanzhof* (Federal Court of Finance) of 18 February 1970.

(Jur., Rec., Samml.XVI (1970), pp.80-81; CMLRev.1970 pp.153-154.)

Notes: Ipsen, *EuR* 1969, *pp.246-248.*

Facts: The Defendant Bollmann had imported into Germany goods from the USA, described as 'turkey tails'. The German Customs Office originally classified these turkey tails under the tariff heading for 'edible turkey offal' and imposed the appropriate levy for this heading. A few months later, however, a new decision was taken, classifying turkey tails under the heading for 'poultry parts' and requesting Bollmann to pay an additional levy.

Bollmann appealed against this decision to the *Finanzgericht* (Court of Finance) Hamburg which annulled the decision. The appellant, the chief Customs Office, lodged an appeal with the *Bundesfinanzhof* against the judgment of the *Finanzgericht*. The *Bundesfinanzhof* requested the Court of Justice to give a preliminary ruling, not only as to whether 'turkey tails' should be considered as falling under the one or the other heading of the Common Customs tariff, but also whether the relevant Community Regulation No.22, establishing the Common Market organization for poultry allowed the national legislature to interpret these definitions autonomously or not. The latter point raised some questions of principle.

The Court held:

....

The first question

'With its first question the Bundesfinanzhof asks the Court of Justice to decide whether Article 14 of Regulation 22 is to be understood as providing that the member

States are entitled and obliged to explain and differentiate from one another the products that are subject to the levy laid down in Article 1 of the Regulation by means of national provisions.

According to Article 14 of Regulation 22, 'the member States shall adopt all measures to adapt their legislative and administrative provisions so that this Regulation, unless therein otherwise provided, may be effectively applied from 1 July 1962'.

Since, by virtue of Article 189(2) of the Treaty, Regulation 22 is directly applicable in all the Member States, in the absence of provisions to the contrary, the Member States are prohibited from adopting measures for the implementation of the Regulation intended to modify its scope or add to its provisions. To the extent that the Member States have assigned legislative powers in tariff matters to the Community in order to ensure the proper operation of the common agricultural market, they no longer have the power to make legislative provisions in this field.

Therefore Article 14 of Regulation 22 must be interpreted to the effect that the Member States are obliged to do all that is necessary to eliminate any obstacles to the application of the Regulation from 1 July 1962 that may arise from their own legislation. Accordingly, this Article does not permit the Member States to make internal provisions affecting the scope of the Regulation itself.

The first question must therefore be answered in the negative.

The second question

If the first question is answered in the negative the Bundesfinanzhof asks the Court of Justice whether Article 1 of Regulation 22, which mentions goods included in the Common Customs Tariff, must be interpreted to the effect that the terms describing these goods may be interpreted by the national legislature because terms describing goods in a customs tariff necessarily require interpretation.

Since description of goods within the meaning of the regulations establishing common organizations of markets form part of Community law, their interpretation can only be regulated if the jurisdiction of the Community is respected. Moreover, common organizations of agricultural markets, such as that which is to be established gradually by Regulation 22, can only fulfil their purpose if the provisions made for their realisation are uniformly applied in all the Member States. The definitions of the goods subjected to these organizations must therefore have the same scope in all the Member States.

This requirement would be jeopardised if, in case of difficulty in the tariff classification of a product, each Member State could fix this scope itself by means of interpretation. Although in case of difficulty in the classification of a product the national authorities may be induced to adopt implementation measures and thus clarify doubts raised by the description of a product, they may only do so in compliance with the provisions of

Community law and they are not empowered to enact binding rules of interpretation. The second question must therefore be answered also in the negative.'[1]

....

Note: The Court of Justice has given similar judgments in further cases, such as the Krohn case (74/69 of 18 June 1970, Jur.XVI (1970) pp.460, 461) and the Bakels case (see below, p.148). For further comment, see the nos concernteing the Krohn case by Ipsen, EuR 1971, pp.39-41; Possen, *SEW 1971, pp.223-228;* Bernhardt, *ZZV 1971 pp.72-76;* Louis, *CDE 1971, pp.633-639.*

(2) RELIABLE IMPORTERS CASE

Norddeutsches Vieh- und Fleischkontor GmbH *v.* Hauptzollamt Hamburg, Case 39/70, Preliminary ruling of 11 February 1971, on the request of the Finanzgericht Hamburg.

(Jur., Rec., Samml.XVII (1971), pp.49-67; CMLR.1971, p.293.)
Notes: AWD, 1971, pp.192-195.

Facts: According to EEC Regulations 805/68, 888/68 and 1082/68, manufacturers exporting tinned meat were exempted from paying the import levy on the frozen meat needed for their export under a number of rather detailed conditions. The German customs authorities required in addition that the importers of frozen meat had to be reliable (*vertrauenswürdig*). The Norddeutsche Vieh- und Fleischkontor was not considered sufficiently reliable and therefore had to pay import levies on the frozen meat which it used for making tinned meat for export. Before the *Finanzgericht* the question arose whether EEC regulations permitted further national requirements or whether they were exhaustive.

The *Finanzgericht* asked for a preliminary ruling.

The Court held:

....

'In all cases where national authorities are responsible for implementing a Community regulation, it should be recognised that in principle this implementation takes place with due respect for the forms and procedures of national law. However, to ensure the uniform application of Community provisions, national rules may only be used to the extent necessary to carry out the regulations.

No such need has been established in the present case, as the regulations, of which interpretation has been requested, fully lay down all conditions necessary to qualify for admission to the system of suspension of levy, as well as all the means and methods of guarantee and supervision designed to prevent fraud.

[1] Translation by CMLR.

National authorities are of course free to make use of all suitable means available in their law to prevent frauds on Community regulations, but this is not the case when internal law is based on criteria which are not in harmony with the system of guarantee and proof set up by Community regulations.

Such national rules should be considered incompatible with these regulations, especially when they are based on such a criterion as the degree of trust worthiness of an importer and leave much too wide a latitude to national authorities.

The application of criteria of this nature may create difference in the treatment of importers between the member States and thus endanger the indispensable uniformity in the implementation of Community regulations in the whole Common Market.

Consequently, the application of national provisions based on criteria not in harmony with those adopted by the Community legislators should be ruled out.'[1]

(3) MAYONNAISE CASE

Firma Gervais-Danone AG *v.* Hauptzollamt München-Schwanthalerstrasse, Case 77/71, Preliminary ruling of 15 December 1971 on request of the *Finanzgericht* München.
(Jur. XVII (1971), p.1136-1140.)

Facts: Gervais-Danone imported different types of Mayonnaise into Germany from Yugoslavia and paid duties appropriate to tariff heading no.21.04 B (sauces, mixed seasoning and similar products, other than Mango chutney) of the International Common Customs Tariff Council in Brussels. In some cases the composition of the Mayonnaise was indicated, in others it was not. The German customs authorities took samples and found an amount of milkfat abnormally high for mayonnaise. They therefore reclassified the product under tariff heading 21.07 (Food preparations not elsewhere specified or included), basing this action on a binding advice (*Zolltarifauskunft*) of the Finance Directorate (*Oberfinanzdirektion*) given in accordance with Article 23 of the German Customs Law (*Zollgesetz*). Gervais-Danone disputed the legality of this reclassification. The *Finanzgericht* asked for a preliminary ruling on several questions; one of which was whether the German Finance Directorates were still competent to issue binding advices after Council Regulation 950/68 on the items concerned became effective.

Translation by CMLR.

The Court held:

ʻ(11)The *Oberfinanzdirektion* may, on request, issue official opinions concerning the tariff heading under which a commodity should be classified. Such opinions may have binding effect upon the administration. On the one hand it is provided that in the event of modification or rescission of an opinion, the applicant may, within 3 months of such an occurrence, still require the application of the former opinion unless the latter is based on defective statements by the applicants. On the other hand it is provided that the authority of an opinion is lost when the legal provisions on which they are based are withdrawn or amended.

(12)The security for importers and the easier application for national authorities may move the latter to apply this procedure provided in their national law. Such application is all the more probable since this procedure contains no normative element and is a part of the usual rules for the application of tariff provisions to individual cases.

(13)As a result it must be concluded that the entry into force of Regulation no.950/68 of the Council did not affect the authority of the binding tariff opinions, issued in accordance with section 23 of the German Zollgesetz.ʼ[1]

(4)SUGAR EXPORT CASE

Firma Schlüter & Maack *v.* Hauptzollamt Hamburg-Jonas, Case 94/71. Preliminary ruling of 6 June 1972 on request of the *Finanzgericht* Hamburg.

Facts. Regulation no.1009/67/EEC of the Council providing for Community regulation on the sugar markets contain in Art.17 a procedure for claiming restitution on export in order to compensate for the difference between the quotations or prices of sugar on the world market and those in the Community.

Restitution, the level of which is fixed by the Council or, in exceptional cases, by the Commission, is paid—at the request of the exporter—by the member State in whose territory the export formalities have been complied with (Art.10 of Regulation no.1041/67 of the Commission).

A request for restitution must be filed within 6 months, from the day on which the customs formalities have been fulfilled, in default of which, any rights otherwise arising, will lapse.

The German authorities required a separate document containing the request for restitution. Schlütter had asked for restitution when he submitted to the customs formalities. The actual export was delayed, however, and when Schlütter forwarded the official document requesting restitution, the six-months period had already elapsed. The question arose whether Germany was permitted to require a separate document in

[1]Translation by Europe Institute.

respect of the request for restitution in the absence of such a requirement in the EEC Regulations.

The Court held:

'10.Since, according to Art.10 of Regulation no.1041/67, 'the restitution is paid by the member State in whose territory the export formalities have been carried out', attention should be paid to the view of the government of the Federal Republic of Germany that when—as in this case—the national authorities are charged with the execution of a Community Regulation, the national rules of procedure are, in principle, applicable to such execution.

11.The rule, expressed in such a way, must be reconciled with the demands that a uniform application of Community Law imposes—which is required to prevent unequal treatment of exporters depending on the border that their products cross on export.

Since the act, as understood in Art.1 of Regulation no.1041/67 exhibits every characteristic of the request to be filed by the exporter, in the sense of Art.17 of Regulation no.1009/67, there exists no motive to qualify the right to restitution with different conditions than those stated in Art.1 of Regulation No.1041/67, in sofar as the right to restitution depends on the filing of a request.

As a result, the member States may, on grounds connected with the organisation of their services prescribe that exporters must also file a request in such form as may be stipulated by national law. The member States may not, however, sanction non-fulfillment of this obligation by means of the loss of the right to restitution.'

C. Concurrent Actions before Community and Municipal Courts

CASES

(1) FIRST GERMAN TOEPFER AND KAMPFFMEYER CASE

Maize importers in Bonn *v.* the German authorities, including the Einfuhr und Vorratstelle für Getreide und Futtermittel (EVSt), *Landgericht Bonn* (first civil Chamber), Decision of 3 December 1968, Case IO 223/67.
(CMLR 1969, pp.244-248).

Facts: In the Toepfer Case (see Jud.Rem., pp.55-57), the Court of Justice annulled the Decision of the EEC Commission of 3 October 1963.

In the Kampffmeyer Case (Jud.Rem., pp.97-100), the Court of Justice held the Commission in principle liable—independently of any liability the German authorities had incurred—to grant damages to the plaintiff but had ordered the plaintiff to pro-

¹Translation by Europa Instituut.

duce first, a decision of the German court on its claim for damages from the German authorities.

The plaintiff importers claimed damages before the German authorities. He argued that the Community and Germany were jointly and severally liable and that an eventual division of damages had to be settled between them. The German authorities submitted that the suit was—at least for the time being—unfounded because the plaintiff had not exhausted its possibilities of compensation from other parties (under German administrative law damages may be claimed from the Government only when no compensation may be obtained from other parties). The question arose whether the EEC Commission was another party in the sense of the German law.

The Landgericht held:

'The case is dismissed as being for the present time unfounded, because it has not been proved that there is no possibility of compensation for the alleged damage from another party (section 839(1)(ii) of the German Civil Code) so that it remains undecided whether the plaintiff can avail itself of the other provisions to claim damages for breach of administrative duty under section 839 together with Article 34 of the Constitution. In order to found a claim against an administrative body it is necessary to show that it is impossible to obtain damages from any other party. This, however, is not the case here, because the plaintiff has a possible claim for damages against the EEC Commission. This results from the judgment of the European Court of 1 July 1965 which annulled the Commission's decision authorising Germany to maintain the measure of protection under Article 22 of Regulation 19.

Therefore the plaintiff could have a claim for damages against the Commission under Article 215 of the EEC Treaty. As long as there is no decision about this, the first and second defendants could make reference to the claim for damages from another party in consequence of section 839(1)(ii).

A reference to a possible claim against the EEC would not be possible, if such a claim were also only a subsidiary one. However, that is not the case here.

The EEC Commission's primary liability under Article 215 stems from the fact that the laws of the other five EEC Member States do not provide for possibilities of reference corresponding to section 839(1)(ii). It also results from the European Court's judgment of 14 July 1967, which the plaintiff has not sought to reject, because the claim against Germany under section 830 together with Article 34 of the Constitution precedes the claim under Article 215 of the EEC Treaty. Rather, the possibility of inadequate or excessive damages being awarded, which might result from the application of different criteria of claims in respect of one and the same injury in different courts, must be prevented.

....

In the present case the fact is that the EEC Commission, against which the claim for damages against the other party could arise, is no further removed from the event giving rise to liability than is the defendant Einfuhr und Vorratstelle. In fact it was the Commission, as prime mover, which on 27 September 1963 established what was certainly a materially incorrect 'Free Frontier Price', because it considered only the supplies of maize from the old harvest and not those from the new harvest. Thus the Einfuhr und Vorratstelle's refusal of the import licence came about only after and on the basis of this improper act of the Commission. Also the Commission's second measure, the authorisation of Germany to maintain the measure of protection, was illegal according to the European Court's judgment.'[1]

(2) SECOND GERMAN TOEPFER AND KAMPFFMEYER CASE

Maize importers in Köln against the German authorities, including the Einfuhr und Vorratstelle für Getreide und Futtermittel, *Oberlandesgericht* Köln, Decision of 2 May 1968, 7 W 18/68.

(EuR (1968), pp.405-406).

Note: Ipsen, *EuR 1968, pp.406-408.*

Facts: The facts were virtually the same as in the above-mentioned case of the *Landgericht* Bonn (which is of a later date).

The *Landgericht* Köln decided in the same way as the *Landgericht* Bonn. The present case concerns the appeal against the decision of the *Landgericht* Köln.

The Oberlandesgericht held:

....

'The appeal allowed (Para.252 ZPO) against the suspension decision is well-founded. The decision in this suit does not depend on the existence of a claim for damages against the EEC Commission for the appellant cannot be referred to such a claim as a further possibility for compensation according to Para 839(1), second sentence *BGB*. As the first Civil Senate of the *Bundesgerichtshof* explained in BGHZ Vol.13, p.83, by reference to the background, meaning and purpose of Para 839(1)(2) *BGB;* the state which is responsible for an official's actions only has the possibility of transferring its liability if the other possibilities for compensation are under private law and lead to the obligations of the state—which must be regarded as one economic unit—being discharged.

On the basis of this decision, the *Bundesgerichtshof* developed, for the future, the principle that a department of State cannot—in so far as it is regarded as one unit—

[1]Translation by CMLR.

refer to a possible claim against another department of State as a further possibility for claiming damages, within the meaning of Para 839(1)(2) *BGB*, in so far as the various claims (claim based on the official's repsonsibility and 'further claim for damages') arise from the same set of facts. (*BGB*, LM No.12 on Para 839(E) *BGB*).

Since here, the claims against the respondents and the EEC Commission arise out of the same set of facts and must all be satisfied from public funds, the question is simply whether, for the purposes of application of Para 839(1)(2) *BGB*, the unity of public funds can be taken to include not only German public funds but also the funds of the EEC Commission. The respondents reference to the *Bundesverfassungsgericht*'s decision in DÖV 1967 p.823 is mistaken in this connection. It was decided in that case that the acts of the Council and Commission of the EEC are acts of a special, public, supra-national authority which is clearly separate from the public authorities of the member States. The possibility of transferring liability does not depend on this legal distinction since economic considerations are decisive on that point. In the above-mentioned decisions, the *Bundesgerichtshof* had only considered the public funds as a single unit from an economic point of view. The EEC is also included in this unit.

It is immaterial whether the Commission could, according to internal Community rules, in the present circumstances, require the Federal Republic to settle internally the payment of the damages so that they would in fact have to be met out of the funds of the respondent mentioned in 1. If this was the case, then the application of Para 839(1)(2) *BGB* would clearly not lead to the saving of German public funds and, therefore, the liability of the EEC could not be referred to as a further possibility for damages.

If the burden of paying the damages cannot shifted onto the Federal Republic by the Commission, then German public funds will ultimately have to bear this burden because the EEC budget is partly made up of German contributions. Accordingly, it would be contrary to the nature of the Community to distinguish vis-à-vis the possibility of transferring liability under Para 839(1)(2) *BGB*—between how much of the compensation paid by the EEC was from contributions of the German taxpayer and how much was from the public funds of the other member States.

The Community is an integrated whole whose acts and financial burdens cannot be differentiated according to the share of sovereign rights and finance contributed by the various member States. The task of creating unity in the economic field was a task to be undertaken as a whole by each member State and not just proportionately. Accordingly, it is in the interests of the Federal Republic as part of the Community to save the funds of the Community to as great an extent as possible. From this it appears that the EEC should be regarded as a department in relation to public funds, whose funds should, in the public interest, be dealt with economically, in accordance with Para 839(1)(2) *BGB*, within the framework of official responsibility.

Therefore, in accordance with Article 34 of the Constitution, no German department of state responsible for officials' actions can refer to a claim against the EEC as an alternative possibility for damages.'[1]

II. PRELIMINARY RULINGS

LITERATURE: Hay, Une approche politique de l'application de l'article 177 du Traité CEE par les juridictions nationales, *CDE 1971, pp.503-522;* Lagrange, The European Court of Justice and national Courts, *8 CMLRev.1971, pp.313-325;* Mashaw, Ensuring the Observance of Law in the Interpretation and Application of the EEC Treaty: The Role and Functioning of the Renvois d'Interprétation under Article 177, *7 CMLRev.1970, pp.258-286,* and *pp.423-454;* Ganshof van der Meersch, La juridiction internationale dans l'Union économique Benelux, *AFDI 1969, pp. 245-265;* Merchiers, Rapport sur les problèmes posés par l'application de l'Article 177 du Traité CEE, *Parlement Européen, Commission juridique, Document No.94, 1969-1970 (Resolution Eur. Parliament, 8 October 1969, OJ 1969, No.C 139/19);* Buxbaum, Article 177 of the Rome Treaty as a federalizing device, *Stanford Law Rev.1969, pp.1041-1057;* Dumon, La Cour de Justice. Questions préjudicielles, *Les Novelles, Droit des Communautés européennes—Brussels, 1969, pp. 341-366;* Juilhard, Procédure préjudicielle et renforcement du lien communautaire, *RTDE 1968, pp. 239-331;* Peter Selmer, Zur Entscheidungserheblichkeit der Gültigkeitsfrage bei der Vorlage nach Art.177 des EWG Vertrages. *AWD 1968, pp.424-427.*

Additional EEC-Protocols

On 3 June 1971, two protocols were signed at Luxembourg, conferring on the Court of Justice jurisdiction to interpret conventions concluded under Article 220 of the EEC Treaty.[2]

Under both protocols the supreme courts are obliged to ask for a preliminary ruling if they consider that a decision on the question is necessary to enable them to deliver judgment.

Under the protocol concerning the convention of 29 February 1968 on the mutual recognition of companies and legal persons, any national court may ask for a preliminary ruling. Article 2 of this protocol repeats the relevant wording of Article 177 EEC.

However, in the protocol concerning the convention of 27 September 1968 on the jurisdiction and the enforcement of civil and commercial judgments the competence to invoke a preliminary ruling has been restricted:

Article 2

'The following courts and tribunals shall have the power to ask the Court of Justice to give preliminary rulings on questions of interpretation:

[1]Translation by Europa Instituut. [2]For texts, see *supplement 4/71, Annex to Bulletin 7-1971* of the European Communities and *8 CMLRev. 1971, pp.491-494.*

1. in Belgium: la Cour de Cassation—het Hof van Cassatie and le Conseil d'Etat—de Raad van State,
   in the Federal Republic of Germany: die obersten Gerichtshöfe des Bundes,
   in France: la Cour de Cassation and le Conseil d'Etat,
   in Italy: la Corte Suprema di Cassazione,
   in Luxembourg: la Cour supérieure de Justice, when sitting as Supreme Court of Appeal,
   in the Netherlands: de Hoge Raad;
2. the courts and tribunals of the Contracting States when they are hearing appeals;
3. in the cases provided for in Article 37 of the Convention; the courts and tribunals mentioned in the said article.'

Article 3

'1. Where a question relating to the interpretation of the Convention and the other texts mentioned in Article 1 is raised in a case pending before a court or tribunal indicated in Article 2, point 1, that court or tribunal shall, if it considers that a decision on the question is necessary to enable it to give judgment, be bound to request the Court of Justice to give a ruling thereon.

2. Where such a question is raised before any court or tribunal indicated in Article 2, points 2 and 3, that court or tribunal may, in the circumstances specified in paragraph 1, request the Court of Justice to give a ruling.'

Article 4 of this protocol introduces another novelty. It reads:

Article 4

1. The competent authority of a Contracting State may ask the Court of Justice to give a ruling on a question of interpretation of the Convention and of the other texts mentioned in Article 1 if decisions made by courts or tribunals of that State are in conflict with the interpretation given either by the Court of Justice or by a decision of a court or tribunal of another Contracting State mentioned in Article 2, points 1 and 2. The provisions of this paragraph shall apply only to judgments at law.

2. The interpretation given by the Court of Justice following such a request shall not affect the decisions in respect of which the interpretation was requested.

3. The Attorney Generals at the Supreme Courts of Appeal of the Contracting States or any other authority designated by a Contracting State shall be empowered to lay before the Court of Justice a request for interpretation in conformity with paragraph 1.

4. The Registrar of the Court of Justice shall give notice of the request to the Contracting States, to the Commission and to the Council of the European Communities which, within a period of two months as from this notice, may submit briefs or written observations to the Court.

5. The procedure provided for in this Article shall not involve either the levying or reimbursement of costs or expenses.'

Notes: See the Commentaries on the two protocols by Dumon, *SEW 1972,pp.203-241;* Mok, *8 CMLRev.1971, pp.485-471;* Cathala, L'interprétation uniforme des Conventions conclues entre Etats-Membres de la CEE en matière du droit privé, *Rec. D.1972,pp.31-34 (Chr.).*

A. Nature of preliminary rulings

1. ECSC

ECSC Article 41

'The Court shall have sole jurisdiction to give preliminary rulings on the validity of conclusions of the High Authority and of the Council, where such validity is in issue in proceedings brought before a municipa court or tribunal.'

CASES

(1) BELGIAN BAUFFE CASE

Bauffe and Servais v. Openbaar Ministerie. *Cour de Cassation* (2nd Chambre), Decision of 1 June 1970.

(GP 1970, pp.343-345. JT 1970, pp.509-511. Pas.Belge 1970, pp.352-359. Revue de Droit International et de Droit Comparé 1970, pp.263-264. RTDE 1970, pp.534-537. RW 1970, pp.1366-1372.)
Notes: GP 1970, p.8.

Facts: Plaintiffs, Belgian truck operators, objected that they had been condemned by the *Tribunal correctionel* of Charleroi, for non-observance of certain Belgian transport-regulations, in particular a Royal Decree of 3 March 1966 which provided for a standard contract for the transport of certain products. They claimed that the lower court had refused to classify the products which they had transported as ECSC-products to which these regulations did not apply. The question thus was one of interpretation of the products concerned; did they or did they not fall within the competence of the ECSC Treaty?

The Cour de Cassation held:

....

'Contrary to what the EEC Treaty and the Euratom Treaty provide in their Articles 177 and 150 respectively, the ECSC Treaty does not contain any provision and does not organise any procedure compelling the municipal courts of the Member States, whenever a question of interpretation of this Treaty is raised before them and there is no possibility of appeal under internal law from their decision to refer the question to the Court of Justice of the European Communities.

Therefore this Court has the power to express itself on the meaning and significance (*sens et portée*) of the provisions contained in the ECSC Treaty.'[1]

....

(After a review of the relevant provisions of the ECSC Treaty, the *Cour de Cassation* concluded, that the lower court had rightly classified the products concerned as falling under the Royal Decree).

[1] Translation by Europa Instituut.

(2) BELGIAN SIDERO CASE

S.A.Aciers Sidero *v.* Fagersta Brucks Aktiebolag, *Cour d'Appel* (Court of Appeal) of
Brussels (2nd Chambre), Decision of 4 May 1970.
(RTDE 1970, pp.538-539; JT 1970, pp.496-497.)

Facts: The Plaintiff had concluded with the defendant, a Swedish manufacturing
company, an exclusive sales agreement for the sale of the latter's goods in Belgium. The
Plaintiff was bound thereunder to sell only goods produced by the Swedish company.
When in his submission the Swedish company unilaterally and without sufficient
notice abrogated the agreement, the plaintiff instituted a claim for damages under a
Belgian law of 27 July 1961. He lost this suit. On appeal the defendant claimed that if
there was an exclusive sales agreement, it should be declared null and void as violating
the provisions of Article 65 of the ECSC Treaty.

The question before the *Cour d'Appel* was whether it had the power to do so.

The Cour d'Appel held:

....

..., 'pursuant to Article 65 para 4(2) of that Treaty, the High Authority alone is competent—apart from the possibility of appeal to the Court of Justice—to pronounce on
the conformity of agreements between enterprises which tend to prevent, restrict,
or distort, either directly or indirectly, the normal working of competition within the
Common Market with the provisions of the abovementioned Article.

.... the respondent has disputed certain points by the abovementioned means and
accordingly the court ought to postpone judgment until the Commission of the
European Communities, exercising the powers and competence of the High Authority
of the ECSC by virtue of the Treaty of 8 April, 1965 which came into force on 1 July,
1967, has given a preliminary ruling on this point.

... the Commission of the European Communities ought to determine the effects of the
'gentleman's agreements' concluded by the appellant in connection with the exclusive
sale of certain of the respondent's products in Belgium.

... the appellant's pleas as to the partial validity of these agreements should not be
taken into account. If the respective obligations undertaken by the parties not to have
dealings with competing enterprises would be held to be void the appellant could no
longer invoke the law of 27 July, 1961.'[1]

....

The *Cour d'Appel* thereupon suspended the proceedings while awaiting the reply of
the Commission.

[1]Translation by Europa Instituut.

2. EEC

CASES

(1) AIR-HOSTESS CASE

Gabrielle Defrenne *v*. Belgium, Case 80/70, Preliminary ruling of 25 May 1971 at the request of the Belgian Council of State.
(Jur.XVII (1971), p.453.)

Facts: Miss Defrenne, a former Belgian air-hostess, had been pensioned at the age of 40 according to a Belgian Royal Decree of 24 October 1967. The level of the pensions of air-hostesses differed from that of other flying personnel. Miss Defrenne submitted that this was in violation of Article 119 of the EEC Treaty. The Council of State asked for a preliminary ruling on three questions:
a. Is a pension part of the renumeration for work?
b. Is it permitted to use different age-limits in pensioning male and female personnel?
c. Do air-hostesses perform the same work as male air-stewards?
The Court answered the first question in the negative. Unlike the practice in many other cases the Council of State had not posed the other questions on the condition that the answer to the first question must be affirmative. Was the Court obliged to answer the other questions as well?

The Court held:

....

'After the reply to the first question, the other questions are without ground' (they were not answered).[1]

(2) HENCK CASE

Günter Henck *v*. Hauptzollamt Emmerich, Case 14/17, Preliminary ruling of 14 July 1971, at the request of the *Bundesfinanzhof* (German Federal Court of Finance).
(Jur.XVII (1971), pp.750, 751.)

Facts: The *Bundesfinanzhof* asked for a preliminary ruling as to what was understood by the term 'cracked grains of millet' in regulation No.19/62 EEC. This regulation had been replaced on 1 July 1967. The *Bundesfinanzhof* had presented such detailed information on the composition of the product concerned that, according to Henck, the question was apparently one of application, rather than of interpretation.

---

[1] Translation by Europa Instituut.

The Court held:

....

... 'the Court of Justice cannot, when asked to interpret Community law, derive competence from Article 177 of the Treaty to make decisions in cases which deal with particular factual situations but if, on the other hand, an interpretation of the texts which are the subject of litigation is to be of any practical use then the national court should have the possibility of defining the legal scope of the requested interpretation;

..., on the basis of facts stated along with the question, it is possible to decide both in general and in abstracto the category of products which came under the contested provision;

..., the firm of Günter Henck further pleads—in connection with the fact that Regulation No.19/62 of 1 July, 1967 has been repealed and replaced by other Community legal provisions—that the Court of Justice, in answering the question put to it, may not take as a starting point provisions which were not applicable at the time when the imports which are the subject of litigation were made;

... the principle of legal security requires that the law which was valid when the disputed provision was applied be taken as the starting point;

... the wording of the question does not prevent the Court respecting that principle in its interpretation.'[1]

....

(3) CHANEL CASE

SA Chanel *v.* Cepeha Handelsmaatschappij N.V., Case 31/68, Preliminary Ruling asked by the Court of Rotterdam, Decisions of 3 June 1969 and 16 June 1970.
(Jur.XVI (1970), pp.404-405; 1971 CMLR, pp.403-419.)

Facts: In the Bosch Case (13/61 of April 6, 1962; see Jud.Rem.pp.182-186) the parties lodged an appeal against the judgment of the Court of Appeal of The Hague in which a preliminary ruling was requested. The Court of Justice decided that such an appeal was irrelevant for its competence to reply to the questions asked. It gave its preliminary ruling before the Netherlands' Supreme Court had decided on the question whether the preliminary ruling was correctly requested (see Jud.Rem., p.183).

In the present case, the Rotterdam District Court, by its judgment of 3 December 1968, asked for a preliminary ruling on Article 85 of the EEC Treaty. On 29 January 1969 the registrar of the Rotterdam Court notified the Court of Justice that an appeal had been lodged against the judgment of 3 December 1968. Nevertheless the Court of Justice decided on 23 March 1969 that the oral proceedings would be held on 29 April 1969. The Advocate-General concluded on 20 May 1969 that no valid request

[1] Translation by Europa Instituut.

for a preliminary ruling had been as long as the decision of the Rotterdam Court was not final. He proposed that the Court of Justice should stay the proceedings until the outcome of the appeal before the Dutch Court was known.

The Court held: (3 June 1969)

. . . .

'A decision in the present case will be postponed until the Court has been notified that a decision in appeal has been taken.'

. . . .

Further facts: On 6 May 1970 the Court of Appeal in The Hague annulled the decision of the Rotterdam Court by which the preliminary ruling had been requested.

The Court held: (16 June 1970)

. . . .

'The request for an interpretation has become without object. The Court in Rotterdam will have to decide on the costs made. Case No.31/68 is removed from the roll.'[1]

B. Jurisdiction of the Court of Justice

CASE

(1)SALGOIL CASE

Salgoil *v.* Ministry of Foreign Trade of Italy, Case 13/68, Preliminary ruling of 19 December 1968, at the request of the Court of Rome.
(Jur.XIV (1968), pp.641-642; Rec.XIV (1968), pp.672-674; 6 CMLRev.1968, pp.478-481.)
Notes: Brinkhorst, 6 CMLRev.1968, pp.481-488.

Facts: The Court of Rome had asked for a preliminary ruling on the direct effect of Articles 30 and 31 of the EEC Treaty. The Italian Ministry of Foreign Trade contended that the request for a preliminary ruling was inadmissible as the referring court had neglected to specify that the dispute in the proceedings concerned trade between the Member States. It alleged that the case actually concerned imports of products from third countries. The Court had to decide whether it could give the rulings requested.

The Court held:

. . . .

'However, Article 177, which is based upon the principle of a clear separation of

[1]Translation by Europa Instituut.

functions between municipal courts and the Community Court, does not allow the latter either to investigate the facts of the case or to criticize the reason and objects of the request for an interpretation. It must, therefore, be accepted that whenever a municipal court requests the interpretation of a Community provision, it considers the interpretation necessary for the adjudication of the dispute. Consequently the Court may not ask the municipal court for a specific declaration that it considers the text, the interpretation of which it deems necessary, to be applicable. Unless the reference to the text concerned is manifestly erroneous the Court is validly seized of jurisdiction.

The question, whether a provision, the interpretation of which is requested, is applicable to the case at bar, does not fall under the jurisdiction of the Court of Justice but under that of the municipal court. It follows that the objection raised cannot be admitted.'[1]

....

C. Function of National Courts

LITERATURE: Mok, Should the first paragraph of Article 177 of the EEC Treaty be read as a separate clause? *5 CMLRev.(1968), pp.458-464.*

1.Courts entitled to ask preliminary rulings

*a.*Courts within the term of EEC Article 177

(i) Arbitral Tribunals

....

(ii) Summary proceedings

CASES

(1)GERMAN TAPIOCA CASE

Bundesfinanzhof (Federal Court of Finance), Decisions of 6 December 1967, No.VII B 48/66, and of 9 January 1968, No.VII B 104, 134/67.
(AWD 1968, p.284; CDE 1970, p.186).

Facts: The question arose whether the *Bundesfinanzhof*, which is a court of the highest instance in the sense of Article 177, para 3, was obliged to ask for a preliminary ruling in summary proceedings before it.

[1]Translation by CMLR.

The Bundesfinanzhof held:

....

'Because in the summary proceedings pursuant to § 69, para 2, clause 2, and para 2 of the FGO, only the prospects of success of a plea were considered, but no final decision was made on the questions that are important for deciding the main issue and hence not on the question mentioned in Article 177, para 1, of the EEC Treaty either, the *Bundesfinanzhof* is not obliged by Article 177, para 3 of the Treaty, to obtain a preliminary ruling from the Court of Justice of the European Communities, in this procedure.'[1]

....

(2) GERMAN RECORDS CASE
Oberlandesgericht Hamburg, Decision of 8 October 1970, No.3 U 108/1970.
(AWD 1971, p.40. See also AWD 1970, p.562.)

Facts: Before the *Oberlandesgericht*, which is in principle the highest Court in the free-state of Hamburg, the question was raised whether the court was obliged to ask for a preliminary ruling in summary proceedings before it.

The Oberlandesgericht held:

....

'The obligation under Article 177, paragraph 3 of the EEC Treaty to request a preliminary ruling from the Court of Justice also exists, in the Senate's opinion, in relation to summary proceedings for an interim injunction; for, there is no appeal under municipal law from the Senate's decision. True, it is possible to examine the same legal questions again in subsequent, main proceedings but the petitioner is not obliged, however, to institute such proceedings. In a concrete case, the *Oberlandesgericht* will make a final decision. The influence of this decision on domestic case law requires that the Court should basically comply with the obligation to ask for a preliminary ruling.'[1]

....

b. Discretion to invoke preliminary rulings

[1] Translation by Europa Instituut.

CASES

(1) GERMAN REWE-ZENTRALE CASE

Rewe-Zentrale des Lebensmittel-Groszhandels GmbH *v.* Hauptzollamt Emmerich, *Finanzgericht* Düsseldorf, Decision of 15 July 1970, No.IV 42/702.
(AWD 1970, p.377.)

Facts: After the German revaluation of 27 October 1969, the EEC Council adopted several regulations permitting protective measures for the German agricultural market. The validity of these regulations was disputed. It was suggested that the *Finanzgericht*—as a lower court—could refuse to apply the regulations, if it considered them invalid (compare the German Exportbond Case, Jud.Rem.p.205).

The Finanzgericht held:

....

'The Senat did not follow the suggestion to refer to the European Court of Justice for a preliminary ruling the question whether national courts that are not of the last instance, are not only entitled, but also obliged to submit their question to the Court of Justice when they deem a legal act of a Community organ invalid.

The senat was not presented with this question because (in accordance with the other courts of finance) it considers it advisable, as a general rule—especially when other questions on whose preliminary decision the decision concerned could depend are inconceivable—to submit the questions of factual relevance in the main decision for a preliminary ruling in the earliest possible stage of the judicial proceedings. It is in the interest of the economy of the proceedings that in the earliest possible stage the European Court of Justice gets the opportunity to answer questions that concern the validity and direct applicability of decisions of the Commission.'[1]

Note: The requested preliminary ruling was given on 11 February 1971 (Case 37/70, Jur.XVII (1971), p.23).

(2) GERMAN IMPORT LICENCE FOR OATS CASE

Verwaltungsgericht Frankfurt a/M., Decision of 15 June 1966-II/1-780/63.
(AWD 1967, p.269; Ehle, No.II H c.10 CMLR 1968, pp.117, 118.)

Facts: Plaintiff disputed the validity of Article 7, para 2, of Regulation No.87 of the EEC Commission. The Court had to consider whether it ought to ask for a preliminary ruling.

---

[1]Translation by Europa Instituut.

The Verwaltungsgericht held:

....

'Article 177 of the Treaty does not lay down the exact conditions under which a court must make use of its right to refer a case to the European Court. It is therefore necessary to start from the general principles of administrative law, which suggest that recourse to the European Court is a matter within the court's discretion. The main matters to be considered in its exercise are the purpose of Article 177, the effects of and the grounds for a request for a ruling, and the parties' interests.

Article 177 of the Treaty is meant to ensure legal unity within the EEC. It is sufficient for that purpose that courts from which there is no further appeal have a duty to refer to the European Court where necessary. It was desired to give other courts the right to request a ruling as well; but it was appreciated that the European Court must not be overwhelmed by requests for rulings as a result. This viewpoint should induce courts to exercise their right sparingly. A reference to the European Court must not become an automatic reaction, and ought only to be made if serious difficulties of interpretation occur, or if there are serious doubts about the validity of an act of a Community institution. That does not apply to the present case, as explained above.

....

In deciding whether or not to request a ruling from the European Court of Justice the parties' interests in obtaining an authorative decision quickly must be considered. Costs would be thrown away if parties had to go through the whole hierarchy of courts within the German Federal Republic in order finally to obtain a decision from the European Court. But in the Court's view there are no serious and well-founded doubts in the present case such as to make a reference to the European Court a proper course. In all probability the European Court's ruling, if obtained, would reject the applicant's view of the law. It is therefore directly in the parties' interests to avoid the detour of having recourse to it, and to have an effective decision of the present matter forthwith.'[1]

....

(3) GERMAN ASBACH URALT BRANDY CASE
Landgericht Wiesbaden, Decision of 10 July 1967. CMLR 1969, pp.177, 178.
Notes: Johannes, *AWD 1968, pp.58-60;* Eichler, *NJW 1968, pp.1049-1050.*

Facts: The plaintiff operated a brandy distillery manufacturing 'Asbach Uralt' brandy. By means of price agreements with all its customers it prescribed fixed retail prices. The defendant sold below that price. During the proceedings in court the plaintiff obtained an interlocutory injunction restraining defendant from selling 'As-

---

[1] Translation CMLR, footnotes omitted.

bach Uralt' brandy. The defendant appealed against this interlocutory injunction. In his submission the price-fixing agreement violated Article 85 of the EEC Treaty and was therefore void. The question arose whether a preliminary ruling should be asked.

The Landesgericht held:

....

'Article 85 is directly applicable in each of the member States. The courts of the member States are empowered to interpret the normative provisions of the EEC Treaty, unless the court is a final appellate court with a duty to refer a question to the European Court of Justice for a preliminary ruling under Article 177(3) of the Treaty. Courts of first instance are not obliged by Article 177(2) to submit a question for a ruling. Moreover, a reference to the European Court would be incompatible with the urgency of the matter in proceedings for the issue of an interlocutory injunction.'[1]

....

2.Courts obliged to ask preliminary rulings

LITERATURE: Goffin, Qui sont les juridictions belges qui sont tenues au renvoi préjudicié devant la Cour de Justice des Communautés européennes, *JT 1968, pp.541-543.*

*a.*Courts of highest instance.

CASE

(1)GERMAN STATUTORY JUDGE CASE

Bundesverfassungsgericht (Federal Constitutional Court), Decision of 13 October 1970, No.2 BvR 618/68.
(AWD 1970, p.516; ZZV 1971, pp.19-24; Der Betrieb 1970, pp.2155-2156; NJW 1970, pp.2155-2157).

Facts: A German wheatimporter had lost his case before the *Bundesfinanzhof* (Federal Court of Finance). In that case the *Bundesfinanzhof* had interpreted Regulations Nos. 19 and 55 of the EEC Council without asking for a preliminary ruling. From decisions of the *Bundesfinanzhof* no appeal lies. Only the jurisdiction of the *Bundesverfassungs-gericht* may be invoked for alleged violations of the German constitution. Plaintiff submitted before this Court that by not asking for a preliminary ruling the *Bundes-finanzhof* had denied him the constitutional right granted by Art.101, para 1, of the German constitution, which provides that no one may be removed from the juris-diction of his lawful judge.

[1]Translation by CMLR.

The Bundesverfassungsgericht held:

'It may be left indecided whether the European Court of Justice—in so far as courts in the Federal Republic of Germany have to submit the questions mentioned in Article 177, para 1, of the Treaty to it for a preliminary ruling pursuant to Article 177, para 3—is a 'lawful' court (= provided by law, (Authors)) in the sense of Article 101, para 1, clause 2, *GG*. Someone is deprived of his lawful court by an act, an omission or a decision of a court only when this act, omission or decision is founded on arbitrariness (*B.Verf.GE* 19, 38(43); 23, 288(320)). This applies also when a court neglects its duty to refer to another court that should decide a certain issue of law (*B.Verf.GE* 3, 359(363); 9, 213 (215ff); 13, 132(143); 18, 441(447); 23, 288(319)). Article 101, para 1, clause 2, *GG*, does not offer protection against faults in the proceedings that occur as a result of a mistake by the court, but solely against arbitrariness. (*B.Verf.GE* 3, 359(364ff); 17, 199(104); 23, 288(320)).

Arbitrariness, however, comes into consideration only when the decision, in applying and interpreting the competence rules—whereto in a larger sense also the regulations on submission to another court belong—has strayed so far from the principle of the lawful court which governs these rules, that the court's decision is not justifiable anymore (judgment of the 2nd panel, of 30 June 1970—2 BvR 48/70—). Article 101, para 1, clause 2, *GG*, is violated only by such judicial decisions as appear no longer understandable on reasonable appreciation of the governing idea of the Constitution, and are obviously indefensible (*B.Verf.GE* 6, 45(53); 19, 38(43)).

The *Bundesgerichtshof* did not arbitrarily refrain from submission to the European Court of Justice.

a) According to Article 177, para 1-b, in connection with para 3 of the Treaty, a court of a member State whose own decision cannot be appealed with domestic means of redress, is obliged to call upon the European Court of Justice when the question arises—in a lawsuit pending before it—whether the act of a Community organ is valid or how it must be interpreted. The *Bundesfinanzhof* is a supreme federal court, whose decisions cannot be further appealed.

The Regulations, issued by the Council of the EEC belong as well to the acts of Community organs (Article 189, para 1, of the Treaty).

In the grounds for the judgment no express position is taken on the question, whether it is necessary to obtain a preliminary ruling of the European Court of Justice on the interpretation of those provisions of Regulation No.19, that contain the principles, decisive for the fixing of the threshold prices.

The explanations of the *Bundesfinanzhof*, however, show that the court was not in doubt as to the content and scope of the applicable provisions of Regulation No.19.'[1]

. . . .

[1] Translation by Europa Instituut.

b. Limitations on the obligation to ask for preliminary rulings

(*i*) *Prior preliminary rulings*

....

(*ii*) *Theory of the 'Acte Clair'*

> LITERATURE: Lagrange, The European Court of Justice and national courts, the Theory of the Acte Clair: a bone of contention or a source of unity, *8 CMLRev.1971, pp.313-325;* Pescatore, L'attitude des juridictions nationales, *RTDE 1970, pp.299-301.*

CASES

(1) GERMAN DURUM WHEAT CASE

Bundesverwaltungsgericht, Decision of 14 February 1969—VII C 15/67, B.Verw.GE, Bd 31 279f.

(Ehle II, H a 1.)

Facts: Before the *Bundesverwaltungsgericht* (the highest court for administrative law cases) a question of interpretation of Article 23, para 4, of Regulation Nr.19/62/EEC had arisen.

The *Bundesverwaltungsgericht* had to decide whether to ask for a preliminary ruling.

The Bundesverwaltungsgericht held:

....

This question must be answered in the negative. An interpretation of Article 23(4) of EEC Regulation No.19/62 has no place in the present case because the provisions thereof do not require interpretation. They provide that a member State, notwithstanding the origin of the grain in question, may only grant a uniform subsidy for domestic use. The adjective 'uniform' only refers to the origin of the grain in question, a point which is particularly apparent from the appeal court's comparison with the French and Italian texts of these provisions. That also follows from the sense of the whole Regulation, which primarily seeks to prevent discrimination on the basis of origin but which besides aims at an eventual stopping or limiting of the payment of domestic subsidies.'[1]

....

[1] Translation by Europa Instituut.

(2) GERMAN WIDOW'S PENSION CASE

Bundessozialgericht (Federal Social Court), decision of 22 January, 1970, CMLR 1971, p.534.

Facts: The Bundessozialgericht had to decide whether the EEC provisions applicable to pensions also apply to gratuities in lieu of widow's pensions and whether it should ask for a preliminary ruling (being a court of last instance).

The Bundessozialgericht held:

'The plaintiff received a widow's pension from the workers' pension insurance fund of her deceased first husband. She remarried in August 1965. The defendant social security office dismissed her application for a gratuity because the plaintiff, who is a French national, lives permanently in France and residence abroad disqualifies a person for a payment.

The Sozialgericht and the Landessozialgericht allowed the claim. They consider that there is authorisation for payment abroad in Article 10(1) of EEC. Regulation 3 whereby pensions and death benefits do not lapse if the recipient resides in a member-State of the European Communities.

. . . .

This Chamber considers itself empowered to give a decision in this case without being compelled to submit to the Court of Justice of the European Communities the question of how Articles 1(s) and 10(1) of EEC Regulation 3 are to be interpreted. There is no obligation to obtain a preliminary ruling from the European Court under Article 177(3) of the EEC Treaty in every case of interpretation of measures of the organs of the Community. For even clear provisions are capable of interpretation even if they do not necessarily need to be interpreted. But it is necessary to invoke the jurisdiction of the European Court if the question of interpretation arises. This must be considered if several meanings have to be taken into account, even if the weights of the various interpretations must be differently distributed. On the other hand, the decision remains within the scope of the jurisdiction of the national court if it cannot find that doubts may arise with regard to the meaning and scope of a provision of Community law. This is the case here. Not only the pension insurance law of Germany but also the provisions of international and supranational law agree in distinguishing between pensions, capital payments in substitution for pensions and other lump-sum payments. There are no indications of any divergent solutions. The decisions of the lower courts to the opposite effect do not conflict with this view. Those courts did not at all see the distinctions discussed here between different types of payment. Only on the basis of such a finding could possible doubts arise as to the judgment delivered.

Accordingly, the claim to have the widow's pension settlement remitted abroad could not be upheld. The decisions of the lower courts must be quashed and the decision of the defendant office confirmed.'[1]

....

(3) GERMAN EXPORT-TAX CASE

Bundesfinanzhof (Federal Court of Finance), Decision of 12 February, 1970. (AWD 1970, pp.231-233.)

Facts: The exporter claimed that the special turnover-tax on exports was in violation of Article 12 of the EEC Treaty and therefore void. The *Bundesfinanzhof*, as a court of highest instance, had to determine this allegation.

The Bundesfinanzhof held:

....

...'No customs duty on exports is involved in the special turnover tax. Export charges with equivalent effect, within the meaning of Article 12 of the EEC Treaty are not included in the special turnover tax.

According to the judgment of 4 April, 1968 of the European Court of Justice in Cases 7/67 and 20/67 (Samml. XIV pp.267, 297, HFR 1969 p.317, BZBl 1968 pp.343 and 346) a charge on the import of goods is not a charge having an equivalent effect to a customs duty of such charge is a component part of the domestic system of turnover tax.

These decisions can also be applied by analogy to export charges having equivalent effect to customs duties. The system of special turnover tax is, however, a part of the domestic system of turnover tax. This view of the Senate follows from the definition of 'charge' made by reference to definitive terms used in the UStG e.g. entrepreneur and export delivery (par.2).

The *Absicherungsgesetz* refers to the law on turnover tax to settle the questions of how tax liability arose and procedure. It does not, therefore, allow of a breach of Article of the EEC Treaty being established in summary examination.

In these circumstances, the request for suspension and quashing of execution was refused.'[2]

....

---

[1]Translation by CMLR, footnotes omitted. [2]Translation by Europa Instituut from CDE.

D. Effects of preliminary ruling

LITERATURE: Gutsche, *Die Bindungswirkung der Urteile des europäischen Gerichtshofes*, Göttingen 1967, 232 pp.

Note: The binding force of preliminary rulings has been expressly accepted in several cases. The German constitutional court did so in the constitutional appeal of the German Lütticke Case on 9 June, 1971 (see above, p.70).

In Advance Transformer Co, *v.* Bara (Arméal) *et al.* the Belgian *Cour de Cassation* on 24 December 1970 held that the interpretation by the Court of Justice in a preliminary ruling could be qualified as a *normative rule* (Pas.Belge, 1971, pp.392-403); see also the conclusions of the procureur-général Ganshof van der Meersch. For a note see Suetens, *SEW 1971, pp.719-724.*

CASE

(1)ITALIAN SALGOIL CASE (FINAL JUDGMENT)
Salgoil *v.* Ministry of Foreign Trade. *Corte d'Appello* (Court of Appeal) of Rome, Judgment of 24 September 1969.
(Foro It.(1969), I Col.3282; Repertario Gen. del Foro It.1969, p.553; CMLR 1970, pp.320-325; CDE 1971, p.55; EuR 1970, p.341).

Facts: This is the final judgment of the Court of Appeal rendered after the Court of Justice of the EC had given a preliminary ruling on the interpretation to be given to Articles 31, 32 and 33 EEC (Case 13/68), reported above, p.132). The Court of Appeal merely had to draw the necessary conclusions from the ruling, notably that 'Article 31, para 2, and Article 32, para 1, have direct effect in the relations between a member State and its citizens and create, in favour of the latter, rights which municipal courts must safeguard'. The Court of Justice had added that 'the legal order of each member State must designate the competent court and, to this end, qualify these rights according to criteria of municipal law'. In its reasoning the Court of Justice had indicated that 'Articles 36, 224 and 226 of the Treaty do not provide an argument to the contrary. Even though these provisions attach a special importance to the interests of the member States, it has to be observed that they concern exceptional situations which are carefully circumscribed and may hence not be interpreted exclusively'.

The Corte d'Appello held:

....

'When the proceedings were resumed before this Court, after the Court of Justice of the European Communities had issued its judgment of 19 December 1968 (13/68), the Ministry for Foreign Trade did not raise again the question of illegality of the reference to the European Court which they had argued in the course of the preliminary hearing before that Court.

In fact, such question could not be raised again particularly after the (negative) answer which was given to it by the Court that considered it, since such answer had—as must be accepted—a fully binding effect upon the court from whom the reference emanated.
...It is a matter for Community law to ascertain 'whether' and if so 'to what extent' any protection is accorded by it to substantive interests of individual citizens vis-à-vis not only one another and other States, but also as regards other States as having their own rights (whether public or private according to the organization which is typical of each) within the ambit of their own legal systems. Once that is done, the question as to which court (where there should be more than one according to the nature and extent of the legal protection afforded by the Treaty provision to the substantive right of the individual) is bound to take cognisanze of possible controversies arising between different subjects, belongs to the moment in which the provisions, as so interpreted, and in the light of the criteria for this purpose brought into being by each individual state, become applicable.

....

As regards Article 32(1) there is no question of any jurisdiction problem since it is quite clear from the very judgment of the European Court that the circumstances adduced by Salgoil (namely the introduction '*ex novo*' of quantitative restrictions and of equivalent provisions as regards goods freely marketable at the time the Treaty came into force) fall within the framework of Article 31 and are excluded indeed by Article 32 which deals only with goods already subject to restrictions at the time the Treaty came into force.

This last hypothesis therefore is inapplicable to the facts of this case...

We are therefore left with Article 31 with respect to which two ideas unequivocally expressed in the judgment of the European Court seem to this Court to be relevant and decisive. The first one is to the effect that the provisions of Article 31... the second one reinforces and explains the foregoing in the sense that 'Articles 36, 224 and 226 cannot supply any contrary consideration'...

...the first statement clearly expresses the belief of the European Court that the interest of individuals, even in those cases where they might possibly conflict with considerations which the State may have to express from time to time in the effectuation of its administrative procedure and in compliance with the needs of the national community as a whole, are nevertheless protected 'directly and immediately'; which is tantamount to saying that they are protected for themselves, and as subjective situations of those who are entitled to them, and not as a mere indirect reflection of a protection primarily directed to guaranteeing the public interest...

...the second statement excludes that the public administration itself has power to infringe the substantive advantages which have been raised to the height of subjective rights, except in those exceptional cases where such a right of minimisation is expressly allowed by the provisions of the Treaty.

....

Therefore, in conclusion, reversing the guiding criterion laid down by the court of first instance, it is the judgment of this Court that the provisions of the Treaty for the purposes that are of interest to us in this case are to be interpreted and applied in the sense that, as a rule, they tend to a direct and autonomous protection of individual interests and therefore, in terms of legalistic qualification which are typical of the national system, to their elevation to the class of subjective rights. It follows from this that the opposite conclusion can be reached only in the presence of an unequivocal legislative intention which, in the case before us, cannot possibly be deduced from the diversity of the general discipline of the subject matter since the contrast is already accounted for by the exceptional nature of the whole of the Community legal system vis-à-vis the national organisation, at any rate as concerns international trade in general.

....

We conclude by saying that the judgment of the court of first instance is to be partially amended by asserting the jurisdiction of the ordinary courts to decide upon the claim for damages by Salgoil...'[1]

[1]Translation by CMLR.

Chapter Five

The law applied by the Court of Justice

LITERATURE: See the statement by Pescatore before the Parliamentary Conference on Human Rights, Vienna 1970, *9 CMLRev.1972, pp.73-79;* Zuleeg, Fundamental Rights and the Law of the European Communities, *8 CMLRev.1971, pp.446-462;* Martens, Die rechtsstaatliche Struktur der EWG, *EuR 1970, pp.209-231;* Rupp, Die Grundrechte und das europäische Gemeinschaftsrecht, *NJW 1970, pp.353-359;* Zieger, *Das Grundrechtsproblem in den Europäischen Gemeinschaften,* Recht und Staat, Vol.384/385, Tübingen 1970; Kropholler, Die Europäischen Gemeinschaften und der Grundrechtsschutz, *EuR 1969, pp.128-146;* Pescatore, Les droits de l'homme et l'interprétation européenne, *CDE 1968, pp.629-673 = Integration 1969, pp.103-136.* A summary has been published in *AJIL 1970, pp.343-351* under the title 'Fundamental rights and freedoms in the system of the European Communities'; Scheingold, *The Rule of Law in European Integration, 1965* pp.273-309.

A. Law derived from the Community Treaties

CASES

(1) SABBATINI CASE

Mrs. Sabbatini-Bertoni *v.* European Parliament, Case 20/71, Decision of 7 June 1972.

Facts: Miss L.Bertoni, of Italian nationality, worked with the European Parliament in Luxembourg and received an *expatriation* allowance. On 4 November 1970 she married Mr.Sabbatini, who did not work for the Communities. Article 4 of Annex VII of the Statute of Personnel provides that the civil servant looses the right to the *expatriation* allowance at marriage unless he becomes the head of the family. Mrs. Sabbatini-Bertoni therefore lost her allowance.

Mrs.Sabbatini-Bertoni submitted that Article 4 of Annex VII of the Statute of Personnel was void as being contrary to the general principle of equality of sexes and contrary to Article 119 of the EEC Treaty obliging the member States to ensure equal pay for men and women.

The Court had to decide whether the actual difference in treatment of men and women following from the Article of Annex VII would affect the validity of that Article.

The Court held:

. . . .

'11.The Refusal to grant a bonus on the occasion of the marriage of the prospective

grantee may be equitable in those cases where such a change in personal status results in a failure to satisfy the condition of *displacement*—the ratio of the grant of the bonus.
12. To that extent, the Statute cannot discriminate against civil servants on the grounds of sex since identical standards, irrespective of sex, must apply as regards the non-fulfillment of the condition of displacement.
13. As a consequence of providing that retention of the bonus shall depend on the acquisition of the status of 'householder'—as defined in Art.1 para 3—the Treaty thereby permits discrimination against civil servants.
14. The decisions (made with respect to the plaintiff) are therefore without a legal basis and must be nullified as provided by Art.184 of the EEC Treaty.'[1]
....

Note: The Court decided similarly in case 32/71 (Mrs.Chollet-Bauduin).

(2) STAUDER CASE
Erich Stauder *v.* City of Ulm, Case 29/69, Preliminary ruling of 12 November 1969 on the request of the *Verwaltungsgericht* Stuttgart.
(Rec.XV, p.419.)
Notes: Ehlermann *EuR 1970, pp.41-47;* Meier, *DVBL 1970, pp.614-615; 7 CMLRev.1970, p.342.*

Facts: The Commission decision of February 12, 1969, OJ No.L 52, 3 March, 1969, authorizes the Member States to make butter available at reduced prices to certain groups of consumers receiving social assistance where their income does not permit the use of butter at normal prices.

Article 4 of this decision, in its German version, provides as follows:

'The Member States shall take all the measures necessary to ensure that... the beneficiaries of the measures provided for in Article 1 receive the butter only upon the presentation of a voucher issued in their name.'

In the French version, the butter can be obtained only upon the presentation of a *'bon individualisé'* (individualized coupon).

The Dutch version says that it can be obtained only upon presentation of an *'op naam gestelde bon'* (coupon made out in the name of a person), and the Italian version says *'buono individualizzato'* (individualized coupon).

The Federal Republic made use of this authorization. Vouchers were distributed under the 'directives for the distribution of butter at reduced prices to recipients of certain social assistance' of March 11, 1969 (*Bundesanzeiger* No.52 of March 11, 1969,

[1] Translation by Europa Instituut.

page 3). These vouchers consisted of detachable coupons and a stub, which, in order to be valid, had to bear the name and address of the holder.

Under Chapter V of these directives, retailers selling butter at reduced prices could accept coupons only if they were still attached to the stub, on which, among other things, the name of the beneficiary had to appear.

The plaintiff is a recipient of aid to war victims and as such is entitled to receive the low-cost butter. He, however, considers it unlawful to condition the receipt of the butter on the requirement that the name of the beneficiary be entered on the stub.

On June 18, 1969, the Administrative Court at Stuttgart issued the referral decision with the question which is now before the Court of Justice.

On August 9, 1969, i.e., after the referral decision, a Commission decision of July 29, 1969, was published in the Official Journal of the European Communities (69/244, Official Journal No.L200, August 9, 1969), in which Article 2 provided that in the German and Dutch versions of Article 4 the word 'individualized' was substituted for the words 'issued in their name', effective as of 17 February 1969.

A question before the Court was whether the German authorities had to take into account the German texts only.

The Court held:

....

...'Article 4 in two of its versions, among them the German, says that the Member States are to take all the measures necessary to ensure that those entitled to the goods receive them only upon the presentation of a 'voucher made out in their name.' The other versions, on the other hand, speak only of the presentation of an 'individualized voucher', so that they permit possibilities for control measures other than the designation of the beneficiary by name. Thus, it is necessary first to clarify what method of control the disputed provision provides for.

Where a decision is addressed to all the member States, the need for a uniform application and thus a uniform interpretation prevents one version of the provision from being viewed in isolation; rather, it requires that the provision be interpreted in light of its version in all four languages so as to give effect to the true intent of its drafter and the purpose he sought to accomplish.

In a case such as the one before us, the interpretation that is the least onerous is the one that is to be preferred, provided that it suffices to attain the goals sought in the decision in issue. Furthermore, it cannot be assumed that the drafters of the decision intended to impose obligations that were more far-reaching in some Member States than in others.

This interpretation, moreover, is confirmed in the declaration of the Commission to the effect that a revision to eliminate the requirement of a voucher made out to the name of the party had been proposed by the Management Committee, to which the draft of Decision No.69/71 had been presented for an opinion. Also, the last consideration of this decision indicates that the Commission had intended to adopt his proposed change.

....

Accordingly, the provision in issue is to be interpreted as not requiring an indication of the name of the beneficiary, although it does not prohibit this.'[1]

(3)BAKELS CASE

Deutsche Bakels GmbH *v.* Oberfinanzdirektion München, Case 14/70, preliminary ruling of 8 December 1970 at the request of the *Bundesfinanzhof.*
(Jur.XVI, p.1009-1010; CMLR 1971, pp.188ff.)

Facts: Bakels imported a product called Voltem and claimed that it should be classified in tariff group 38.19 (chemical products). The German customs authorities however, classified it in tariff group 21.07 (products for human consumption) which led to a higher tariff. The EEC tariff classification was not clear so that the *Bundesfinanzhof* considered to apply the further interpretation given by the German authorities or that given by the Customs Cooperation Council, a world wide organization in which all EEC Members take part. A preliminary ruling was asked on the question whether such interpretations could be used.

The Court held:

....

'For it follows from the nature of the Common Customs Tariff that the individual tariff headings must have the same scope in all the member States. This requirement would be jeopardised if when difficulties arose in the tariff classification of a product each member State was able to regulate this scope itself by means of interpretation.
(4)However, in the event of difficulties in the classification of a product the national authorities may feel compelled to issue implementary measures and thereby clarify the doubts that have arisen because of a product definition; nevertheless, they may only do so subject to the provisions of Community law and are not empowered to issue binding rules of interpretation.
(5)Accordingly, the first question posed by the Bundesfinanzhof must be answered to the effect that even in the absence of interpretative provisions issued by the Community the effect of a binding interpretation cannot be attributed to provisions of the

[1]Reproduced by permission from Common Market Reports, published by and copyright 1965, Commerce Clearing House, Inc., Chicago, Illinois.

national authorities elucidating headings of the Common Customs Tariff.

(7)The Brussels Nomenclature, which was established by the Convention regarding nomenclature for the classification of goods in customs tariffs of 15 December 1950, to which the member States were signatories, is undeniably the basis of the Common Customs Tariff annexed as an appendix to Regulation 950/68.

(8)In order to ensure the uniform interpretation and application of the Nomenclature Articles III and IV of the Convention provide that a committee for the Nomenclature under the supervision of the Council for Co-operation in the Field of Customs is to prepare explanatory notes and tariff notices.

(9)These explanatory notes and notices are a means of interpretation for the original and present meaning and scope of the individual tariff headings. In the absence of relevant provisions issued by the Community, therefore, the authorities competent to apply the Community law provisions in which the Brussels Nomenclature was adopted should not ignore the meaning attributed to these explanatory notes, and notices for the interpretation of the Nomenclature.

....

(11)Accordingly, the aim and the structure of the Common Customs Tariff necessitate that in the absence of relevant provisions of Community law the above-mentioned explanatory notes and tariff notices should be regarded as an authoritative source of information for the interpretation of the tariff headings contained in Regulation 950/68. The second question posed by the Bundesfinanzhof must therefore be answered in the affirmative.'[1]

....

Note: In Case 30/71 of 24 November 1971 (Siemers) the Court had decided that in absence of Community interpretations the informations and advises of the International Customs Council had the standing of valuable auxiliary means of interpretation.

B. The national law of a member State

See Handelsgesellschaft case, consideration 2 and 3, below p.150.

C. General Principles of law

LITERATURE: Rupp, Die Grundrechte und das Europäische Gemeinschaftsrecht, *NJW 1970, pp.353-359;* Ziegler, *Das Grundrechtsproblem in den Europäischen Gemeinschaften,* Tübingen, 1970; Louis, *Règlements de la Communauté Economique Européenne,* p.88 Brussel 1969; Kropholler, Die Europäischen Gemeinschaften und der Grundrechtsschutz, *EuR 1969, pp.128-146;*

[1]Translation by CMLR.

Pescatore, *1978 CDE pp.629-673; Idem, AJCL 1970, pp.343-351;* Lorenz, General Principles of Law: Their Elaboration in the Court of the European Communities, *AJCL 1964, pp.7-12.*

CASES

(1)STAUDER CASE

Erich Stauder *v.* City of Ulm, Case 29/69, Preliminary Ruling of 12 November 1969 on the request of the *Verwaltungsgericht* Stuttgart.

(Jur.XV, p.419. See also above p.146.)

Facts: See above p.146.

Another question before the Court was whether the original version of the German text violated basic human rights of Mr.Stauder (the right not to be humiliated), and in particular whether the Court of Justice would have to apply such human rights.

The Court held:

....

...'the provision in issue contains nothing that could jeopardize the basic personal rights contained in the general principles of Community law, *whose observance the Court of Justice must ensure.*'[1]

Note: Another reference to human rights can be found in case 11/70 (*Jur.XVI 1970, p.1135,* consideration No.4). In that case as well no violation was found.

(2)HANDELSGESELLSCHAFT CASE

Internationale Handelsgesellschaft mbH *v.* Einfuhr- und Vorratstelle für Getreide und Futtermittel, Case 11/70. Preliminary ruling of 17 December 1970 on the request of the *Verwaltungsgericht* Frankfurt a/M.

(Jur.XVI (1970), pp.1134-1139; CMLRev.1971, pp.250-263; CMLR 1972, pp.282-286.)

Facts: See above p.72, Second German Exportbond Case, first decision, which was rendered before the present case, and p.74, Second German Exportbond Case, second decision, rendered thereafter.

The *Verwaltungsgericht* disputed the validity of two EEC Regulations for reason of violation with basic principles of the German Constitution.

The Court held:

....

'(2)It appears from the reasoning of the jugdment making reference that the Administrative Court has hitherto refused to admit the validity of the provisions in

---

[1]Reproduced by permission from Common Market Reports, published by and copyright 1965, Commerce Clearing House, Inc., Chicago, Illinois, italics added.

question and for that reason considers it indispensable to put an end to the existing legal uncertainty.

(3)In the view of that court the deposit system is contrary to certain structural principles of the national constitutional law which should be protected in the framework of Community law, such that the primacy of the supranational law should give way before the principles of the German Constitution. More particularly, the deposit system is thought to infringe the principles of freedom of action and disposition, economic liberty and proportionality which follow from Articles 2(1) and 14 of the German Constitution.

The validity of such instruments can only be judged in the light of Community law. In fact, the law born from the Treaty, the issue of an autonomous source, could not, by its very nature, have the courts opposing to it rules of national law of any nature whatever without losing its Community character and without the legal basis of the Community itself being put in question. Therefore the validity of a Community instrument or its effect within a member State cannot be affected by allegations that it strikes at either the fundamental rights as formulated in that State's constitution or the principles of a national constitutional structure.

(4)An examination should however be made as to whether some analogous guarantee, inherent in Community law, has not been infringed. For respect for fundamental rights has an integral part in the general principles of law of which the Court of Justice ensures respect. The protection of such rights, while inspired by the constitutional principles common to the member States must be ensured within the framework of the Community's structure and objectives. We should therefore examine in the light of the doubts expressed by the Administrative Court whether the deposit system did infringe fundamental rights respect for which must be ensured in the Community legal order.

....

(20)It follows from all these considerations that the certificate system involving an undertaking, by those who apply for one, to import or export guaranteed by a deposit, does not infringe any right of a fundamental character. The deposit system constitutes an appropriate means, within the meaning of Article 40(3) of the Treaty, of the common organisation of the agricultural markets, and also conforms to the requirements of Article 43.'[1]

(3) WALT WILHELM CASE

Walt Wilhelm and others *v.* Bundeskartelamt, Case 14/68. Preliminary Ruling of 13 February 1969 on the request of the *Kammergericht* Berlin.

(Jur.XV (1969), p.16; CCH p.7867, See also above p.111.)

[1]Translation by CMLR.

Facts: The German Cartel authorities had imposed a fine on Walt Wilhelm for violation of German anti-trust laws while the possible application of community anti-trust law was pending.

The *Kammergericht* had asked for a preliminary ruling on the question whether German and Community prohibitions could be cumulatively applied for the same set of facts.

The Court held:

....

'The possibility of cumulative penalties would not preclude the admissibility of parallel proceedings introduced for different purposes. Notwithstanding the conditions and limitations stated in answer to the first question, the admissibility of such a dual prosecution in fact results from the special system of division of jurisdiction between the Community and the Member States in cartel matters.

If, however, the possibility of a dual prosecution were to result in a cumulation of penalties, general considerations of equity, which moreover are found at the end of para.2 of Art.90 of the ECSC Treaty, imply that in determining a penalty, account shall be taken of any prior penal sanction. In any event, until such time as a regulation is issued under Art.87, para.2(e), there is nothing in the general principles of Community Law to prevent such a possibility...'[1]

....

(4) PORTELANGE CASE

N.V.Portelange *v.* N.V.Smit Corona and others, Case 10/69; Preliminary Ruling of 9 July 1969 on request of the Commercial Court of Brussels.
(Jur.XV p.317; CCH p.8095; 7 CMLRev. (1970) pp.234-236.

Facts: In the dispute between Portelange and Smit Corona the validity was involved of a mutual agreement which had been notified to the EEC Commission, but which had not yet taken a decision. Was Article 85 para.2 (declaring such agreements void) applicable? The court had to decide on a question of legal security.

The Court held:

....

'15.Since the parties do not have any effective legal means for speeding up the issuance of a decision under Article 85, para.3,—the more serious the effects, the more time is needed to issue the decision—it would be contrary to the general principle of legal

---

[1] Reproduced by permission from Common Market Reports, published by and copyright 1965, Commerce Clearing House, Inc., Chicago, Illinois.

security to conclude from the fact that the validity of registered agreements is not final that so long as the Commission has not issued a decision based on Article 85, para.3, of the Treaty they are not fully valid.

16.The fact that these agreements are fully valid could under certain circumstances result in practical drawbacks, but the difficulties that could arise from the uncertainty of the legal relationships based on registered agreements would be even more harmful.'[1]

(5)QUININE CARTEL CASE

AFC Chemifarma N.V. *v.* Commission of the European Communities, Case 41/69, Judgment of 15 July 1970.

(Jur.Rec.Samml.XVI, p.686; CCH pp.8175-8201; 82 CMLRev.pp.86-92. See also above, pp.39 and 115.)
Notes: Baardman, *8 CMLRev.pp.89-92;* Le Gros, *86 JT no.4733, pp.148, 149;* Mulder, *SEW 1971, pp.204-214;* Tizzano, *Foro it, 1971, pp.33-38.*

Facts: AFC Chemifarma N.V.—and two other firms, see cases 44 and 45/69—had been found guilty of violating Article 85 of the EEC Treaty and had been fined by the Commission.

All three firms had appealed against the fine.

Besides other arguments the AFC Chemifarma suggested that because the Commission had waited so long after the violations had taken place it had lost its right of pursuit, according to the general principle of the laws of the member States which forbid actions to be taken after a reasonable period of time.

The Court held:

....

'(17)Plaintiff accuses the Commission of having failed to take into account the fact that the alleged violations was prescribed by the statute of limitations, considering the time that elapsed between the happening of the events themselves and the time the Commission started the administrative proceeding.

(18)The provisions governing the Commission's power to impose fines in the case of a violation of the rules of competition do not contain a statute of limitations.

(19)To fulfill their purpose of ensuring legal security, periods of limitations must be set in advance.

(20)Setting the length and the terms of application of a statute of limitations are the province of the Community legislators.

(21)The plea, therefore, is without merit.'[1]

---

[1]Reproduced by permission from Common Market Reports, published by and copyright 1965, Commerce Clearing House, Inc., Chicago, Illinois.

Chapter Six

Procedure before the Court of Justice

LITERATURE: Mario Berri, The Special Proceedings before the Court of Justice of the European Communities, 8 *CMLRev.1971, pp.5-28;* Plouvier, 'Le recours en révision devant la Cour de Justice des Communautés Européennes', *CDE 1971, pp.428-445;* Günther, *Die Präklusion neuer Angriffs-, Verteidigungs- und Beweismittel im Verfahren vor dem Gerichtshof der Europäischen Gemeinschaften*, Kölner Schriften zum Europarecht, Band 12, Carl Heymans Verlag KG, 1970, 149 pp.; Van den Heuvel, De omvang van het kort geding van het Hof van Justitie van de Europese Gemeenschappen, *SEW 1970, pp.131-142;* Chevallier, La procédure devant la Cour de Justice, *Les Novelles, Droit des Communautés Européennes*, Brussels, 1969, pp.391-405; Donner, Het kort geding bij het Hof van Justitie, *SEW 1969, pp.655-658;* Gand, Composition, organisation, fonctionnement et rôle de la Cour de Justice, in *Les Novelles, Droit des Communautés Européennes*, Brussels 1969, pp.295-308; Van Der Sanden, Le recours en intervention devant la Cour de Justice des Communautés Européennes, *RTDE 1969, pp.1-27; idem*, Le recours en tierce opposition devant la Cour de Justice des Communautés Européennes, *CDE 1969, pp.666-682;* Hammes, Gedanken zur Funktion und Verfahren des Gerichtshofes der Europäischen Gemeinschaften, *EuR 1968, pp.1-9;* Grementieri, Le statut des juges de la Cour de Justice des Communautées Européennes, *RTDE 1967, pp.817-830.*

A. Sources

....

B. Language

....

C. Procedure

CASES

(1) THE ASSISTANT CONTROLLER CASE

X, former assistant of the Commission of Control of the EC *v.* Commission of Control of the EC, Case 12/68, Judgment of 7 May 1969.
(Jur.XV 1969, p.115.)

Facts: X had been dismissed as a civil servant on the proposal of the disciplinary board. He maintained that the disciplinary board had not heard him before taking its decision and therefore had violated Article 87 of the Statute. The Commission replied that the obligation to hear Mr.X could not be derived from Article 87. He should have invoked Article 7 of Annex IX for this purpose. His claim being imprecise it should be declared inadmissible.

The Court held:

....

'(7)An error, committed by the aplicant in indicating the applicable text, cannot result in the inadmissibility of this ground of appeal.'
(As X had been given sufficient opportunity to appear before the disciplinary board the claim was unfounded).

(2)ICI CASE

Imperial Chemical Industries Ltd. *v.* Commission of the EC, case 48/69, Judgment of 14 July 1972, Considerations nos.34-44. See also above, pp.30.
(not yet published)

Facts: The Commission had notified its decision imposing a penalty of 50.000 E.U.A. on ICI at the registered office of its subsidiaries within the Common Market. ICI disputed the validity of this notification.

The Court held:

....

On the plea relating to the notification of the decision

'(The applicant contends that the Commission, by providing in Article 4 of the decision challenged that notification thereof may be made at the registered office of the subsidiairies of the applicant established in the Common Market, and by proceeding accordingly, violated the Treaty, or at least essential procedural requirements. The German subsidiary of the applicant, to whom the decision was notified by the Commission, had received no mandate in this respect from the parent company, and under German law it was under no obligation to bring the documents in question to the latter's notice.
Article 191 of the Treaty, second paragraph, provides that decisions shall be notified to the persons to whom they are addressed and shall take effect upon such notification'. Article 4 of the decision challenged could not in any event alter this rule, and hence could not affect the applicant's rights.
Irregularities in the procedure of notification of a decision are external to the legal act and therefore, cannot vitiate it. In certain circumstances, these irregularities might prevent the time for bringing an action from starting to run. The final paragraph of Article 173 of the Treaty provides that the time for bringing an action for annulment

against individual acts of the Commission starts to run upon the notification of the decision to the applicant, or, failing that, from the data on which the latter had knowledge of it.

In the present case, it is apparent that the applicant had complete knowledge of the text of the decision and made use, within the time limits, of its right to bring an action. In these circumstances, the question of any irregularities of notification becomes immaterial.

The above-mentioned pleas are, therefore, inadmissible on the ground that they are immaterial.

D. Time Limits

By Regulation No.1182/71 of 3 June 1971[1] the Council of the European Communities provided *inter alia* that working days are all days excluding Saturdays, Sundays and the public holidays of the member State or institution where the action must be performed (Art.2). Periods of time begin on the day following that on which the event took place (Art.3, para 1) but acts of the Council and the Commission enter into force at the beginning of the day mentioned therefore (Art.4, para 2). They loose force at the end of the day mentioned for that purpose (Art.4, para 3). Periods mentioned in months end at the end of the last day which bears the same number as the day on which they begun (Art.3 para 2).

CASES

(1) REDISCOUNT RATE CASE

Commission of the EC *v.* French Republic, Consolidated cases 6 and 11/69, Judgment of 10 December 1969.
(Jur.XV 1969, p.540; CMLR 1970, pp.43-69; 7 CMLRev.1970, p.480.)
See also above pp.7 and 29.

Facts: In an action of the Commission against France under Art.169 (see above p.29) France submitted that the discount policy of the Commission was not based upon the treaty as only the member States were competent in the monetary field.

The Commission's Decision of 23 July 1968 was therefore legally inexistent. The Commission maintained that France could have lodged an appeal for annulment against that Decision but had not done so.

The Court held:

....

'The French Government, while not disputing that it let the time limit pass, submits

O J8 June 1971, No. L 124, pp.1, 2.

nevertheless that this decision was taken in a field which falls within the exclusive competence of the member States, invoking on the one hand Community public policy (*ordre public communautaire*) and arguing on the other hand that 'too close an attachment to forms would be just as contrary to the true Community spirit as their neglect'. If that submission were founded, the above-mentioned decision would lack all legal basis in the Community order and, in proceedings where the Commission, in the interests of the Community, brings any action against a State for violation of the Treaty, it is a basic requirement of the legal order that the Court should examine whether this is the case.'[1]

. . . .

(The Court subsequently studied the submission of the French Government and concluded that it did not justify the French unilateral measures under consideration).

(2) MULDERS CASE

Th.Mulders *v.* Commission of the EC, Case 8/69, Judgment of 10 December 1969. (Jur.XV 1969, p.567).

Facts: By decision of 21 May 1968 Mulders was nominated in grade A3; by decision of 30 July 1968 he was appointed to the function of accountant which carried, in his submission, the grade A1. On 14 October 1968 Mulders lodged an administrative appeal with the Commission against his grade. When he did not receive any reply he lodged an appeal under Article 175 with the Court on 7 February 1969. The Commission maintained that the appeal was actually addressed against its decisions of 21 May 1968 and 30 July 1968 and therefore tardy.

The Court held:

. . . .

'4.Plaintiff maintains further that his appeal concerns neither the decision of 21 May nor that of 30 July 1968 but, rather, the implicit negative decision on his request for reclassification.
5.Consequently the dispute regards the question whether plaintiff derives a right to appointment to the grade A1 from the decision of 30 July 1968.
6.Since the time limit for appealing against the decision of 30 July had not expired at the moment the administrative appeal was filed, the plaintiff, when filing on appeal against the implicit dismissal of his administrative appeal, was entitled to demand a ruling concerning the legality of this decision.
7.Consequently, the plaintiff's appeal is admissible.'

[1]Translation by CMLRev.

Note: In the *Lacroix Case* (30/68, Jur.XVI 1970, p.309), the Court confirmed that a letter to the Commission which can be seen as an administrative appeal, suspends the time limits.

(3)ASSESSMENT FOR SOCIAL FUND CASE
Federal Republic of Germany *v.* Commission of the EC, Case 2/71, Judgment of 6 July 1971.
(Jur.XVII 1971, pp.676-677; CMLR 1972, pp.443-444.)

Facts: On 2 and 6 March 1970, the Commission had informed Germany of its financial obligations to the Social Fund for the budgetary year 1969. On 25 March 1970 the German Government raised objections against the calculations of the Commission.

On 6 November 1970 the Commission rejected these objections.

On 11 January 1971 Germany lodged an appeal against the letter of 6 November 1970. The Commission submitted that the appeal actually concerned its decisions of March 1970 and was therefore tardy.

The Court held:

....

'(5)As far as the legal basis of the computation of the accounts and the notifications is concerned, the Budget Ordinance of 31 January 1961 states in Article 17: 'On 31 December each year the Commission shall determine (a) the balances of the accounts specified in Article 16, and (b) the amounts required to be transferred in order to clear the positive or negative balances respectively'. The above-mentioned regulation lays down in Article 18: 'Immediately after the determinations in accordance with Article 17, and not later than on 31 January following, the Commission shall advise (a) a debtor Member State as to the amount due to the Commission, and (b) a creditor Member State as to the amount due from the Commission'. From these decrees it is apparent that both the computation of the accounts and also the notification to Member States must be carried out within fixed periods, which incidentally have been exceeded. In view of this legal position these actions must be regarded as final decisions and not as provisional views.

(6)Nor can they be regarded as provisional on the basis of their substantive character, because the administrative procedures relating to the computation of European Social Fund accounts are complicated and apply equally to all Member States, as decisions and opinions relating to one Member State automatically affect the balances of the others. Thus a computation of accounts notified to all Member States cannot be regarded as provisional in connection with any one of these States.

7.Accordingly the communications by the Commission of 2 and 6 March 1970, constitute final decisions of a legal nature which may be objected to in accordance with Article 173 of the EEC Treaty. The claimant, having failed to object within the period of two months laid down, cannot remedy its omission by appealing against a later communication, whereby a variation of the above-mentioned legal procedure is refused.

8. For these reasons the claims are rejected as inadmissible.'

(4) MÜLLERS CASE

H. Müllers v. Economic and Social Committee of the EEC and Euratom, Case 79/70, Judgment of 7 July 1971.
(Jur.XVII 1971, pp.696-698.)

Facts: On 5 December 1969 the applicant had made a detailed and reasoned request to the administration for a school allowance of Bfr.4410 for the period September up to and including 31 December 1969. The amount was largely based on the cost of transport to and from the school. In a document of 12 December 1969, signed on 15 December by the financial controller, the requested allowance was settled at Bfr.3250 for the period in question.

In a statement, dated 19 February 1970, the applicant informed the head of the competent department that he wished to protest against the calculation of his allowance, maintaining his petition of 5 December 1969.

On 31 March 1970 he received the answer that the Secretary-General of the Economic and Social Committee had requested a decision of principle concerning the problem raised by the applicant, this being given as a reason why 'some patience' was requested on his part for a final settlement of his case and he was promised a further answer when the heads of administration had taken their standpoint. After they had made their decision in a manner which was unfavourable to the applicant, the Secretary-General of the Economic and Social Committee rejected the applicant's protest in a decision of 10 September 1970 which was communicated to him on 15 September.

The applicant then instituted proceedings in the present appeal on 11 December 1970.

The Court held:

. . . .

'6. Although the defendant has not disputed that the appeal is admissible, it must be examined, ex officio, whether the appeal was lodged in good time;

. . . .

13. The document of 15 December 1969, drafted by the authority competent at that time, is to be regarded as a decision, since it indicates clearly and concisely that

transport costs must be calculated on a basis other than that as the applicant had requested in his reasoned letter of 8 December 1969.

14.Consequently, the applicant had the choice either to lodge an appeal directly within the period of three months as provided in Art.91, sect.2, subsect.1, of the Statute of Personnel, or to lodge a complaint within that period, with the appropriate appointments authority,—while retaining the right of appeal—against the decision concerning him, in accordance with Art.90 of the said Statute.

15.The applicant availed himself of the second possibility by his memorandum of 19 February 1970, which—even though he himself refers to it as an 'objection' and the conditions for filing of a complaint as provided by Art.90 had not been fulfilled—must be considered as a complaint as understood by that article, since its purpose, evidently, was to evoke a decision on the issue of the appropriate appointments authority.

16.According to Art.91, sect.2, subsect.2, of the Statute 'if, within two months of the day on which a complaint or a request is filed by a person to whom this Statute applies, the competent authority of the institution has not made a decision, this silence must be regarded as a decision to dismiss', and 'appeal against this... (must) be filed within a further two months'.

17.The memorandum of 31 March 1970, which only announced that a future final answer would be given, did not constitute a decision, with the result that the defendant —on the basis of the said provision—is considered to have dismissed the complaint of 19 February 1970 by an implicit decision of April 1970.

20.The present appeal, directed against the explicit decision to dismiss has been filed, it is true, in good time. However, this decision is no more than a mere confirmation of the implicit decision and therefore cannot be regarded as an injurious act.

21.The argument fails that the explicit decision contained a new element in so far as the defendant allegedly had not yet finally decided, at the time of the implicit dismissal, to dismiss the complaint so that the factual or legal situation had charged to that extent.

22.In fact, the defendant has always been of the opinion that the complaint would not be viewed favourably on the basis of the existing regulations.

23.Consequently, the appeal is inadmissible.

E. Effect of Proceedings

CASE

(1)FOURNIER CASE

B. Fournier *v.* Commission of the EC, Case 39/69, Judgment of 13 May 1970.
(Jur.XVI 1970, p.273.)

Facts: Fournier claimed damages with the legal interests for lost holidays.

The Court held:

....

'Plaintiff therefore has a right to payment of the said account (77093 Bfr.) and there is reason to allow him interests for delay, estimated for this case at 4.5 percent from the day of the submission of the appeal.'[1]

....

F. Costs

CASE

(1) GERMAN COSTS OF PRELIMINARY RULINGS CASE

Bundesfinanzhof (Federal Court of Finance), decision of 29 October 1968, BFH VII B 106/67.
(Sammlung der Entscheidungen 94 p.49; NJW 1969, 1135; AWD 1969, pp.37, 38.)

Facts: In Germany the costs of the procedure to which the loosing party may be condemned depend on the value of the issue at stake.

In the present case the lower court had decided that the value of the case itself was 1324 DM but that the value of the preliminary ruling, asked during the process, should be separately estimated. Since this preliminary ruling was of great general importance its value was estimated at 500.000 DM.

The Hauptzollamt appealed.

The Bundesfinanzhof held:

....

'In the case of Art.177 of the EEC Treaty the national court concerned can only make a decision on the question of costs when the proceedings before the European Court of Justice do not constitute an independent procedure with regard to costs, but are part of the principal action pending before the national court.

This is the case. The procedure of a preliminary judgment on validity and interpretation of rules of European law arises from the lawsuit pending before the national court. It is not initiated by actions of the parties, but by a decision of the national court. Its subject matter corresponds with that of the principal procedure, the trial and decision by the European Court of Justice are limited to certain points of law, which are of importance for the decision of the national court.

The resulting unity of both proceedings as to costs is also assumed by the European

[1] Translation by Europa Instituut.

Court of Justice, when it declares in its judgment, given in the present dispute, that the procedure conducted before it, has the character of an incident as far as the parties to the action pending before the Finanzgericht are concerned and that consequently the decision about the costs is the province of that court.

Since as a result no special value of the issue at stake should be fixed for the proceedings before the European Court in the present case, the decision of the *Finanzgericht* should be altered, in conformity with the demand of the Hauptzollamt, to the effect that the value of the issue at stake which is fixed for the action before the Finanzgericht at 1324 DM. will also be decisive for the proceedings before the European Court.'

G. Special Proceedings

CASE

(1) WONNERTH CASE

G. Wonnerth *v.* Commission of the EC, Case 12/69, Judgment of 10 December 1969. (Jur.XV 1969, pp.577.`

Facts: The Commission had appointed Mr. Arning to head of the section labour-safety; a position to which Mr. Wonnerth claimed to have better rights. Wonnerth appealed for the annulment of Arning's appointment and he asked the Court to require Mr. Arning to intervene in the case.

The Court held:

....

'The appeal is inadmissible to the extent that a compulsory intervention of Mr. Arning is requested, as such intervention is not provided for in the Court's Rules of Procedure.'

....

(the rest of the appeal was declared admissible and granted; the appointment of Mr. Arning was annulled).

APPENDICES*

I—Cases submitted to the Court of Justice:
analysis by subject matter (situation at 31 December 1971)

Type of case	ECSC				EEC										Total
	Scrap compensation	Transport	Competition	Other¹	Customs union	Right of establishment, freedom to supply services	Tax cases	Competition	Social security and free movement of workers	Agricultural policy	Transport	Euratom	Privileges and immunities	Proceedings by staff of the institutions	
New cases	169	36	55	19	53	1	26	38	37	99	3	3	6	268	813
(1971)		1			7			5	7	28	1	1		46	96
Cases struck off	22	5	15	9	8	1	5	2	2	4	—	1	—	60	134
(1971)					1	1	1	1	1	1				5	11
Cases decided	147	30	40	10	42	—	21	26	34	73	3	2	6	163	597
(1971)	4		1		5		1	5	6	23	2	1		30	78
Cases pending	—	1	—	—	3	—	—	10	1	22	—	—	—	45	82

¹Levies, investment declarations, tax charges, miners' bonuses.

II—Cases submitted to the Court of Justice:
analysis by type (EEC Treaty)* (situation at 31 December 1971)

Type of case			Proceedings brought under Articles										
			173					177					
	169 and 93	170	By Governments	By individuals	By the institutions	Total	175	Validity	Interpretation	Total	184	215	Grand total
New cases	27	—	14	52	1	67	8	11	134	141	3	20	259
Cases struck off	7	—	4	3	—	7	—	—	8	8	—	—	22
Cases decided¹	19	—	10	35	1	46	7**	11	114	121	3	9	201
In favour of plaintiff³	16	—	1	7	—	8	—				—	—	
Dismissed on the merits³	3	—	8	9	1	18	—				—	9	
Dismissed as inadmissible	—		1	19	—	20	6				3	—	36
Cases pending	1	—	—	14	—	14	1	—	12	12		11	36

**Excluding proceedings by staff and cases concerning the interpretation of the Protocol on Privileges and Immunities (see Table 25). ***Including one non-suit.
¹The number of judgments is smaller than the number of cases decided, because some cases were joined during the procedure. ²In respect of at least one of the plaintiff's main claims. ³This also covers proceedings dismissed partly as inadmissible and partly on the merits. ⁴The total may be smaller than the sum of cases listed, since some cases were based on more than one Article of the Treaty.
*Source: Fifth General Report on the Activities of the Communities, Tables 25-28, Brussels-Luxembourg.

III—Cases submitted to the Court of Justice:
analysis by type (ECSC and Euratom Treaties)* (situation at 31 December 1971)

Type of case	Number of proceedings brought						Total	
	By Governments		By the institutions		By individuals (undertakings)			
	ECSC	Euratom	ECSC	Euratom	ECSC	Euratom	ECSC	Euratom
New cases	22	—	1	2	257	1	280	3
Cases struck off	9	—	—	1	42	—	51	1
Cases decided[1]	13	—	1	1	214	1[4]	228	2
In favour of plaintif[2]	5	—	—	1	48	1[4]	53	2
Dismissed on the merits[3]	7	—	—	—	117	—	124	—
Dismissed as inadmisisble	1	—	1	—	49	—	51	—
Cases pending	—	—	—	—	1	—	1	—

*Excluding proceedings by staff and cases concerning the interpretation of the Protocol on Privileges and Immunities (see Table 25).
[1]The number of judgments is smaller than the number of cases decided, because some cases were joined during the procedure. [2]In respect of at least one of the plaintiff's main claims. [3]This also covers proceedings dismissed partly as inadmissible and partly on the merits. [4]Terminated by order of the Court.

IV—Decisions by national courts concerning Community law[1]

Subject matter[2] / Country	EEC Treaty														Total
	Free movement of goods			Agriculture	Free movement of persons and right of establishment	Social security law[3]	Transport	Competition			Tax provisions	Other[4]	ECSC Treaty[5]		
	Customs duties	Quantitative restrictions	Monopolies					Restrictive agreements, monopolies	Dumping	Aids					
Belgium	1			1	1	9		36				3	2		53
Germany (FR)	20	2	2	53	12	2	1	43	2		34	12	4		187
France	5	1	1	4	3	12	1	16	1	1		2	2		49
Italy			1	3	1	3		1		2			13		24
Luxembourg								1							1
Netherlands	4		1	1	1	7		34				4			52
Total	30	3	5	62	18	33	2	131	3	3	34	21	21		366
Previous totals	28	3	5	50	17	29	2	124	3	3	34	13	20		331
New judgments	2	0	0	12	1	4	0	7	0	0	0	8	1		35

[1]Figures are for decisions published up to 15 November 1971, excluding cases which give rise to a reference to the Court of Justice for a preliminary ruling. [2]The breakdown of subject matter is asccording to the main aspect of the judgment. Thus cases referring to tax questions in agriculture are classified under 'tax provisions'. [3]Cases concerning social security and Article 119. [4]Cases concerning Article 7, Article 169 (effects of a judgment by the Court of Justice), Article 177 (costs, examination by a national court of its obligation to lay a request for interpretation before the Court of Justice), Articles 215, 220, 227, Protocol 1, 7, and association agreements with Turkey and the AAMS. [5]Prices, financing, social security, competition, transport, obligation to pay, and forced execution.

CUMULATIVE TABLE OF CASES — ALPHABETICAL

Pages marked *J* refer to the main work; those preceded by *S* to the Supplement

CUMULATIVE TABLE OF CASES — BY NUMBER

Pages marked *J* refer to the main work; those preceded by *S* to the Supplement

	Reported	Reference
1/54 First Monnet-Rabat Case	*J* 27, 67	
2/54 Second Monnet-Rabat Case	*J* 243	
3/54 Assider Case	*J* 49	*J* 67
6/54 Kingdom of the Netherlands *v.* High Authority		*J* 19, 234
7, 9/54 Steel Industries in Luxembourg Case	*J* 36, 45, 71	*J* 37
8, 10/54 Coal Consumers in Luxembourg Case	*J* 37	
5/55 Assider Case		*J* 259
8/55 Fédéchar Case	*J* 41, 50, 223	*J* 22
2/56 First Geitling Case	*J* 29	
7/56 (3-7/57) Algera Case	*J* 237	
8/56 ALMA Case	*J* 101	
9/56 First Meroni Case	*J* 61, 77	*J* 93, 234
1, 14/57 Tubes de la Sarre Case	*J* 21, 62	
(7/56), 3-7/57 Algera Case	*J* 237	
8/57 Hauts Fourneaux Case	*J* 66	
13/57 Ruhrstahl et al. *v.* High Authority		*J* 67
15/57 Hauts Fourneaux de Chasse Case	*J* 68	
18/57 First Nold Case	*J* 38, 43, 231, *J* 245	
1/58 Stork Case	*J* 229	
19/58 The Federal Republic of Germany *v.* High Authority		*J* 6
24, 34/58 Chambre Syndicale de l'Est de la France Case	*J* 47, 73	*J* 249
32-33/58 SNUPAT Case	*J* 83	
1/59 First Dalmas Case	*J* 101	
3/59 Railway Tariffs Case	*J* 6, 79, 87	*S* 3
14/59 Fonderies de Pont à Mousson Case	*J* 245	
19/59 Geitling et al. *v.* High Authority		*J* 248
23/59 Feram Case	*J* 89	*J* 88, 97
25/59 First Publication of Transport Tariffs Case	*J* 7, 224, 254	*J* 16
30/59 Limburg Coalmines Case	*J* 47, 69, 252	
43, 45 and 48/59 Lachmüller Case	*J* 238	
44/59 Fiddelaar Case	*J* 95	

	Reported	Reference
2-3/60 N.B.A. Case	*J* 33	
6/60 Humblet Case	*J* 229	
9, 12/60 Vloeberghs Case	*J* 39, 91, 257	
13/60 Geitling Case		*J* 222
19, 21/60 (2, 3/61) First Fives Lille Cail Case	*J* 93, 245	
(19, 21/60) 2, 3/61 First Fives Lille Cail Case	*J* 93, 245	*J* 97
7/61 Pork Case	*J* 10	
10/61 Radio Tubes Case	*J* 225	
13/61 Bosch Case	*J* 182, 186, 236	*J* 202, 216, 249; *S* 131
14/61 Hoogovens *v.* High Authority		*J* 64, 236
16/61 First Modena Case	*J* 102	
5-11, 13-15/62 San Michele Case	*J* 74	
16-17/62 Fruit and Vegetables Case	*J* 40, 57	*J* 249
19-22/62 Féderation nationale de la boucherie en gros *v.* Council of the EEC		*J* 41
24/62 Brennwein Case	*J* 63	
25/62 Plaumann Case	*J* 52, 96, 225	
26/62 Van Gend en Loos Case	*J* 109, 187, 195	*J* 114, 209
28-30/62 Da Costa-Schaake Case	*J* 209	*J* 213, 216
31, 33/62 Wöhrmann Case	*J* 80, 195	
32/62 Alvis Case	*J* 238	
1/63 First Dalmas Case		*J* 64, 76
15/63 Lassalle Case	*J* 255	
29, 31, 36-47, 50, 51/63 Société anonyme des laminoirs, hauts fourneaux, forges, fonderies et usines de la Providence et al. *v.* High Authority		*J* 95
53-54/63 First Lemmerzwerke Case	*J* 22	*J* 83
55-59, 61-63/63 Second Modena Case	*J* 44	
66/63 Kingdom of the Netherlands *v.* High Authority		*J* 31
70/63-bis Collotti Case	*J* 259	
73-74/63 Internatio Case	*J* 191, 196	
75/63 Hoekstra Case	*J* 232	
90-91/63 Dairy-products Case	*J* 12	*S* 14, 15
101/63 Fohrmann/Krier Case	*J* 249	*J* 222
106-107/63 Toepfer Case	*J* 55	*J* 97, 100; *S* 28, 122
108/63 Merlini Case	*J* 230	
111/63 Second Lemmerzwerke Case, Klöckner intervention	*J* 253	
1/64 Glucoseries Case	*J* 53	
6/64 Costa-ENEL Case	*J* 105, 189, 207, *J* 256	*J* 111, 167, 168; *S* 68
12, 29/64 Ley Case	*J* 28	*J* 248

	Reported	Reference
30/68 Lacroix Case		*S* 158
31/68 Chanel Case	*S* 131	
4/69 Third Lütticke Case	*S* 36	
6/69; 11/69 Rediscount Rate Case	*S* 7, 29, 156	*S* 3, 4
7/69 Wool Imports Case	*S* 8	
8/69 Mulders Case	*S* 157	
10/69 Portelange Case	*S* 152	
26/69 Olive Oil Case	*S* 10	
29/69 Stauder Case	*S* 146, 150	
31/69 Export Rebates Case	*S* 11	
40/69 Turkey Tail Case	*S* 117	
41/69 Quinine Cartel Case	*S* 153	
45/69 Boehringer Case	*S* 39	*S* 153
48/69 ICI Case	*S* 30, 155	
64/69 Compagnie Française Case	*S* 27	
69/69 Alcan Case	*S* 20	
74/69 Krohn Case		*S* 119
77/69 Wood Case	*S* 5	
9/70 Grad Case	*S* 48	
11/70 Handelsgesellschaft Case	*S* 150	
14/70 Bakels Case	*S* 148	*S* 119
22/70 ERTA Case	*S* 18	
33/70 Sace Case	*S* 53	
39/70 Reliable Importers Case	*S* 119	
41-44/70 Apples Case	*S* 22	
59/70 Steel Subsidies Case	*S* 32	
62/70 Chinese Mushroom Case	*S* 23	
79/70 Müllers Case	*S* 159	
80/70 Air-Hostess Case	*S* 130	
2/71 Assessment for Social Fund Case	*S* 158	
5/71 Zuckerfabrik Schöppenstedt Case	*S* 38	
8/71 Composers Case	*S* 34	
14/71 Henck Case	*S* 130	
18/71 Eunomia Case	*S* 43	*S* 13
20/71 Sabbatini Case	*S* 145	
30/71 Siemers Case		*S* 149
43/71 Politi Case		*S* 55
48/71 Second Art Treasures Case	*S* 12	
77/71 Mayonaise Case	*S* 120	
93/71 Slaughtered Cow Case	*S* 54	
94/71 Sugar Export Case	*S* 121	

CUMULATIVE TABLE OF CITATIONS TO TREATY ARTICLES

(Parts of) texts of the Articles are inserted on the pages printed in italic type
Pages marked *J* refer to the main work; those preceded by *S* to the Supplement

ECSC Treaty

Art.	2	*J* 66
	3	*J* 62, 66
	4	*J* 17, 66; *S* 33
	5	*J* 66
	8	*J* 4, 229
	14	*J* 8, 20, 181, 225
	15	*J* 2, *62*, 244
	31	*J* 229, 230
	32	*J* 36
	32bis	*J* 166
	32ter	*J* 166
	33	*J* 20, 21-29, *30*, 31-40, *45*, 48, *49*, 60, 61, 88, 92, 192, 231, 234 246; *S* 33
	34	*J 69*, 91, 92
	35	*J* 37, 38, *70*, 92; *S* 33, 34
	36	*J 76*, 100, 102
	37	*J 32*, 33, 34, *69*, 86, 88
	38	*J 30*, 192
	39	*J* 248
	40	*J* 85, *89*, 259
	41	*J* 181
	43	*J* 2, 181, 182
	48	*J 36*
	50	*J* 42
	53	*J* 62, 66, 68
	54	*J* 22, 62
	58	*J* 70
	59	*J* 68, 70
	60	*J* 49, 67, 182
	61	*J* 67, 70
	64	*J* 102
	65	*J* 38, 43, 44, 67, 181; *S* 129
	66	*J* 38, 86, 181, 182
	67	*S* 33

69	*J* 2
70	*J* 6, 7, 8
80	*J 36*, 37, 38, 39, 253
86	*J* 87; *S* 4
87	*J* 1, *2*
88	*J 5*, 6, 8, *16-17*, 48, 71, 85, *87*, 88, 224, 230, 255; *S* 1, 2, 3, 33
89	*J* 2, *5*
90	*S* 152
92	*J* 78, 143, 231
96	*S* 92
98	*S* 88, 89

EEC Treaty

5	*J 104*, 107; *S* 4, 55, 99
7	*S* 53
9	*J* 110; *S* 43, 50, 54
10	*J* 159, 215
12	*J* 13, 109, 187, 196, 210, 225; *S* 14, 15, 16, 57, 58, 141
13	*S* 53, 54
14	*J* 225
16	*J* 191; *S* 8, 12, 13, 43
25	*J* 17, 64
26	*J* 17
29	*J* 199
30	*J* 215; *S* 132
31	*J* 159, 215; *S* 132, 142, 143
32	*S* 142, 143
33	*S* 142
36	*S* 142, 143
37	*J* 106, 169, 214, 257
40	*J* 146; *S* 151
43	*J* 13, 108; *S* 151
44	*J* 59
48	*J* 233; *S* 46

CUMULATIVE INDEX

Pages marked *J* refer to the main work; those preceded by *S* to the Supplement

180

— Antwerp   *S* 62
— Berchem   *S* 62
Jus standi   *J* 254
    see also *capacity to lodge an appeal*
Justice of the peace Milano *J* 105, 167-170,
              189, 207; *S* 85, 86

Lack of powers *J* 60, 61-62, 193; *S* 29-32
Landgericht Bonn   *S* 122, 123
Landgericht Wiesbaden   *S* 136
Languages *J* 21, 212, 222, 241, 241, 242, 252;
                        S 147
Language laws (Belgium)   *J* 138
Law violating EEC treaty *J* 14, 15, 107, 157,
159, 161, 167; *S* 4, 5, 8, 9, 10, 12-14, 15, 16-17,
43, 46-47, 51-52, 53-54, 57-58, 63, 64-66, 71, 79,
                  84, 86, 130
Legal aid   *J* 248
Legal guarantees   *J* 26, 153
Legal order (Community —) *J* 14, 106, 107,
110, 153, 157, 166, 183, 230, 235; *S* 58, 104,
                 112, 151, 157
Legal personality *J* 228, 231, 256; *S* 31-32
Legal (in) security *J* XXI, 116, 194, 197, *237*,
           245, 258, *S* 131, 152, 153
Legal situation (change in —)   *J* 25
Legality (compared to validity) *J* 191, 192, 193
Letters (appeal against —) *J* 22-25, 44, 60, 63,
        72, 84, 238; *S* 158, 159
Liability see *non- Contractual liability*
Liberia   *J* 31
Lucrum cessans   *J* 98, 99
Luxembourg (judicial organization) *J* 131-132
Luxembourg (constitution)   *J* 170-172

Member States
    action against — *J* *1-17*, 70, 75, 255; *S* *1-18*
    See also *breach of obligation by State*
    capacity to lodge an appeal *J* 30-35; *S* 20
    — as persons   *J* 226
Misuse of powers *J* 16, 49-51, 59, 60, *67-69*, 78,
                  127, 135, 158
Modification of judgment   *J* 257
Monist theory   *J* 157, 171, 173
Motion (court action of its own —) *J* 96. 199,
              244, 245, 248, 253

Motivation   *J* 10, 21, *62-66*, 238, 244
Municipal, see *national*

National competences (Community competen-
ces and residual —)   *S* 111, *117-122*
National constitution *J* 136-176; *S* 56-87
National Courts
    obligation to apply Community law *J* 17,
          103-117, 177-186; *S 42-55*
    Competence   *J* 89, 156, 199-216
    relation to Court of Justice *J* 80, 85, 97, 100,
    183, 185, 186, 195, 198, 205, 251; *S* 114, 122-
         126, 128, 132-133, 138
    task   *S* 68
National law
    see also *Community law, relation to national*
    law
    — used by Court of Justice *J* 224, 228-233,
              234; *S* 151
National legal systems *J* 18, *117-135*; *S* 104,
                       112
Ne bis in idem   *J* 239; *S* 116
Negative duty   *J* 110, 114
Negligence   *J* 97-99
Netherlands (judicial organization) *J* 132-135,
                       201
Netherlands Constitution *J* 172-176, 187, 188;
                       S 14

New Member States, see *accession*
Non-contractual liability *J* 84, 85, *88-100*, 246;
              S 35-39, 123, 124, 125
Non-member State   *J* 40, 66
Normenkontrolle   *J* 124
Norwegian Constitution   *S* 100-103
Notification of decisions   *J* 21; *S* 155

Oberlandesgericht Hamburg   *S* 134
Oberlandesgericht Köln   *S* 124
Objectives of the Communities *J* 67; *S* 112, 151
Office Commercial du Ravitaillement (Luxem-
bourg)   *J* 71
Official Journal   *J* 21, 104, 258, 259
Officials, see *staff members*
Officio (court acting ex —) *J* 96, 199, 244, 245,
              248, 253
Opinons   *J* 20, 21, 22, 25, 76